Ruby A. Keator

THE MOTHER TONGUE

BOOK I
LESSONS IN SPEAKING, READING, AND WRITING ENGLISH

BY

SARAH LOUISE ARNOLD
DEAN OF SIMMONS COLLEGE
FORMERLY SUPERVISOR OF SCHOOLS IN MINNEAPOLIS AND IN BOSTON

AND

GEORGE LYMAN KITTREDGE
PROFESSOR OF ENGLISH IN HARVARD UNIVERSITY

REVISED NEW YORK STATE EDITION

GINN AND COMPANY
BOSTON · NEW YORK · CHICAGO · LONDON

The Athenæum Press

GINN AND COMPANY · PRO-
PRIETORS · BOSTON · U.S.A.

PREFACE

TO THE REVISED NEW YORK STATE EDITION

Book I of " The Mother Tongue " is designed to guide children to an intelligent appreciation and enjoyment of good English, to help them to speak and write correctly, and to introduce them to the study of grammar. The book is divided into three Parts, intended for use in the Fourth, Fifth, and Sixth Years of school respectively. This edition has been carefully revised so as to meet the requirements of the latest Syllabus of the Education Department of the State of New York.

To appreciate the power and beauty of any language, a child must become familiar with well-written prose and verse in selections that shall be interesting from his own point of view as well as acceptable to the critical scholar. By familiar association with such writings, and wisely directed study of them, the child's taste is cultivated and a love of literature is fostered.

With this in view, the book provides in each Part selections from good authors, in prose and verse, together with full instructions for their use in different ways. Exercises for reading, study, discussion, and learning by heart accompany the selections. A similar study of the material contained in the pupil's reading book should follow as a natural result, and thus these

iii

lessons form an introduction to the elementary study of literature. Frequent reference is made to library books in which the pupil is likely to be interested and to the topics which he is studying in history and geography. A considerable list of subjects for composition may be found on page 334. This is meant to be merely suggestive.

Accuracy in speaking and writing can be secured only by a process of *imitation*, and for this the essentials are a " copy " and occasions for practice. Such copies or patterns are therefore provided in sufficient quantity and variety to direct attention to accepted usage and to arouse the child's interest and observation. The necessary repetition is ensured by a variety of exercises, each of which will be recognized by children as practical and useful.

In Part One punctuation marks and capital letters are reviewed, so that the oral instruction of earlier years is brought together and sufficient instruction is added to complete the requirements of ordinary practice. It is hoped that this review and summary will lead to the conscious recognition of the meaning and purpose of such fixed customs, — and the section on Punctuation therefore explains with care this essential element of correct writing.

At the end of the Fourth Year the pupils should gather together and summarize for themselves the rules of writing to which they have been accustomed. Selections from the required exercises should illustrate each rule.

Letter writing is developed in its natural order, beginning with the child's own friendly notes (in Part I) and continuing through all its essential phases, including business letters and formal notes of invitation and acceptance or regret. Here, again, full provision has been made for continuous practice. The subjects are adapted to the interests and experiences of the pupils.

Inasmuch as usage in many matters of detail is far from being absolutely fixed, the authors have presented only the latest accepted forms, or the general rule which may always be followed with safety. For example, commas have been omitted in addresses on envelopes, in accordance with a custom which is rapidly gaining ground; and only those rules for the use of the comma which are supported by general usage have been brought to the pupil's attention.

In Part Two the attention of the pupil is directed to the construction of the sentence, and he is taught to separate it into its main elements, — the subject, predicate, and modifiers. He is thus made ready for a more specific analysis of the thought in the sentence, in Part Three, and a systematic study of "The Work which Words Do."

Although errors of speech are not emphasized by undue comment, such constructive exercises are introduced as will tend to correct common mistakes. Tense forms and number forms of verbs, and the much-abused personal pronouns, are frequently employed in exercises which will serve as types for the correction of prevalent errors.

Part Three continues the elementary study of grammar in systematic fashion. At the same time this portion of the book specifically directs the student to a methodical analysis of his own thoughts and of the words in which his thoughts are expressed. To such study of the "thought in the sentence" formal rules and definitions have been subordinated. Thus in the summary of the "work which words do" and in the sections that lead up to it, emphasis is laid upon the functions rather than the definitions of the parts of speech, and it is not until the following sections that technical definitions are given. It is hoped that the lessons will be used as they are intended, since the common failure of grammatical study comes chiefly from the propensity to learn definitions by rote before one has acquired that power to analyze thought which alone renders the definitions valuable.

Part Three, then, not only provides for an elementary study of grammar, but serves to develop that power of weighing one's words on which depends, in a high degree, the ability to speak and write forcibly and well and to appreciate similar merits in the style of another. Thoughtful reading is a direct result of such study. The pupil who leaves school with only such instruction in grammar as this book affords, will be well grounded in the essential principles and well practised in the customary forms observed in writing.

Abundant exercises in description, narration, explanation (or exposition), and character study have been included in each of the three Parts.

Extracts from Longfellow, Whittier, Lowell, Bayard Taylor, Celia Thaxter, Alice Cary, and John Burroughs are used by permission of and by special arrangement with Houghton Mifflin Company, publishers of the works of those authors. Acknowledgments are also due to the E. W. Noyes Co. for authority to reproduce Mr. Eldred's etching of "The Caravan," to Miss Mary C. Judd for permission to use extracts from "Wigwam Stories," to Mrs. Charlotte V. Gulick for an extract from "Emergencies," to Miss L. E. Poulsson for a passage from "Lisbeth Longfrock," and to Dr. William J. Long for a page from "Secrets of the Woods." The publishers of Burkett, Stevens, and Hill's "Agriculture for Beginners" (Messrs. Ginn and Company) have allowed the reproduction of an extract from that book.

The following pictures have also been used by permission: "The Queen's Birthday" (page 36), by Mrs. Woodbury (from a Copley Print, copyright, 1904, by Curtis & Cameron, publishers, Boston); "A Summer Day" (page 54), by Jules Breton (from a Copley Print, copyright, 1899, by Curtis & Cameron, publishers, Boston).

The Selections to be Committed to Memory prescribed for the Fourth, Fifth, and Sixth Years by the Education Department of the State of New York are printed at the end of the volume, where particular acknowledgments to several authors and publishers will be found.

CONTENTS

PART ONE

CAPITAL LETTERS AND PUNCTUATION MARKS

CONTENTS

PART TWO

CONSTRUCTION OF SENTENCES AND PARAGRAPHS

CONTENTS

CONTENTS

PART THREE

THE WORK WHICH WORDS DO

CONTENTS

xvi CONTENTS

CONTENTS

LESSONS IN SPEAKING, READING, AND WRITING ENGLISH

PART ONE

SECTION 1

FOR READING ONLY

To the Boys and Girls:

This book will tell you about something which you have always used, but which you have never studied. You know something about it; yet probably that something is very little. You have breathed air all your life; yet you do not know what air is made of and what it does for you. You have walked and played upon the earth; yet you do not know the earth's story. You have eaten bread: do you know how it is made? You drink water: do you know whence it has travelled?

All these common things, if they could talk, might ask you a hundred questions about themselves. But to every question you would give the same answer: "I do not know." Yet the common things are the most interesting, after all, and are best worth studying.

One of the common things which serve you every day is **the English language.** You have used this language ever since you began to talk. You have spoken it everywhere — at home, at school, at play. You are constantly using it. It is your servant. Do you know what it does for you? How much do you know about it?

Tell me this : Do all children speak the same language? No. You say in English, "I go to school." The German boy says, "Ich gehe in die Schule." The French boy says, "Je vais à l'école." You speak in the English language, the German boy in the German language, the French boy in the French language. Every language has names of its own for all common things. You often speak of your house. Were you French, you would say "ma maison"; if you were German, you would say "mein Haus" instead.

Have you ever thought why your language is called **the English language,** and why it is different from other languages? Were you to think about this, you would ask many questions, some of which would be hard to answer.

Think of your games without language. Can you imagine yourself playing "I spy," or baseball, without speaking? You must have words and speak them, or the game would soon come to an end. Can you imagine yourself remaining silent an entire day, from morning till night, speaking to nobody? How much you would miss that now makes your day pleasant! You begin talking as soon as you are awake in the morning. At the breakfast table, at play, at school, at dinner, at the afternoon games, at supper, by the fireside in the evening, you are constantly talking with your friends and playmates. You make known your wants and express your thoughts in spoken language, and through the spoken words of your friends you learn their thoughts and feelings and wishes. You would be very lonely and unhappy if you could not thus make your thoughts known and understand the thoughts of others.

This book is meant to help you to know more about this language of yours. Perhaps you think you know enough already. It would not be strange if you were to say, "I can talk. I know how to use my language now, for I have used it nearly all my life." What you say is partly true. It is as if you were to say, "I have seen the earth; I have lived upon it all my life." But when I ask you to go with me to visit the wide prairie, or the high mountains, or the changing sea, you are glad to go. How much there is upon the great earth which you know nothing about! How you would like to know all its story!

So it is with our **mother tongue,** — the English language. You use some of its words every day. It is always ready to help you. It helps you to let your friends know when you are hungry, or happy, or tired. By its aid, you tell stories to your little brother or sister. Without it you could not tell your mother to-night what has happened at school to-day.

Do you not care to know more about this language which is so necessary to you? Should you not like to write it easily, as well as to speak it, so that you may talk to your friends who are far away, as well as those who are near? When you grow older and go away from home, shall you not wish to tell your mother what you are doing, just as you tell her to-day? But then you must speak with pen and ink, in written words. Do you not wish to learn how to write letters which others will like to read?

There is a right way of doing everything, as well as several wrong ways. There is a right way to spin a top, to set a table, to harness a horse, to write a letter, to express a thought. This book will help you **to speak and write correctly.** It will help you to choose words which will express just what you desire to say, and to put those words together properly. That is, it will help you to make an intelligent use of your **mother tongue.**

SECTION 2

FOR READING AND STUDY

THE STORY OF A LESSON

The lesson was not a reading lesson, nor a writing lesson, nor a drawing lesson, nor a music lesson. I wonder if you can guess what kind of lesson it was?

The children stood near the teacher, Miss Brown, looking at an apple which she held in her hand. "See," said Miss Brown, "what a beautiful apple I have! Look at it. Think about it. Now tell me some of your thoughts about the apple."

This is what the children said in reply : —

Jamie. The apple is round.
Kate. The apple is green.
Mary. The apple is good to eat.
Joe. The apple grew on my apple tree.
Frank. The apple has brown seeds.

"I will write your thoughts as you have told them to me," said Miss Brown. "And now I will tell *you* something.

"Each of you thought about the apple and told me his thought. Your thoughts were different, and so you chose different words in which to tell them. Each one has told his own thoughts in his own words.

"A group of words which tells one's thought is called a sentence.

"Who can find and read Jamie's sentence? and Joe's? and Mary's?"

Of course every child could find and read his own sentence. Before long the children were making and reading other sentences about the apple, and these were so easy and pleasant to make that more sentences followed, sentences which told other thoughts, about the chestnut which Joe had brought to school, the dog that Frank had at home, the game which the children played at recess. The children laughed when they found that it was so easy to tell their thoughts in sentences.

"You see," said Mary, "we really have been making sentences ever since we began to talk, only we never knew it."

Perhaps you can tell now what the lesson was about, — and perhaps you can make **sentences,** just as Frank, and Joe, and Jamie did.

You cannot remember when you began to use sentences.

When you first spoke you used single words as the baby does to-day. "Sugar!" he says when he wants some sugar to eat. "Baby wants some sugar," you say to mamma. The baby uses the

single word only, naming or pointing at the thing
he wishes to get, but you have learned to express
the complete thought in a sentence.

Learn : —

**A sentence is a group of words which expresses a
complete thought.**

*Look at something in the room and tell your
thought about it. Then write, on the blackboard or
on paper, the sentence which expresses your thought.*

SECTION 3

ORAL EXERCISE

1. *Tell your thoughts about* —
Honey, gold, pencils, bricks, the schoolhouse,
the playground.

2. *Tell your thoughts about* —
Horses, dogs, cows, cats, birds, fishes.

SECTION 4

WRITTEN EXERCISE

Write your thoughts about —
The dandelion, the elm tree, the rose, the violet,
the golden-rod, the lilac.

Or, if you prefer, write about —
Grapes, apples, plums, peaches, corn, potatoes.

Do not try to write about anything unless you first know something about it.   Sentences have no use except to tell what one knows or thinks.

First know, then tell.   Tell your own thoughts.

SECTION 5

WRITTEN EXERCISE

Write sentences about —

Your father, your mother, your sister, your brother, your house, your pets, your playthings, your work.

SECTION 6

EXERCISE FOR STUDY

PROVERBS

Look at these sentences : —

A soft answer turneth away
    wrath.

Haste makes waste.

Birds of a feather flock to-
    gether.

Wilful waste makes woful
    want.

Where there's a will there's a
    way.

These sentences are **proverbs.** That is, they express thoughts which have been remembered and repeated for hundreds of years because they were worth keeping.

Every nation has many proverbs. Even among savage tribes, where reading and writing are unknown, such sayings are common, and are much valued for their wisdom.

Read the proverbs and see if you can tell what they mean. Why do you think people have kept them in mind and taken pains to hand them down to us from old times?

Copy the proverbs just as they are written.

Look at them carefully, and tell where you find capital letters.

The sentences which you have been studying are written correctly. They follow a rule which you must learn if you do not already know it. Here is the rule:—

Every sentence should begin with a capital letter.

Copy the proverbs that follow. Remember the capital letter at the beginning.

A new broom sweeps clean.

Still waters run deep.

It is never too late to mend.

Make hay while the sun shines.

Straws show which way the wind blows.

SECTION 7

PLAYING INDIAN

1. Here are two little boys who have been " playing Indian." This is their tent.

2. The two boys are named Malcolm and Dwight. The older boy is Malcolm. Can you tell which boy he is in the picture?

3. Their father once went away for a long time. He promised to bring them something they would like very much, if they would be good boys while he was gone.

4. They must have been very good, for when he came home he brought them a large box. They wondered what it held, and could hardly wait to open it.

5. What do you think they found in the box? Two Indian suits, two caps with feathers, and two hatchets, besides bows and arrows. But the greatest surprise was the tent or wigwam, all ready to set up.

6. The boys thanked their father. Then they ran away at once to set up their tent, put on their suits, and play Indian.

SECTIONS 8-9

EXERCISES

8. *Tell the story of Malcolm and Dwight.*
Tell all that you see in the picture.
Tell how you have played Indian.

9. *Copy the story in Section 7.*

What does each part tell you about?

SECTION 10

WRITTEN EXERCISE

Write your thoughts about some dog that you know.

Tell his name; his color; what he can do; what he likes to eat; how he is cared for.

SECTION 11

STUDY OF A PICTURE

SAVED.   BY LANDSEER

Here is a copy of a well-known picture.

What do you see in the picture?

Where are the dog and the child?

What shows you where they are?

What do you think happened to the child?

What did the dog do then?

What is he doing now?

What kind of dog is this?   What can you tell about him?

Make a story to tell about the dog and the child. Make it in three parts. Tell (1) what happened to the child; (2) what the dog did; (3) what the child's father did.

SECTION 12

WRITTEN EXERCISE

Tell all that you see in the picture " Saved."

Tell (1) about the place; (2) about the dog; (3) about the child; (4) about anything else in the picture.

SECTION 13

WRITTEN EXERCISE

Copy the poem "September" (Selections, pages 9–10). Learn the poem by heart.

SECTION 14

ORAL EXERCISE

Read "September" line by line.

Tell what you know about each thing mentioned in the poem.

When you come and go to and from school, try to see some of the things mentioned, and say the poem to yourself.

Find words or expressions in the poem which you do not use in your everyday speech.

SECTION 15

Pattern Sentences

Copy the following sentences.
Make other sentences like them, using the italicized words.

1. Frank *likes* to play ball.
   Boys *like* to play ball.
2. Mary *sews* neatly.
   Girls *sew* and knit.
3. The general *rides* a black horse.
   The soldiers *ride* well.
4. Mr. Jackson *makes* boxes.
   Bakers *make* bread.
5. My canary *sings* beautifully.
   Canaries *sing* beautifully.
6. The blacksmith *shoes* the horse.
   Blacksmiths *shoe* horses.
7. The horse *draws* the cart.
   Two horses *draw* the carriage.
8. A brook *runs* down the hill.
   Still waters *run* deep.
9. The lily *is* white.
   Violets *are* blue.
10. The apple *is* red.
    Some apples *are* red.
11. The elephant *has* a trunk.
    Elephants *have* large ears.
12. James *has* a hard lesson to learn.
    The boys *have* hard lessons to-day.
13. Alfred *has* a silver watch
    James and Alfred both *have* watches.

SECTION 16

How Names are Written

My name is
    Helen Louise Watson.
My sister's name is
    Kate Watson.
My brother's name is
    James Dwight Watson.

Look at the names which are written above.
With what kind of letter does *Helen* begin?
Louise? Watson? Kate? James?

Copy the three names, taking care to place the capital letters correctly.

Names of persons begin with a capital letter.

~~~~~~~~~

Write your full name.
Write the names of three pupils in your class.
Write the names of three other persons whom you know.
Write the names of three persons of whom you have read.

SECTION 17

FOR READING AND STUDY

FAMILY NAMES

Everybody that you know has at least two names, — a **given name** and a **family name**. Mary Meade, Harold Pierson, Helen Stuart, John Hancock, — all have two names. The last name is always the family name. Thus, *Meade* is the name which belongs to every one in Mary's family, while *Mary* is the given name which belongs to her alone. You can easily think of many family names, and can remember all the given names in the families that you know best.

In old times family names were unknown, for one name was thought to be enough for one person. But it often happened that there were many Johns or Marys or Williams in a single neighborhood. To prevent mistakes a word was sometimes added to a person's name to describe him. Thus he might be called *Thomas the Baker*, if baking were his trade ; or *John the Strong*, if he were stronger than his neighbors ; or *John at the Wood*, if his cottage stood near a forest. Sometimes, too, this added name contained the name of the person's father. Thus Thomas the son of Peter might be called *Thomas Peterson*, while Thomas the son of Jack would be called *Thomas Jackson*.

In time these nicknames, as we may call them, were attached to whole families and so became what we now call family names. Every family name once meant something. John Goldsmith was a goldsmith, — Thomas Field lived in a field, — George Farmer lived on a farm, — and Henry Long was a long man. But now-a-days the early meaning of the name is seldom thought of. William Farmer may be a merchant; Thomas Field may live in the heart of the city ; and John Little may be six feet tall.

It is interesting to think about the family names that we know. Often we can readily guess what meaning they used to have ; but many names have been so changed in the course of years that we cannot tell what they meant when they were first used.

~~~~~~~~

Try to find out the meaning of the family names that follow.

Smith	Carpenter	Brooks
Baker	Mason	Wiseman
Townsend	Miller	Stevenson
Weaver	Cook	Wilson
Thomson	Short	Brown

SECTION 18

WRITTEN EXERCISE

Write full names in answer to these questions : —

1. What is your name ?
2. What is the name of your father ?
3. What is the name of your mother ?
4. What is the name of your teacher ?
5. Who is the President of the United States ?
6. Who is the Governor of your State ?

SECTION 19

WRITTEN EXERCISE

Write ten sentences in which you use names of persons whom you know.

SECTION 20

FOR STUDY

INITIAL LETTERS

A person's name may be written in full, as *John Kingman, Edith Otis Grant, George Alfred Peabody;* or it may be shortened by writing merely the first letter of the given name or names.

Thus, John Kingman may prefer to write his name *J. Kingman;* Edith Otis Grant may sign herself *Edith O. Grant;* while George Alfred Peabody may choose to shorten his name, or signature, by writing it simply *G. A. Peabody.*

The first letter of a name is the **initial** or beginning letter.

When the initial stands alone, it is always a capital letter, and is always followed by a period.

~~~~~~~~

Write the names that follow, using initials for all but the family names.

> John James Curtis.
> Wallace White Noyes.
> Charles Simpson Sprague.
> Amos Alden Abbott.
> Mary Lowe Smith.
> Jane Ellen Perry.
> Eleanor Eldredge Eaton.
> Clara Louise Burnham.

SECTION 21

WRITTEN EXERCISE

1. *Write your own name, using initials for all but the family name.*

2. *Write the names of ten persons whom you know, using initials instead of their given names.*

3. *Make a list of names, first writing the full name, and then using the necessary initials.*

SECTION 22

STUDY OF A PICTURE

THE HELPING HAND.   BY RENOUF

This picture has something to tell you.   What do you see in it?

Tell all you can about —

    1. The little girl.   3. The boatman.

    2. The boat.   4. The sea.

See if you can tell a story that will fit the picture.
Tell —

    1. Who the little girl is.

    2. What she is doing.

    3. How she happened to go out in the boat.

SECTION 23

WRITTEN EXERCISE

THE DAYS OF THE WEEK

*How many days has the
baby to play?
Saturday, Sunday, Monday,
Tuesday, Wednesday,
Thursday, Friday,
Saturday, Sunday, Monday.*

Copy carefully, then write from memory. Compare what you have written with the text and see if you have used capitals where they are required.

Learn : —

The names of the days of the week always begin with capital letters.

SECTION 24

WRITTEN EXERCISE

Write a sentence telling one thing that you did on Monday of last week. Use the word Monday.

Do the same for each of the other days of the week.

SECTION 25

FOR READING AND STUDY

A NIGHT WITH A WOLF

Little one, come to my knee;
    Hark! how the rain is pouring
Over the roof, in the pitch-black night,
    And the wind in the woods a-roaring!

Hush, my darling, and listen,
    Then pay for the story with kisses:
Father was lost in the pitch-black night,
    In just such a storm as this is,—

High up on the lonely mountains,
    Where the wild men watched and waited,—
Wolves in the forest, and bears in the bush,
    And I on my path belated.

The rain and the night together
    Came down, and the wind came after,
Bending the props of the pine-tree roof,
    And snapping many a rafter.

I crept along in the darkness,
    Stunned, and bruised, and blinded—
Crept to a fir with thick-set boughs,
    And a sheltering rock behind it.

There, from the blowing and raining,
　Crouching, I sought to hide me;
Something rustled, two green eyes shone,
　And a wolf lay down beside me.

Little one, be not frightened;
　I and the wolf together,
Side by side, through the long, long night,
　Hid from the awful weather.

His wet fur pressed against me;
　Each of us warmed the other;
Each of us felt, in the stormy dark,
　That beast and man were brother.

And when the falling forest
　No longer crashed in warning,
Each of us went from our hiding-place
　Forth in the wild, wet morning.

Darling, kiss me in payment;
　Hark! how the wind is roaring!
Father's house is a better place
　When the stormy rain is pouring.

BAYARD TAYLOR.

*Read the poem over and over until you can tell
the story in your own words without book.*

SECTION 26

FOR CONVERSATION

Who is telling the story in the poem in Section 25?

To whom is he telling it? When? Where?

On what kind of night?

How and where was the father lost?

What were some of the dangers of the night?

What does "in the bush" mean?

What were the "props of the pine-tree roof"?

What were the "rafters"?

Why did the fir seem safer than the pine?

What happened in the fir-tree house?

What do you think is strange in the story?

SECTION 27

WRITTEN EXERCISE

Copy the sentences and fill the blanks.

1. I lost my path on the —— mountains, and was ——.

2. The wind bent the —— of the pine-tree roof, and —— many a rafter.

3. I crept behind a —— rock.

4. The falling —— crashed in warning.

SECTION 28

For Conversation

The Emperor's Messenger. By Schreyer

This picture was painted by an artist named Schreyer, whose pictures of horses are very much admired.

The man with a gun is a messenger who has been sent by the emperor on an important errand. He must carry his letter through a wild, snow-covered country. On the way he is attacked by wolves.

Study the picture.
Look at the horses and the driver.
Tell all you can about them.
Tell the story which the picture tells you.

Are these wolves like the one in the poem in Section 25? What makes the difference?

SECTION 29

Oral Exercise

What can you tell of the character of the man who is driving the horses in Schreyer's picture (page 25)?

Do you know other men who are brave and strong, and perform brave and strong deeds? *Tell about them.*

SECTION 30

Oral Review

1. What is language good for? Why are you studying language? What have you learned this term? What have you liked best?

2. What is a sentence?

3. What rules for writing sentences have you learned?

4. What kind of letter do you use at the beginning of a sentence?

5. What are family names? What do you know about them?

6. How are names written?

7. What is a proverb? How long are proverbs usually?

8. Recite one rule for the use of a capital letter.

9. Recite a rule for writing initials.

10. Tell the story of " A Night with a Wolf."

FOR READING AND STUDY

PUNCTUATION

Do you know what is meant by the word **custom?** I think you do. Custom is the way in which a thing is usually done. It is your custom to come to school at nine o'clock. To eat butter with bread is a common custom. It is Frank's custom to run home from school. It is customary to say " Good-morning ! " or " How do you do ? " in greeting a friend. We say " Thank you ! " when any one does us a favor. It is customary in driving to turn to the right when we meet another carriage. It is customary to place a postage stamp in the upper right-hand corner of an envelope. It is customary to begin a written sentence with a capital letter.

I am sure that every one in the class will readily think of many common customs. See how many customs you can mention or describe.

One of the hardest things for us to learn in writing our thoughts is to remember **the rules,** or **customs, of writing.** There are certain ways in which our thoughts must be written if we would make them plain to those who read them. You would find it easy enough to write down what you think or know, if it were not for the many little customs which must be remembered; but if you were to neglect these customs, it would be hard for others to read what you had written. One use of this book is to teach you the rules or customs that we follow in writing.

There are certain **signs** or **marks** which it is customary for us to use in writing in order to make the meaning plain. These are called **marks of punctuation.**

For example, when you write your name, it is your custom to begin every word with a capital letter and to put a period after each initial. That is right. It is a common custom, and if you should forget to put either the capital or the period in its proper place, you would be thought ignorant. Some one who read your letter might say, " Whoever wrote this must have learned very little at school."

A person who forgets to say " Thank you !" to one who shows him a kindness is regarded as rude and untaught. In the same way, one who does not follow the rules of writing, who neglects to use the customary signs, is regarded as ignorant. More than this, he makes it difficult for others to find out his meaning.

In order that you may see how helpful such little **marks of punctuation** are, and how difficult it is to get the meaning of a sentence when they are omitted, try to read the next paragraph. It is written without the marks of punctuation.

the fox and the grapes

a fox went out to walk early in the morning one fine day in summer by the side of the road he saw a tree beside the tree grew a beautiful vine which had fastened itself to the sturdy boughs the fox saw the purple grapes hanging from the vine and wished to get some for he was very fond of grapes he jumped and jumped but could not reach even the lowest cluster what do you think i care he said as he went away disappointed everybody knows that your old grapes are sour

Do you find it easy to read this story? If you do not, turn to page 93. There you will have the help of **punctuation marks** in reading it, and by their aid you will easily get the sense.

Punctuation marks are used to make the thought in the sentence plain.

The punctuation marks which you will learn to use this year are the period (.), the comma (,), the interrogation point (?), the exclamation point (!), and the apostrophe (').

SECTIONS 32–33

FOR STUDY

HOW QUESTIONS ARE WRITTEN

32. You have already used the period at the end of sentences which you have copied. This was a

sign that the thought was finished or complete.
You have used the period after the initial of your
middle name, and have learned that it is always
customary to put the period after initials. There
is another common mark of punctuation which
many of you have already learned to use correctly.
You will find it in the sentences below.

Do foxes like grapes ?
Did the fox in the fable reach his grapes ?
Why could he not reach them ?
What did he say when he found they were out of reach ?
Were the grapes really sour ?
What do people mean by saying "sour grapes" when
they are not talking about real grapes at all ?

You already know the sign which has been
used in these questions. What does it tell you?
What is it a sign of ? When should it be used?

Ask a question about apples.
Write your question on the blackboard.

What mark do you place after the question ?

33. *Ask questions about objects in the room.*
*Ask a question about a wolf ; about the fox ;
about grapes ; about your schoolhouse.*
Write these questions on paper.
*Make the sign of the question very plainly, so that
no one can mistake it.*

SECTION 34

ORAL EXERCISE

THE GAME OF QUESTIONS

Play the game of questions.

[In this game one player thinks about some object in the room. The others question him, in order to guess what he is thinking about. All the questions must be such as may be answered by "Yes" or "No."]

Here is an example of the game : —

John.   I am thinking about something in the room.

Mary.   Is it on the floor ?

John.   No.

Susan.   Is it near the blackboard ?

John.   Yes.

Charles.   Is it in the chalk-tray ?

John.   Yes.

George.   Do we use it to write with ?

John.   Yes.

Ella.   Is it the crayon ?

John.   Yes.

Ask some pupil to think about an object in the room, and let the others ask questions in order to guess what he is thinking about.

SECTION 35

WRITTEN EXERCISE

THE INTERROGATION POINT

Play the question game; but write your questions on the blackboard, instead of asking them aloud.

Do not forget to use the question mark. Its longer name is **interrogation point.** "Interrogation" is a word that means "question." Use this name hereafter.

Make the interrogation point carefully, so that it shall be like those in your book.

SECTION 36

WRITTEN EXERCISE

Write questions about these objects: —

your pencil,	the weather,	baseball,
your desk,	the lesson,	marbles,
your book,	recess,	dolls,
your ruler,	vacation,	kites.

Choose some other pupil to answer each of your questions.

SECTION 37

FOR READING AND TELLING

THE WONDERFUL CRADLE

Last summer there lived a little caterpillar in my grape-vine. He fed upon the green leaves, and ate so many that I wondered if there would be any left. One day, after a very large dinner, the caterpillar began to spin. I saw a strong silk thread that seemed to come from his mouth, and it was fastened to the grapevine.

Then a strange thing happened. He moved his head to and fro and twisted it round and round, until he was wrapped in a beautiful soft silk blanket which he had made for himself. Soon there was no caterpillar to be seen, — nothing but this curious silken cradle. There lay the cradle tied close to the grapevine stem all through the fall. Thanksgiving came, then winter, with its snow and ice and bitter winds; the Old Year went and the New Year came, but the cradle lay quietly in its cranny. It did not even rock in the wind.

At last the cold winds died away, and the warm days came. The little sleeper awoke with the May sunshine, and rustled inside his brown cradle. I watched to see the caterpillar come forth from his winter nest; but what do you think I saw? A beautiful butterfly, that clung to the grapevine stem, and slowly unfolded his velvety wings.

"Oh!" cried the children, "a butterfly! a butterfly! Did you ever see anything so beautiful?"

I wonder if they knew that the baby caterpillar had changed into a beautiful butterfly in his winter cradle?

Read the story on page 33.

After reading, close your book and tell the story to the class.

Try to tell everything in its proper order, and so well that all your hearers will enjoy the story.

SECTIONS 38–41

WRITTEN EXERCISES

STATEMENTS

38. *Write some fact about —*

a top,	a tree,	a cradle,
a marble,	a house,	a caterpillar,
a kite,	a road,	a butterfly.

You have learned to write questions correctly. Some of the sentences which you use are questions, but most of them are **statements**.

A sentence which tells or states something as a fact is called a statement.

Read the statements which you have written.

Every written statement should end with a period.

39. *Write ten statements about things which grow in a garden.*

40. *Write ten statements about yourself, and what you do in school.*

41. *Write five questions about the city of New York, and answer them in written statements.*

SECTION 42

WRITTEN EXERCISE

A RULE FOR CAPITALS

You have copied and committed to memory many pieces of poetry. Have you observed that every line of poetry which you have copied began with a **capital letter** ?

Here is a rule for you to remember : —

Every line of poetry should begin with a capital letter.

Write from memory the poem in Section 42. Remember your new rule.

SECTION 43

STUDY OF A PICTURE

THE QUEEN'S BIRTHDAY

The children in this picture live in Holland. Their queen is named Wilhelmina, and they love her very dearly. To-day they are celebrating the queen's birthday.

Tell all that you see in the picture.
Name the children.
Tell about their dress, their shoes, their caps.

The Dutch live in Holland. These are Dutch children, and they are carrying the Dutch flag.

THE QUEEN'S BIRTHDAY

SECTION 44

Draw a picture of the American flag; of the Dutch flag.

Write a little story called "The Queen's Birthday."

SECTION 45

FOR READING AND CONVERSATION

ORANGES

1. Oranges grow only in a warm climate. They need warmth and sunshine. Their native home is in eastern Asia, but they are cultivated in Florida and California.

2. The orange tree is very beautiful. It has thick glossy green leaves all the year round. Its white blossoms are very fragrant. They are often used in bridal wreaths. The deep yellow fruit is an ornament to the tree.

3. The ripe oranges are carefully picked, wrapped in tissue paper, and packed in wooden boxes, or crates, to be shipped to all parts of the country. When you eat an orange you may think you are drinking the sunshine of Florida or California, which the sweet juicy fruit has hoarded for you.

SECTION 46

FOR STUDY

ABOUT PARAGRAPHS

Read again the lesson in Section 45. You find it divided into three parts. The first part tells you where oranges grow ; the second part describes the orange tree; the third tells how the fruit is shipped.

Prose writings are divided in this way, into **paragraphs.** Each paragraph usually contains several sentences, all telling about the same thing. When we have written about the places where oranges are found, and wish to tell how the orange tree looks, we begin a new **paragraph,** and in this way give notice of the change in our thinking, or thought.

In order that every new paragraph may be easily recognized, it is "indented," that is, its first sentence begins at a little distance from the even margin of the page.

This custom in the arrangement of paragraphs helps to make clear what we read, much as punctuation does.

In your own writing, follow this custom. Your letters, unless they are very short indeed, should be divided into paragraphs. Always indent each paragraph.

SECTION 47

WRITTEN EXERCISE

Answer these questions about apples. Arrange your answers in paragraphs, and indent each paragraph.

PARAGRAPH 1

What are apples? Where do they grow?

PARAGRAPH 2

What do you know about apple trees? How do they look in blossom time? in harvest time? What is an apple orchard?

PARAGRAPH 3

What are apples good for? How are they cooked? What is the juice of the apple called? What article of food is made from cider?

SECTION 48

Study this old rhyme until you can write it from dictation or from memory: —

WEATHER SONG

When the weather is wet,
We must not fret.
When the winter is cold,
We must not scold.
When the weather is warm,
We must not storm, —
But be thankful together,
Whatever the weather.

Write a paragraph, telling in prose what the rhyme tells you.

SECTION 49

For Talking or Writing

1. My father *works* on a farm.
   His men *work* with him.
2. He *plants* seeds in the spring.
   They *plant* corn, beans, and peas.
3. My father *makes* hay in June and July.
   We *make* it, too, or help to make it.
4. Jack *rakes* behind the cart, but the horses *rake* the big field with a large rake.
5. Father *fills* the barn with the sweet hay.
   We *fill* the day with fun.

Make as many statements like the patterns as you can, using the words works, work; plants, plant; makes, make; rakes, rake; fills, fill.

SECTION 50

Pattern Sentences

Copy these sentences. Then make others like them.

1. This book belongs to Robert. I gave it to *him.*
2. Show the pictures to *Mary and me*, Robert.
3. The book is *his* to keep, Mary.
4. *Mary and I* shall like to read it, Robert.
5. *You and I* will let Mary read it first, John.
6. This boat belongs to *you and me.*
7. *You and I* own the boat.
8. That boat belongs to *Harry and me.*
9. *He and I* own the boat.

SECTION 51

FOR READING

This piece of poetry is a part of the "Song of Hiawatha," by Henry Wadsworth Longfellow. It describes little Hiawatha, the Indian boy, as he sits at the door of his wigwam, listening and watching. Longfellow has been called "The Children's Poet."

Read the selection carefully.

> At the door on summer evenings
> Sat the little Hiawatha;
> Heard the whispering of the pine trees,
> Heard the lapping of the water,
> Sounds of music, words of wonder;
> Saw the firefly, Wah-wah-taysee,
> Flitting through the dusk of evening,
> With the twinkle of its candle
> Lighting up the brakes and bushes.
> And he sang the song of children,
> Sang the song Nokomis taught him:
> "Wah-wah-taysee, little firefly,
> Little, flitting, white-fire insect,
> Little, dancing, white-fire creature,
> Light me with your little candle,
> Ere upon my bed I lay me,
> Ere in sleep I close my eyelids!"
> Saw the rainbow in the heaven,
> In the eastern sky, the rainbow;
> Whispered, "What is that, Nokomis?"

And the good Nokomis answered:
" 'T is the heaven of flowers you see there;
All the wild flowers of the forest,
All the lilies of the prairie,
When on earth they fade and perish,
Blossom in that heaven above us."

SECTION 52

ORAL EXERCISE

CONVERSATION

Who was Hiawatha?   Was he young or old?
How can you tell?

Where was he?

What did he hear?   What is the voice of the
pine tree called?   Why?   Did you ever hear it?
What is the sound of the water called?   What
other sounds and other names have you heard?
What were the " sounds of music " ?   What were
the " words of wonder " ?

Who do you think Nokomis was?

What is the firefly?   What is its candle?   Have
you ever seen one?   Where?   Do you know the
difference between a firefly and a glowworm?

What are brakes?   Where have you seen them?

What is a prairie?

What part of the verses do you like best?
Repeat them.

SECTION 53

FOR STUDY

A RULE FOR CAPITALS

1. Here is an old rhyme which children like to recite.

Copy it carefully.

> Star light, star bright,
> First star I see to-night,
> I wish I may, I wish I might
> Have the wish I wish to-night.

2. *Observe the capital* I's.

The word "I" stands for the person who is speaking. It is always written with a capital letter.

3. *See if you can write the rhyme from memory. Follow the rule for capital* I.

SECTION 54

WRITTEN EXERCISE

ACCOUNT OF A DAY

Write, in order, a full account of what you did yesterday.

Remember the rules for the use of capital letters and marks of punctuation.

SECTION 55

A RULE FOR CAPITALS

1. In March we find the pussy-willow.
2. April showers bring May flowers.
3. June is the month of roses.
4. Water lilies float on the ponds in July.
5. In August comes the golden-rod.
6. Asters, the star-flowers, bloom in September.
7. October turns maple leaves to gold.
8. November winds blow the leaves from the trees.
9. Through December, January, and February the flowers are asleep in their warm earth-houses.

You have learned how to write the **names of persons.** You know that such names always begin with **capital letters.**

Read the sentences above.

1. Which words begin with capitals because they stand at the beginning of sentences?

Write these words in a column.

2. What other words begin with capitals?

Write them in a column.

3. Do you discover from this second column another use for capital letters?

Write the rule which you have made.

By such study all rules are best learned.

SECTION 56

WRITTEN EXERCISE

Here is an old rhyme which has been recited by children for many years : —

Thirty days hath September,
April, June, and November;
All the rest have thirty-one,
Excepting February alone,
Which has just eight and a
    score,
Till leap-year gives it one
    day more.

Copy the rhyme, then write it from memory.

Fill the blanks and copy : —

In January there are —— days.

There are —— days in February.

Once in four years February has —— days.

The third month, ——, has —— days.

April has —— days, but May has ——.

June has one less day than ——.

My birthday comes in ——.

SECTION 57

WRITTEN EXERCISE

1. *Write the names of the days of the week.*
2. *Write the names of the months.*
3. *Write the names of six holidays.*
4. *Answer, in written sentences, the following questions:* —

In what month do we celebrate Washington's Birthday? Independence Day? Thanksgiving? Christmas? New Year's Day? What holiday do you like best? Why?

SECTION 58

WRITTEN EXERCISE

Copy the following sentences: —

The capital of Virginia is Richmond.
Coffee is brought from Arabia.
The ship sails for London to-morrow.

Virginia, Richmond, Arabia, and *London* are names of places. Each of them begins with a capital letter.

Learn: —

Names of places begin with capital letters.

SECTION 59

WRITTEN EXERCISE

Write ten statements or questions in each of which you use the name of one of the places in the following list : —

Asia, New York, Washington, England, Paris, China, Boston, Chicago, Cuba, Atlantic Ocean.

SECTION 60

REVIEW

Write all the rules you can for the use of capital letters. Make an example for each rule.

SECTION 61

STUDY OF A PICTURE

On page 48 is a copy of a very famous picture. It represents the child of an English king of the Stuart family and is known as " Baby Stuart."

1. What do you like about the picture ?

2. After studying the picture and talking about it, you may write a description of some baby whom you know.   You should tell his age, and his first name ; what he likes to do, and what you can do for him.

SECTION 62

BABY STUART. BY VAN DYCK

1. *Tell a story about some child.*

The anecdote should recite something interesting which the child has done. It should be told as simply and naturally as if you were talking to a friend.

2. *Write your story.*

You should be careful to arrange your story in an orderly way and to write it neatly and plainly. Be careful about periods and capital letters.

SECTION 63

FOR READING AND WRITING

A FABLE

A hungry dog once found a large piece of meat. He was very glad to get it, you may be sure, for he had had nothing to eat for a long time. He seized the meat with his teeth and ran to find a quiet place where he might eat it all himself. On his way he crossed a plank which served as a bridge over a quiet brook. Down in the water he saw another dog with another piece of meat. So greedy was he that he opened his mouth, snapping at the piece of meat which belonged to the other dog, when behold! his own meat fell into the brook and was carried down the stream where he could not reach it. Too late he saw that the other dog was simply his own reflection. His greed had cost him his breakfast.

Read the fable. Think about it.
Write it in your own words.

SECTION 64

Fables are written about animals, but are meant to teach us about men.

What character does the dog show in the story? Have you seen anything like it in persons?

Tell a story about a child who lost something by being selfish and greedy.

SECTIONS 65-67

65. *Copy these prose sentences and learn them :* —
Never be discouraged by trifles. If a spider breaks his thread twenty times, he will mend it as many. Patience and perseverance will accomplish wonders.

Have you ever watched a spider? What can you tell about him? *Make notes of three things which you have observed.*

66. *Write five questions about spiders. Be careful about punctuation.*
Write five sentences in answer to your questions.

67. *Write a short composition about spiders.*

SECTION 68

ORAL REVIEW

1. What do we mean by "customs in writing"? Name one of *your* customs.

2. Why do we learn about these customs?

3. What rules for writing sentences can you remember?

4. Recite a rule for the use of the period; the interrogation point.

5. What is a statement? How is it written?

6. What is a paragraph? How are paragraphs written?

7. Who was Hiawatha? Tell about him.

8. What is a fable? Recite one.

9. Write a name which means "George who lives near the wood."

SECTION 69

Copy " Sweet and Low" (Selections, page 3).
Learn the poem by heart.

This is a song which a mother is singing to her baby. The father is a fisherman, out at sea in his boat. The wind of the western sea is a favoring wind, which will bring him home. The poem tells you of the rolling waters of the sea, of the silver sails under the silver moon, of the absent father in his boat, and of the loving mother at home, watching, waiting, cradling her baby in her arms, and singing "Sweet and Low."

SECTION 70

ORAL EXERCISE

1. What did you do with the glass *yesterday?*
   I *broke* it when I *fell.*
2. What did you do in school *last Monday?*
   I *wrote* a letter and *drew* a picture.
3. How did you spend your *last vacation?*
   I *went* to Saratoga.

Use these sentences as patterns, and make other sentences like them.

Every one of your questions must speak of past time; every answer must contain one of the words in the list below.

wrote	took	drew	spoke
gave	saw	broke	stole
came	found	did	shook

SECTION 71

Copy the sentences and make others like them, using the italicized words.

1. Can you *write*, James?
   Yesterday I *wrote* a letter to my mother.
   I *have written* a hundred letters.
2. Did you *break* this window?
   I *broke* it with my ball *yesterday.*
   I *have* never *broken* a window before.
3. *Will* you *give* me some candy?
   I *gave* you some a little while ago.
   I *have given* you enough for to-day.

SECTION 72

Write a paragraph about the house you live in.
Tell (1) where it is; (2) what it is made of, and
(3) what its color is. (4) Then tell whether it is a
city house, a village house, or a house in the country.
(5) Add something about the yard, if it has one.
Do not forget to indent the paragraph.

SECTION 73

ORAL EXERCISE

THE CROW AND THE PITCHER

A thirsty crow one morning sought far and wide for water to quench his thirst. He flew north, south, east, and west. At last he found a long-necked pitcher which was partly filled with water. "Now, at last," he said, "I can have water to drink." But when he tried to drink, he found that he could not reach the water, it stood so low in the pitcher. He tried and tried in vain.

At last a happy thought came to the crow. He found a pebble near by, brought it in his bill, and dropped it into the water. Then he flew to get another, and another, and another, dropping them into the pitcher one by one. The water rose higher and higher with every pebble, until at last he could reach it easily. Then he drank his fill. Do you not think that he earned all that he drank?

"Where there's a will there's a way."

~~~~~~~~~~~~~

Read this fable to yourself.

Close your book, and tell the story of " The Crow and the Pitcher " in your own words. Make three parts, or paragraphs, in telling the story.

What does this fable tell you about the character of the crow? What is it meant to teach? How can you become patient and persevering?

SECTION 74

WRITTEN EXERCISE

A DESCRIPTION

Copy the following description. Then write a paragraph like it, describing something you have at home.

I know something that I have at home. It is made of wood. It has four legs, but it cannot walk. It stands in the middle of the floor. We sit around it when we eat breakfast. What is it?

SECTION 75

STUDY OF A PICTURE

A SUMMER DAY.   BY JULES BRETON

This picture shows you a harvest field in France. See how tall the wheat is. See the blossoms in the wheat. See the high church tower beyond the harvest field.

~~~~~~~~~~

Tell everything that you see in the picture.
Tell what each person is doing.
Describe each one.
Make up a story about the picture.

SECTION 76

FOR READING AND STUDY

THE APOSTROPHE

We have already studied about the **marks of punctuation,** which do so much to make our thoughts plain to the people who read them.

You already know the **period** and the **interrogation point.** To-day you must learn about another little mark, which has a very long name. It is called the **apostrophe.**

Here are some sentences in which the apostrophe is used : —

I 'll do my very best.
You can't lift that heavy book.
Don't cry, little girl, don't cry.

Here are the same sentences written without the apostrophe : —

I will do my very best.
You cannot lift that heavy book.
Do not cry, little girl, do not cry.

1. *Find the apostrophe.*
2. *Write the words which have the apostrophe.*
3. *Opposite each of these words write its meaning. Thus,* — I 'll = I will.
4. *See who can make the shortest and clearest rule telling where the apostrophe is used.*

SECTION 77

FOR STUDY AND WRITING

CONTRACTIONS

In the preceding lesson you learned that the apostrophe is used in certain shortened forms like *I'll, can't,* and *don't.* Such forms are called **contractions.**

They are chiefly used in conversation, but are often found in poetry, and in informal letters.

Here is a list of other common **contractions** in which the **apostrophe** must be used : —

e'er, ever;	don't, do not;
ne'er, never;	does n't, does not;
I'm, I am;	did n't, did not;
you'll, you will;	I've, I have;
ma'am, madam;	we're, we are;
is n't, is not;	I'd, I would;
are n't, are not;	I'd, I had;
was n't, was not;	there's, there is;
were n't, were not;	it's, it is;
has n't, has not;	what's, what is;
have n't, have not;	e'en, even;
had n't, had not;	can't, cannot;
won't, will not;	sha'n't, shall not.

Write ten sentences, using contractions. Put the apostrophe in its proper place.

Read your sentences aloud, using both the contractions and the full forms.

SECTION 78

ORAL EXERCISE

CONTRACTIONS

1. I 'm to be Queen o' the May, mother,
   I 'm to be Queen o' the May!

2. An honest man 's the noblest work of God.

3. A foot more light, a step more true
   Ne'er from the heath-flower dashed the dew;
   E'en the slight harebell raised its head
   Elastic from her airy tread.

4. Where there 's a will there 's a way.

Read these selections and tell why the apostrophes are used in each.

Is n't is a contracted form of *is not*.
Are n't is a contracted form of *are not*.
Ain't is an incorrect form, which is sometimes used when the speaker means "am not," "is not," or "are not."

Avoid the use of " ain't."

Does n't is a contraction of *does not*.
Don't is a contraction of *do not*.

Avoid the use of " don't" when " does not" or " does n't " is required.

Observe your own speech, and correct these errors whenever they occur.

SECTION 79

Give reasons for the use of the apostrophes and the capital letters in the following selections.

1. Up the river and o'er the lea,
   That's the way for Billy and me.

2. O velvet bee, you're a dusty fellow,
   You've powdered your legs with gold.

3. Howe'er it be, it seems to me,
   'T is only noble to be good.

4. Is it raining, little flower?
       Be glad of rain.
   Too much sun would wither thee;
       'T will shine again.
   The clouds are very dark, 't is true;
   But right behind them shines the blue.

SECTION 80

WRITTEN EXERCISE

Answer these questions in written statements, using the italicized word or words in your answer.

1. Where *is* John?
   Where *are* my books?

2. Where *was* the pencil?
   Where *were* the crayons?

3. What books *has* Helen *taken*?
   What books *have* the boys *read*?

4. Who *has* Frank's hat?
   Which colors *have* Belle and Frances *chosen*?

5. What *has* George *found*?
   How many letters *have* you *written*?

SECTION 81

FOR READING AND STUDY

Read the following selection from " The Ugly Duckling," by Hans Christian Andersen.

In a sunny spot stood a pleasant old farmhouse, circled all about with deep canals; and, from the walls down to the water's edge, grew great burdocks, so high that under the tallest of them a little child might stand upright. The spot was as wild as if it had been in the very centre of the thick wood.

In this snug retreat sat a duck upon her nest, watching for her young brood to hatch; but the pleasure she had felt at first was almost gone; she had begun to think it a wearisome task, for the little ones were so long in coming out of their shells, and she seldom had visitors. The other ducks liked much better to swim about in the canals than to climb the slippery banks, and sit under the burdock leaves to have a gossip with her. It was a long time to stay so much by herself.

At length, however, one shell cracked, and soon another; and from each came a living creature, that lifted its head and cried, " Peep, peep!"

"Quack, quack!" said the mother; and then they all tried to say it, too, as well as they could, as they looked all about them on every side at the tall, green leaves. Their mother allowed them to look about as much as they liked, because green is good for the eyes.

"What a great world it is, to be sure!" said the little ones, when they found how much more room they had than when they were in the eggshell.

What is described in the first paragraph of the selection from "The Ugly Duckling" on page 59?

What are you told about the farmhouse? Where did it stand? What grew near it? How tall were the burdocks?

What is described in the second paragraph? What does the paragraph tell you about the duck?

What does the third paragraph tell you? the fourth? the fifth?

SECTION 82

WRITTEN EXERCISE

Use in written sentences the words in the columns below. You have found them in "The Ugly Duckling."

Be sure that the sentences mean something to you, and express your thought clearly.

sunny	burdocks	visitors
pleasant	retreat	slippery
farmhouse	wearisome	allowed

SECTIONS 83–85

ORAL AND WRITTEN EXPLANATIONS

83. *Make an explanation, orally and in writing, on each of the following subjects:* —

1. How to Care for the Teeth.
2. How to Take Care of the Eyes.
3. How to Sweep and Dust a Room.

SECTION 86

STUDY OF A PICTURE

HORSES' HEADS. BY J. F. HERRING

These three horses are named Dobbin, Lady White, and Peter. They have been at work all day on the farm. Now they have been freed from their harness, and may rest. But first they go to the big stone trough for the cool water, which they like as well as you and I do.

Write a paragraph telling what you see in the picture, and a second paragraph about the horses and their work.

SECTION 87

For Conversation and Writing

WHAT ANIMALS DO FOR MAN

Everybody knows something about animals. Some of us have taken care of pet animals, — cats, dogs, hens, horses, or cows. We can easily tell what we do for them. We give them food, water, and shelter. Now let us ask what animals do for us.

1. Horses. — Of what use is the horse to us? Name some kinds of work which he does for the farmer; for the lumberman; for the merchant; for the expressman; for the traveller; for you.

What is a young horse called? How is he taught to work for us?

How should we take care of a horse? What does he need? How should we treat him? Can you give examples of kind treatment which you have seen?

2. Dogs. — What do you know about dogs? Have you a pet dog? Tell how he looks. Describe him so clearly that we should recognize him if we met him.

Of what use are dogs? Tell stories that show in what ways dogs are useful.

Do you know of what use the dog is to the shepherd? to travellers in the mountains? to expressmen?

A large express company has the picture of a dog upon all of its express wagons. Can you tell why?

After talking about the lesson, write about either horses or dogs, using the outline.

SECTION 88

For Reading and Study

Study this story until you can read it well.   Then read it aloud in the class, and talk it over.

KINDNESS TO ANIMALS

The wagon was heavily loaded with bars of iron.   It looked too heavy for a single horse to draw.   The patient creature had strained and tugged, until he succeeded in reaching the top of the hill.   Now he must back the heavy load in at the open door of the barn.

"Back, Jim! back!" said the driver, pulling lightly at the reins.

The horse braced his fore feet and pushed, but the wagon did not move.   The man got down from the seat, went to the back of the truck and pulled.

"Back!" he cried.

The horse strained every muscle.

"Back!" cried the driver again.

The wagon moved this time at least a foot.   Once more the driver pulled and the horse pushed, together.

"Back!"

With the last command, the great horse shoved with all his might.   There was a sound of splintering wood, and the wagon rolled back.   Not a blow had been struck.   Only gentle words had been spoken, and the horse had done the rest.   The man went to the horse's head, took his nose in his hands, patted him between the eyes, and said: —

"Good old Jim! You did it, did n't you? I knew you would."

The horse rubbed his nose against the man's cheek.

Read this poem carefully : —

A CHILD'S THOUGHT OF GOD

They say that God lives very high;
　But if you look above the pines
You cannot see our God; and why?

And if you dig down in the mines,
　You never see Him in the gold;
Though from Him all that's glory shines.

God is so good, He wears a fold
　Of heaven and earth across His face,
Like secrets kept for love untold.

But still I feel that His embrace
　Slides down by thrills through all things made,
Through sight and sound of every place.

As if my tender mother laid
　On my shut lips her kisses' pressure,
Half waking me at night, and said,
　"Who kissed you through the dark, dear
　　guesser?"

Mrs. Browning.

In reading this poem you observe not only that
the name of God begins with a capital letter, but
also that every word which refers to Him is written
with a capital. This is a rule which you should
remember.

**Every word denoting the Deity should begin with a
capital letter.**

SECTION 90

FOR STUDY

OWNERSHIP OR POSSESSION

Mary owns a book. We speak of it as Mary's book. " Mary's book is full of pictures," Jane says. Frank owns a knife. " This is Frank's knife," we say.

In the following sentences are words which indicate ownership. Find them.

Washington's home was called Mount Vernon.
I found Kate's apple.
Henry's book lies on the table.
William's paper is blotted.

In each of these sentences, look for some sign which is found only in the words which indicate ownership.

What sign do you find ?   You already know its name.

Ownership or **possession** is often shown in writing by adding an **apostrophe** and s to the name of the owner or owners.   If the name of the owners ends in s, the **apostrophe only** is added.   Thus, —

A boy owns a ball.	The boy's ball.
Two boys together own a ball.	The boys' ball.
The men own a horse.	The men's horse.
A man owns a horse.	A man's horse.
Mary owns a book.	Mary's book.
John owns a book.	John's book.

SECTION 91

WRITING NAMES OF OWNERS

1. The boat which belongs to John is drifting away.
   John's boat is drifting away.
2. The book which you gave to Mary is lost.
   Mary's book is lost.
3. The house owned by Mr. Brown is burned.
   Mr. Brown's house is burned.
4. That man has a black band on his hat.
   That *man's* hat has a black band on it.

Make five pairs of sentences like these.

The second sentence of each pair must contain the owner's name, written with the **'s**, to show **ownership**.

SECTION 92

OWNERSHIP OR POSSESSION

Mention five objects whose owners you know.

Use the owner's name in describing each of the objects.

Use these names in written sentences, showing the ownership by the use of the apostrophe and s.

SECTION 93

WRITTEN EXERCISE

Write five sentences in which you need to use the apostrophe in contractions, and five in which it marks possession.

SECTION 94

Explain orally the use of the apostrophe in each of the following sentences : —

1. It's a long lane that has no turning.
2. Marion's men were famous soldiers.
3. A cloud has hidden the moon's face from my sight.
4. 'T is November, and the winter is coming on.
5. Hannah's at the window, binding shoes.
6. I've travelled east, I've travelled west.
7. Now that the winter's gone, the earth hath lost
   Her snow-white robes.
8. Notes from the lark I'll borrow.
9. My heart's in the Highlands.
10. In a cowslip's bell I lie ;
    There I couch when owls do cry,
    On the bat's back I do fly.

SECTION 95

PATTERN SENTENCES

Copy these sentences. Make others like them, using the italicized words.

1. John *throws* the ball well.
   He *threw* it over the apple tree yesterday.
   He *has thrown* it over the barn.
2. *May* I *drive* Dobbin to-day, father?
   Jack *drove* him yesterday, and Kate *has driven* him three times.
3. *May* I *take* your pencil, Mary?
   You *took* my blue pencil yesterday, you know, and Robert *has taken* my lead pencil.

SECTION 96

Copy "The Village Blacksmith," by Longfellow (Selections, page 10), and learn the poem by heart.

What does the poem tell you of the character of the blacksmith? How does it describe his appearance? What makes him so strong? How does the poem describe his strength?

What does the second stanza tell you of the blacksmith's character? the third? the fourth? Why do the children come so freely? The fifth and sixth stanzas tell you more yet about what the blacksmith does and how he feels.

In the last two stanzas Longfellow is thinking of others as well as of the smith. Do you know any one whom the seventh stanza describes?

What does the poet think as he sees the smith work at his anvil? "Life has its forge, too. We are hammering out our fortunes. We, too, are shaping, not red-hot iron, but burning deeds and thoughts."

SECTION 97

A FAMOUS LETTER

You have enjoyed reading "Hiawatha" and "The Village Blacksmith," which Mr. Longfellow wrote for you. When he was a little boy, living in Portland, Maine, his father went to Boston, many miles away. He wished to tell his father something; but of course he could not talk to him. So he wrote a letter to tell what he wanted. Here is the letter. When you look at it, you will see that his father could understand the boy's thoughts and wishes by reading the written words quite as easily as if they had been talking together.

PORTLAND, January, 1814.

DEAR PAPA,

Ann wants a Bible like little Betsy's. Will you please buy her one if you can find any in Boston?

I have been to school all the week, and got only seven marks. I shall have a billet on Monday.

I wish you to buy me a drum.

H. W. L.

Could you have done so well?

SECTION 98

FOR READING AND STUDY

LETTER WRITING

Every village, town, or city has its **post-office,** and every one who reads this book knows where the post-office is. Even in the smallest town it is a busy place. Nearly every passing train brings a mail bag, which is thrown out at the station. This bag is made of strong leather, riveted with brass, and fastened by a heavy strap and padlock. It contains **letters** for the people of the town.

A man whose duty it is to carry the mail takes the bag from the station to the post-office. Sometimes a crowd of people await the coming of the mail, every one hoping that the bag contains some message for him.

The postmaster sorts and distributes the treasures, putting every letter in its proper place or box. How eagerly people gather about the little window, when it is opened, and ask for their letters!

If the post-office is in a large city, the mail bags are many and full, and are carried from the station to the post-office in large mail wagons, which are finely painted. An army of clerks is needed to sort and distribute the tons of letters which arrive every day. Machines are used to stamp and count the letters. The post-office is like a busy factory, with many men constantly coming and going.

In the city the letters are taken from house to house by the mail carriers, men in gray uniform with brass buttons. Sometimes these carriers use whistles to announce their coming. A merry sound it is, the postman's whistle. It says, very plainly, "Here is a letter for you. You had better hurry and get it!"

Why are these letters so welcomed? Why are the post-offices so crowded and the mail wagons so heavily loaded? Why are the little folded sheets of paper so carefully borne from town to town, from state to state, from country to country?

"Ah!" you say, "I know why. The letters are *more* than folded squares of paper. They come from our friends to us, bearing messages. They tell us our friends' thoughts."

In old times there were no railroads to carry the mail, but coaches, drawn by prancing horses, rolled merrily into the towns, bringing letters as

The Old Mail Coach. By Charles Hunt

well as passengers. Letters came more slowly then. You may be sure they were warmly welcomed.

Can you imagine what would happen if no letters were sent from friend to friend, or if nobody knew how to write letters? If you can, you will soon discover why so many are written, and why everybody wants to learn how to write them.

Do you know how? Should you like to learn?

SECTION 99

THE POST-OFFICE

Tell what you know about your post-office.
Where is it? Describe the building. Who is postmaster? Did you ever post a letter? How did
you do it? Did you ever receive a letter? How
did it come to you?

Who pays for building the post-office? Who
pays the postman? Who pays the railroads for
carrying the letters? Do you pay anything when
you mail a letter? Suppose you send a letter to
New York or to San Francisco. How far does it
travel? How much does it cost you? Who takes
care of the letter on the way? What more do you
know that the government does for you?

SECTION 100

WRITTEN EXERCISE

POSTAGE STAMPS

*Write a paragraph answering each of the follow-
ing questions :* —

What is a postage stamp? What does it cost?
By whom are the postage stamps made? Describe
the different kinds of stamps which you have seen.
What is a cancelled stamp? Why is it cancelled?

SECTION 101

WRITTEN EXERCISE

A LETTER

This letter was written by Mabel Hood, a little girl eight years old. She was staying at her summer home on an island in a beautiful lake. She wrote the letter to her cousin, whose name was Dorothy, to tell her how she was spending the vacation.

Copy this letter carefully.
See if it obeys all the rules that you have learned about capital letters.

Lakeland, Mass.,
July 10, 1907.

Dear Dorothy,

Papa brought me your letter yesterday. I was glad to get it. We have been here two weeks. Every day is full of fun. We play on the rocks by the lake, and dig in the sand.

The squirrels come to our door, and eat nuts from our hands. Kate and I scatter corn for them. Harold saw a rabbit in the woods yesterday. I think it is the one that ate up our lettuce. A bird has built a nest in a hollow tree near our house. Mamma says it is a woodpecker. A chickadee lives somewhere near us. I hear him every morning.

I wish you were here. Come as soon as you can.

Your loving cousin,
Mabel Hood.

SECTION 102

FOR CONVERSATION

Observe the paragraphs in Mabel's letter.

What does each paragraph tell Dorothy?

SECTION 103

For Study

THE PARTS OF A LETTER

Every letter is written to **carry a message** from the writer to somebody else.

A letter should not only carry the message, but should also tell **by whom** it is written, **to whom** it is written, **when** it is written, and **where** it is written.

Study Mabel's letter in Section 101.

By whom was it written?
To whom was it written?
Where was it written?
When was it written?
What message did it carry?

It is customary to use a certain order in writing letters. By studying Mabel's letter you will learn the usual arrangement of the parts of a letter.

These parts are : —

1. **The Heading.**

Lakeland, Mass.,
July 10, 1907.

This tells **where** the letter was written, and **when** it was written.

2. The Salutation.

Dear Dorothy,

This shows **to whom** the letter was written. Sometimes the salutation is very dignified and formal, but in this letter it is informal and friendly.

3. The Body of the Letter.

This tells **the message.**

4. The Ending.

Your loving cousin,

This is a **polite** or **friendly phrase** which expresses the feeling of the writer toward the receiver of the letter, or shows the relation in which they stand to each other. In this case Mabel is Dorothy's cousin. A friend's letter might use the words, " Yours sincerely" or " Yours with love." A business letter might end with " Yours truly," or " Yours respectfully."

5. The Signature.

Mabel Hood.

This is the **name of the writer.**

SECTION 104

A Pattern Letter

Copy the letter that is given below.

When you are learning to write letters, you may use this as a pattern.

Maywood, Ill.,
March 3, 1908.

My dear Mother,

I reached Maywood safely last night, although my train was an hour late. Uncle Jack met me at the station.

Aunt Kate says she should like to have me stay a month. May I? I should miss you and Baby, but I like to play on the farm.

Please write often, or I shall be homesick.

Your loving son,
Harold May.

The Use of Titles

You have already learned that a person's name consists of his **given name** and his **family name** (p. 16). Besides these it is customary in writing, and often in speaking, to use a **title** when we refer to a person or address him.

Thus, John Smith's name is plain *John Smith;* but a letter written to him should be addressed to *Mr. John Smith,* or *John Smith, Esq.,* and his friends and acquaintances usually call him *Mr. Smith.*

If he were the captain of a military company, his title would be *Captain,* and he would be addressed as *Captain John Smith.* If he were a physician, he would be called *Dr. John Smith,* or *Dr. Smith,* or we might write his name *John Smith, M.D.* If he were a Member of Congress, he would be spoken of as the *Honorable John Smith.*

These **titles,** and others like them, are **terms of respect** and **courteous address.** *Mr.* is used in addressing a man. *Mrs.* is the title of a married woman, and *Miss* is prefixed to the name of a woman who is unmarried. Mr. John Smith's wife is *Mrs. John Smith.* His daughter is *Miss Smith.* His son, if he is too young to be called *Mr.,* is *Master Smith.*

The titles *Mr.* and *Mrs.* are never written in full. *Esquire, Reverend, Doctor,* and military titles are usually shortened (or abbreviated). The same is also true of most titles that follow a person's name, as *M. D.* Other titles are frequently abbreviated in various ways, but it is best to write them out fully in letters and other documents addressed directly to a person.

Every title attached to a person's name should begin with a capital letter. If a title is abbreviated, it should be followed by a period.

A title that follows the name of a person is separated from it by a comma.

NOTE. — The titles *Master* and *Miss* are not followed by periods, since they are not abbreviations.

Study the following examples : —

Capt. John Smith attempted to settle Virginia.

Gen. Garfield was born in Ohio.

Dr. French is a cousin of the Rev. Oliver T. Brooks.

My father's name is Eliot P. Snow, Jr.

Address your letter to Henry T. Barnes, Esq.

Dr. Winthrop's sign reads, "Charles Winthrop, M. D."

SECTION 106

WRITTEN EXERCISE

Write the names and titles of ten persons of whom you have read or heard.

SECTION 107

How to Address an Envelope

Harold May's letter (p. 77) was sent in an
envelope, upon which he wrote the **address**. Here
is a picture of the envelope. In addressing envelopes you may use this as a pattern.*

Mrs. Edwin D. May

West Ottawa

Illinois

Copy the address of Harold's letter.

*Write the addresses of two persons whom you
know.*

*In writing names and titles, remember what you
have learned about the use of capitals and periods.*

* For the omission of commas in addresses, the teacher is referred
to the Preface.

SECTION 108

ORAL EXERCISE

STUDY OF A LETTER

MAYNARD, CONN.,
DEAR COUSIN TED,   Feb. 14, 1910.

To-day is a holiday.   It snows so hard that nobody can get to school.   The drifts are three feet deep.   We all are snow-bound, even papa, who could not plough through the drifts to the station.

I wish you were here.   What fun we might have!   The wind howls down the chimney, and the snow is heaped against the windows.   This is just the time for games and books and candy-making.   Elsie promises to make some caramels this evening.   But the best fun will come when we get out into the snow and dig caves and make forts.

Jack Marlow has gone to the Latin School, and now he tries to put some Latin into everything he says.   He'll get over that.

Dobbin is lame, and old Kate has to do all the work now.   My white Leghorns are beauties.   I am to have a garden next summer.   Come and help me to take care of it. You must have a sorry time living in the city.

Elsie says, "Tell Ted I had to tell you what to say." Perhaps that is so, and perhaps you can guess which parts of the letter are Elsie's.

Don't forget to come.

Your cousin,
GEORGE ELWYN.

Elsie wants me to write a postscript, but I'll do nothing of the sort.   G.

Study George's letter to his cousin Ted.
See if it contains all the parts of a letter.

Where was it written?
When was it written?
To whom was it written?
What message does each paragraph bring?
How does the letter end?
Who wrote it?

Answer the same questions about Harold's letter on page 77.

SECTION 109

For Study

THE DATE OF A LETTER

The **date** of an event is the time when the event occurs. Thus you may say, "Our ball game will take place on the first of September," or "The date of our ball game is September first." "The great snowstorm came last February," or "The date of the great snowstorm was February 15, 1910." In each case you are giving a **date**.

The **date of a letter** shows the time when it was written. The date should tell the **month,** the **day of the month,** and the **year.**

Find the dates in the letters in this book.
Observe the punctuation and arrangement of each line in the headings of the letters.

SECTION 110

FOR STUDY

HOW DATES ARE WRITTEN

For convenience in writing **dates,** we often shorten or **abbreviate** the name of the month. Here are the **abbreviations** commonly used: —

Jan.	= January	Aug.	= August
Feb.	= February	Sept.	= September
Mar.	= March	Oct.	= October
Apr.	= April	Nov.	= November
	Dec.	= December	

May, June, and *July* should never be abbreviated; and it is better to write *March* and *April* in full, although the abbreviations given above are allowed.

Every abbreviation should be followed by a period.

The following dates are correctly written and punctuated: —

July 4, 1776.	Feb. 22, 1723.
Aug. 10, 1793.	Sept. 18, 1845.
Jan. 8, 1815.	April 30, 1789.
Oct. 31, 1899.	Nov. 5, 1897.
Dec. 25, 1890.	March 4, 1909.
June 9, 1875.	Oct. 20, 1910.

Copy these dates carefully.
Be sure to punctuate them correctly.

SECTION 111

Written Exercise

Write the date of your last birthday.

Write the date of to-morrow.

Write the date of last Christmas.

Write the dates of five events which you remember.

Write a sentence in which you name a holiday in the first month, giving its exact date.

Do the same for the second month ; the fifth ; the seventh ; the ninth ; the twelfth.

Write a sentence telling wnen America was discovered by Columbus.

SECTION 112

Written Exercise

Rewrite the following sentences, using abbreviations for the names of the months.

1. Longfellow was born on February 27, 1807.
2. Forefathers' Day is celebrated December 22.
3. New Year's Day comes on January 1.
4. September 4 will be Labor Day.
5. February 12 is the anniversary of Lowell's birthday.
6. Hallowe'en is celebrated on October 31.
7. The Boston Tea Party occurred on December 16, 1773.
8. Thanksgiving Day fell on November 30 in 1899.
9. Washington's Birthday, February 22, is a holiday.
10. Columbus discovered America on October 12, 1492.

SECTION 113

For Reading and Telling

THE LION AND THE MOUSE

A little mouse, who was playing in the woods, carelessly ran so near a sleeping lion that she was caught beneath his heavy paw. The lion could easily have crushed her to death; but the mouse begged so piteously that he lifted his foot and set her free.

Not long after, the lion was caught in a hunter's net. He struggled to free himself, but every movement twisted the cords more tightly about him. He knew that he must lose his life if he could not escape before the hunters arrived. He roared frightfully and struggled wildly, but in vain. Just then a little mouse appeared, ran up across his broad shoulders, and whispered in his ear: "Keep quiet a moment, and I will set you free."

"You?" said the lion, "you tiny creature?"

"Yes, I," said the mouse; "just wait and see."

The lion lay quiet and helpless. The mouse began to gnaw the cords; first one and then another she cut with her tiny, sharp teeth.

"Now stretch yourself," she said to the lion.

With one great bound the lion freed himself from the net. "What can I do for you?" he cried, looking gratefully upon his tiny helper.

"Ah," said the mouse, "you do not remember? There was once a time when you saved *my* life."

Read this fable; then tell the story.

What does the fable tell you of the character of the lion? of the mouse?

SECTION 114

WRITTEN EXERCISE

Write about either the lion or the mouse. Arrange what you have to say in paragraphs.

Where does it live? How large is it? How does it look?

What does it eat? What are its habits? What is it afraid of?

Do you know any proverb about it? If you do, write the proverb.

SECTION 115

WRITTEN EXERCISE

Write a note to your teacher, explaining that you were absent from school yesterday because it was raining and you were not well enough to go out in the rain.

Make an envelope for your note, and write the address upon it.

SECTION 116

WRITTEN EXERCISE

Write a note to a friend, asking him to lend you a certain book to use in getting your lessons. Tell him that you will take good care of the book and will return it to him next Monday.

SECTION 117

FOR STUDY

Mr. Newell lives in a large city, where carriers deliver the mail at the homes or offices of the persons addressed. It is very necessary, in such cases, that the address should include the name of the street and the number of the house. Thus, —

> Mr. John Eliot Newell
> 65 State Street
> Richmond
> Virginia

Mr. Ashton lives in a small town, where everybody is well known. He either calls for his own mail or sends for it. In such cases the name of the street is not included in the address.

If Mr. Ashton is a stranger or a newcomer, he may ask his friends to write upon his letters the number of the post-office box which he has hired. This will prevent any delay in obtaining the letter. The number of the box should be written in the left-hand lower corner of the envelope.

The words *Street* and *Avenue* are often abbreviated in addresses: thus, — *St.*, *Ave.* The name of the State may be abbreviated or written in full, as one chooses.

SECTION 118

ADDRESSES

Cut out ten oblong pieces of paper to represent envelopes. Upon each piece write one of the following addresses, as you would write it upon an envelope.

1. Your father's address.
2. Your teacher's address.
3. Your own address.
4. The address of William O. Pratt, who is a physician living in Ithaca, New York. His office is at 224 Union Square.
5. Walter D. Hyde lives in Germantown, Pennsylvania. His office is Room 49, in the Century Building.
6. H. W. Randolph owns a seed farm at Rockford, Illinois.
7. Miss Anna Carey Dwight lives in Savannah, Georgia, at the Hampshire Arms.
8. Frank Mortimer, Junior, has an office in the Phœnix Building, Grand Rapids, Michigan.
9. Owen H. Hunt lives in Maynard Place, Dorchester, Massachusetts.
10. Mrs. John R. Brainerd lives in Lynn, Massachusetts, at 1308 Marlborough St.

The stamp belongs in the upper right-hand corner of the envelope. It should be fixed in its place neatly and accurately, with its edges parallel to those of the envelope.

Indicate the place for a stamp upon each envelope.

SECTION 119

FOR READING AND CONVERSATION

DAFFYDOWNDILLY

Daffydowndilly
    Came up in the cold,
        Through the brown mould,
Although the March breezes
    Blew keen on her face,
Although the white snow
    Lay on many a place.

Daffydowndilly
    Had heard underground
        The sweet rushing sound
Of the streams, as they broke
    From their white winter chains,
Of the whistling spring winds
    And the pattering rains.

"Now then," thought Daffy,
    Deep down in her heart,
    "It's time I should start."
So she pushed her soft leaves
    Through the hard frozen ground,
Quite up to the surface,
    And then she looked round.

There was snow all about her,
    Gray clouds overhead;
    The trees all looked dead.
Then how do you think
    Poor Daffydown felt,

When the sun would not shine
  And the ice would not melt?

"Cold weather!" thought Daffy,
  Still working away.
  "The earth's hard to-day!
There's but a half-inch
  Of my leaves to be seen,
And two-thirds of that
  Is more yellow than green.

"I can't do much yet;
  But I do what I can.
  It's well I began!
For, unless I can manage
  To lift up my head,
The people will think
  That the Spring herself's dead."

So, little by little,
  She brought her leaves out,
  All clustered about;
And then her bright flowers
  Began to unfold,
Till Daffy stood robed
  In her spring green and gold.

O Daffydowndilly,
  So brave and so true,
  I wish all were like you!
So ready for duty
  In all sorts of weather,
And loyal to courage
  And duty together.

                                MISS WARNER.

The poem on pages 89 and 90 describes a daffodil. Many children know the bright yellow blossom which lifts it head so early in the year. In some mild climates it grows wild and is one of the most beautiful and most welcome signs of spring.

Describe the time when Daffydowndilly came.

What signs of spring had she heard underground ?

What were the " white winter chains " of the streams ?

What words in the poem describe the winds, the rains, and the sound of the storms ?

Why did Daffy think it was time for her to start ?

How did she make her way upward ?

What did she see ? How did she feel ? What did she say ?

How did Daffy look in her spring dress ?

Ask your teacher if she will kindly read Words-worth's "Daffodils" to you.

SECTIONS 120–121

120. *Read "Daffydowndilly" again. Then make sentences, using these words so as to show that you understand their meaning :* — mould, keen, rushing sound, whistling winds, pattering rains, surface, overhead, manage, clustered, unfold, robed, duty, courage, loyal.

121. *Describe the daffodil, if you have seen the flower. If not, study the picture and see what you can learn from it.*

Describe some other flower that blossoms in the spring. Tell where you find it and how you recognize its leaf and its blossoms. Then compare it with the daffodil.

SECTION 122

EXPLANATION *

Children, and grown persons too, are always asking to have things **explained** to them.

You can remember many questions of this kind that you have asked of your friends. "What makes it rain?" "What makes it snow?" "Why do the leaves fall in the autumn?" "How do you make a pudding?" "Why does wood float and iron sink?" are perhaps some of these questions.

You have been making explanations almost all your life. When you tell your little brother or sister how to play a game, you are making an explanation. Your recitations at school are often explanations of what you have learned from books, or of something that your teacher has already explained to you. It is very important to be able to make an explanation clearly. If it is not clear, you can hardly call it an explanation at all.

Try to think (1) of five things that you believe you can explain; (2) of five things that you would like to have explained to you.

Write these subjects down, each in the form of a question beginning with "How," or "What makes."
Thus, —

How do you learn to swim?
What makes it rain?

* Explanation is also called **exposition**.

SECTIONS 123–124

123. *Ask your teacher to explain how rain is caused. Repeat the explanation orally. Write it.*

124. *Repeat the exercise in Section 123, using the question, "How does indoor air often become impure?"*

SECTIONS 125–127

125. *Write a note to your teacher, asking if you may be excused from school at three o'clock. Give your reason.*

126. *Write a note, asking some friend to spend a week with you. Address the note properly.*

127. *Write your friend's reply, explaining why he cannot visit you.*

SECTION 128

THE FOX AND THE GRAPES

A fox went out to walk early in the morning, one fine day in summer. By the side of the road he saw a tree. Beside the tree grew a beautiful vine, which had fastened itself to the sturdy boughs. The fox saw the purple grapes hanging from the vine, and wished to get some, for he was very fond of grapes. He jumped and jumped and jumped, but he could not reach even the lowest cluster.

"What do you think I care?" he said, as he went away disappointed. "Everybody knows that your old grapes are sour."

Read the story; then tell it orally.

SECTION 129

For Study

THE COMMA

One of the commonest **marks of punctuation** is the **comma.** You have seen it many times in books, but you have not yet learned its use. Like other marks of punctuation, it has helped you to understand the sentences which you have read.

Its use is to break up the sentences into parts, so as to make the meaning plainer.

There are many rules for the use of the **comma.** One simple rule you are ready to learn.

Observe the use of the comma in these examples :—

Mary, please lend me your book.
Come here, Frank, and let me brush your coat.
Friends, I come not here to talk.
Come to me, O ye children, for I hear you at your play.
There is your brother on the playground, Jack.

You will discover that each of these sentences is **addressed** to some person or persons named in the sentence. In every case the name of the **person addressed** is set off by **commas.** This is a common custom, and you can easily begin to practise it now.

Find sentences in your reading book which follow the custom which you have just observed.

SECTION 130

Exercise for Dictation

Study the sentences which follow.

Observe the words or phrases which name the persons addressed. See how they follow the custom which you observed in Section 129.

1. Where are you going, my pretty maid?
2. Santa Claus, come down the chimney.
3. So now, pretty robin, you've come to my door.
4. Run, little Bess, and open the door for your father.
5. My fairest child, I have no song to give you.
6. Sing on, sweet thrush, upon the lifeless bough.
7. Boatman, do not tarry.
8. Guard thy lips, my child.
9. Will you buy a paper, sir?
10. Love thy mother, little one.

SECTION 131

Notice the punctuation after yes *and* no *in the following sentences :* —

1. Are you going to New York to-morrow?
   Yes, if it does not rain.
2. Shall you go by boat?
   No, for it takes too much time.
3. Do you not enjoy the journey by boat?
   Yes, for the Hudson is very beautiful.
4. Have you ever travelled by night?
   No, but I should like to try it.

Yes and *no* are set off from the rest of the sentence by a comma.

FOR STUDY

THE COMMA IN A SERIES

Read the following paragraph.

John Jones has a " variety store." He sells butter, eggs, hammers, hooks, linen, cotton, small wares of all sorts, wash-tubs, stoves, carpets, and curtains. Everything that you want may be obtained at this convenient establishment.

In the second sentence of the paragraph you have just read, you find a long list of the articles which John Jones sells. Such a list of words is often called a **series.**

The name of every article in this **series** except the last is followed by a **comma.** You will find a similar **series of words** in each of the sentences which follow.

1. Here are cinnamon, cloves, allspice, and nutmeg for your pudding.

2. Have you your paper, pencil, book, and slate ?

3. Hurry, Joe! it is school time. Here are your coat, hat, overshoes, and muffler.

4. The grocer sells sugar, tea, meal, flour, nuts, and raisins.

5. The carpenter uses hammer, nails, rule, saw, and plane.

6. I saw Grace, Ella, John, Julia, and Frank on their way to school.

7. Europe, Asia, Africa, and Australia are in the Eastern Hemisphere.

The rule for the use of the comma in a **series** applies to every word in the series except the last. This may have no mark of punctuation after it (as in the sixth and seventh examples); but if it ends the sentence, it is of course followed by that mark of punctuation which the meaning of the sentence requires.

SECTIONS 133–134

133. *See if you can find in your reading book, or elsewhere, sentences containing a series of words.*

Observe the punctuation in every such sentence.

Copy the sentences and bring them to school.

134. *Study these passages and observe the use of the commas. Be ready to write the passages from dictation, using capitals and marks of punctuation in their proper places.*

1. Tom, Harry, Jack, and Joe are going to a picnic. They have cake, apples, tarts, and buns in their lunch basket. The picnic is at Island Grove. There are swings, hammocks, ponies, and bicycles at the grove. The boys will have fine sport.

2. Pepper, cloves, nutmeg, and cinnamon are found in tropical countries. Corn, rye, wheat, oats, and potatoes are natives of the temperate zone.

3. Hedge, ditch, meadow, field, and even the very paths and highways, are set thick with primroses.

4. James has been a great traveller. He has visited England, France, Germany, and Italy.

SECTION 135

FOR STUDY

THE HYPHEN

It often happens in writing that for lack of room a word has to be divided at the end of a line. If you look through Section 1 you will find a number of examples. Whenever a word is so divided, a small mark or sign called the **hyphen** (-) is used.

Find in Section 1 words which are divided at the end of the line, and note the use of the hyphen in every such instance.

When a word is divided at the end of a line, that part of the word which remains on the line must be followed by a hyphen. The division must always be made between two syllables.

For example: — *walking* would be divided thus, *walk-ing*. *Company* might be divided thus, *com-pany* or *compa-ny*.

It is plain that you must know how to divide a word into syllables in order to know how to divide it at the end of the line. This you have doubtless already learned in your spelling lessons

A word of one syllable should never be divided.

Find in your reading book ten examples of words divided at the end of the line.

Copy them, showing the position of the hyphen.

Separate ten words on this page into syllables, as you do in oral spelling.

SECTION 136

The **hyphen** is also used in writing many words which consist of two or more words put together to make one: as, — *to-day, to-morrow, three-cornered, father-in-law, thirty-one.*

Such words must be learned from the spelling book or dictionary, and by observation in reading.

See if you can find examples of such words in your reading book, or in the " Selections to be Committed to Memory."

SECTION 137

Use these words in written sentences.

take	write	do	go
took	wrote	did	went
taken	written	done	gone

SECTION 138

Ask questions in each of which you use a word from the following list. The questions may be answered orally by the class.

do	come	tear	show
did	came	tore	showed
done	stand	torn	shown
sing	stood	break	forget
sang	win	broke	forgot
sung	won	broken	forgotten

SECTIONS 139-140

139. *Study the following sentences. Notice how the italicized words show the time of the action.*

1. The wind *blows* hard to-day.
2. It *blew* almost as hard yesterday.
3. I think it *will blow* forever.
4. It *has blown* hard for a week.
5. It blew harder last Tuesday than it *had blown* for a month before.
6. I hope it soon *will have blown* enough.

140. *Find similar words, or groups of words, in the sentences below : —*

1. Sarah has broken her arm.
2. I have not seen Jack since Monday.
3. My dog has been stolen.
4. The wind shook the house.
5. The balloon had risen to a great height.
6. He was thrown from my horse.
7. You and I have seen each other seldom.
8. Tom had drawn a picture of a tiger.
9. I don't know who did it.
10. The earthquake has done much damage.
11. Does n't he remember where he saw me ?
12. The children's carriage has not yet come.
13. Gertrude came to Utica last Friday.
14. Sarah will come to school to-morrow.
15. I shall learn a poem next Friday.
16. Tom has known me for five years.

After *have, has, had, am, are, is, was, were,* say *written, taken, broken,* and so on, not *wrote, took, broke.*

SECTION 141

*Copy the passage from Whittier's " Barefoot Boy "
beginning " Oh for boyhood's time of June," and
ending " Fashioned for a barefoot boy " (Selections,
pages 21–22).*

Commit the extract to memory.

Talk about the poem.

*Tell what you learn from it about the boyhood of
the poet who wrote it.*

*Tell anything that the poem shows you about the
poet's character.*

SECTIONS 142–144

LETTER WRITING

142. Your mother is visiting her sister in Utica.

*Write a letter to her, telling her what you are doing in
school, and what has happened at home since she went away.
Arrange your letter in paragraphs, telling one kind of thing
in each.*

You must not forget to tell her that you miss her at
home, and that you often speak of her.

Make an envelope for your letter and address it neatly.

143. *Write a note of thanks to your Uncle Horace, who
sent you a bicycle yesterday as a birthday gift.*

144. *Write a letter to your friend Frances Aiken, telling
her how you learned to row a boat.*

*Explain to her how you sat in the boat, how you held the
oars, and so on. Make your explanation as clear as you can.*

SECTION 145

STUDY OF A PICTURE

THE PET BIRD

The name of the picture on page 103 is "The Pet Bird," but the artist means to show you something more than the canary.

Study the picture.
Tell all that you can about the children.
Tell all that you can about the room and its furniture.

Meyer von Bremen was a German artist who lived from 1813 to 1886. He loved to paint pictures of children. Every one who likes children enjoys his pictures.

The children whom you see in his pictures are German children, and the houses which he painted are German houses. Do you see anything in the dress of the children, or the furniture of the room, which is unlike our dress and our furniture?

Turn back to the picture of "The Queen's Birthday" (page 36). The children in that picture are Dutch children. Do they look different from the German boys and girls in "The Pet Bird"? How?

Turn to the picture of "Playing Indian" (page 10), and notice the dress of the two boys in front of the wigwam.

THE PET BIRD. BY MEYER VON BREMEN

SECTION 146

ORAL EXERCISE

OBSERVATION OF THE CANARY

Look at the canary closely, to see what he can do.

Describe his movements. Are they slow or rapid? Does he move often or seldom? Does he walk or hop? Does he jump or fly?

What use does he make of his wings? How do they help him?

Observe the canary as he uses his bill. Is it hard or soft? long or short? pointed or blunt? stout or slender? What does he do with it? How is the bill suited to such work?

Observe the canary's foot. Describe it. Draw it. Look at it as it clasps the perch. How many toes has it in front? How many behind? What can the canary do with his feet?

Observe the canary when he drinks. Describe his movements in drinking.

Watch the bird while he dresses his feathers. What are his tools?

What does the canary eat? What does he drink?

Compare the canary with some other bird which you know well. In what ways are the birds alike? In what respects are they different?

SECTION 147

Study of a Poem

On pages 18–19 of the Selections you will find " The Sandpiper," a poem by Celia Thaxter. You should read it carefully two or three times until you think you understand it.

Read the poem again and think of the place which it describes.

Find all the words or phrases which help you to see the beach and to feel the coming storm. Have you ever been on the seashore ?

Read the poem again, thinking about the sand-piper. Have you ever seen a sandpiper ? What does the poem tell you about him ?

In the last stanza the poet tells you the thought which sustains her in the storm, and you learn the secret of her sympathy for the little sandpiper. What is the truth which she means to suggest ?

Commit the poem to memory.

SECTION 148

Pattern Sentences

Copy the following sentences.

Use the italicized words in other sentences, telling what the persons or animals do.

1. The *girl* runs.
   Girls run.
2. The *boy* skates.
   Boys skate.
3. The *dog* barks.
   Dogs bark.
4. The *bird* flies.
   Birds fly.
5. The *teamster* drives his horse.
   Teamsters drive horses.
6. The *farmer* ploughs his field.
   Farmers plough their fields.

SECTION 149

Copy these sentences. Then make others like them, using one of the italicized words in each sentence.

1. Mary *comes* to school every day.
   The children *come* for their dinner.
2. John *goes* to the store for a book.
   The boys *go* to the playground to play.
3. Ethel *runs* fast.
   Boys *run* faster than girls.
4. Jack *drives* the cows home.
   The lumbermen *drive* the logs.
5. The book *lies* on the table.
   The books *lie* on the table.
6. The bricklayer *lays* bricks.
   Bricklayers *lay* bricks.
7. Mary *sits* at the window.
   The pupils *sit* at their desks.
8. Rachel *sets* the table.
   Physicians *set* broken limbs.

SECTION 150

FOR STUDY

QUOTATION MARKS

We have learned the use of the **period,** the **interrogation point,** and the **apostrophe** in making clear the sense of what we read. In this lesson we shall study other marks of punctuation, called **quotation marks.**

You will find such **quotation marks** in the following selection. By studying the poem you will discover their use.

" Lady Moon, Lady Moon, where are you roving ? "
        " Over the sea."
" Lady Moon, Lady Moon, whom are you loving ? "
        " All that love me."

" Are you not tired with rolling, and never
        Resting to sleep ?
Why look so pale and so sad, as forever
        Wishing to weep ? "

" Ask me not this, little child, if you love **me;**
        You are too bold ;
I must obey my dear Father above me
        And do as I 'm told."

LORD HOUGHTON.

In this poem a child is talking with the moon.

Read the first question. Who asks it ?

Copy the first question, carefully noting the marks of punctuation at the beginning and the end.

What is the reply? Who says " Over the sea "?

Copy the reply, noting every mark of punctuation.

What new marks of punctuation do you find? Where do you find them?

The marks which enclose the question are **quotation marks.** Those which enclose the reply are also **quotation marks.**

Find other quotation marks in the selection, and tell what they enclose.

The poem recites the exact words of a conversation between the moon and the child. If the quotation marks were omitted, we should find it hard to tell what part is the moon's and what part is the child's.

Whenever, in writing, the exact words of a person are used (or *quoted*), these words are enclosed in **quotation marks.** The quoted words are called a **direct quotation.**

SECTION 151

WRITTEN EXERCISE

Copy the poem on page 107 carefully, inserting all the quotation marks.

Write it correctly from memory.

SECTION 152

For Study

THE BABY

" Where did you come from, baby dear ? "
" Out of the everywhere into the here."

" Where did you get your eyes so blue ? "
" Out of the sky as I came through."

" What makes the light in them sparkle and spin ? "
" Some of the starry spikes left in."

" Where did you get that little tear ? "
" I found it waiting when I got here."

" What makes your forehead so smooth and high ? "
" A soft hand stroked it as I went by."

" What makes your cheek like a warm white rose ? "
" Something better than any one knows."

" Whence that three-cornered smile of bliss ? "
" Three angels gave me at once a kiss."

" Where did you get that pearly ear ? "
" God spoke, and it came out to hear."

" Where did you get those arms and hands ? "
" Love made itself into hooks and bands."

" Feet, whence did you come, you darling things ? "
" From the same box as the cherub's wings."

" How did they all just come to be you ? "
" God thought about me, and so I grew."

" But how did you come to us, you dear ? "
" God thought of you, and so I am here."

GEORGE MACDONALD.

Read the poem on page 109.

The poet asks questions, and the baby replies.

Find the quotation marks, and tell why they are used.

What do they make plain to you?

SECTION 153

ORAL EXERCISE

CAPITALS IN QUOTATIONS

Find the quotations in the following sentences.
Observe the first letter of every quotation.

1. King Alfred said, " While I have lived I have striven to live worthily."

2. You remember the old proverb, " Where there's a will there's a way."

3. A voice was heard through the forest, saying, " Behold your king!"

4. John called to me as I ran, saying, " I have your ball."

5. The fox went away, saying, " The grapes are sour."

6. Poor Richard says, " Lost time is never found again."

7. Up spoke our own little Mabel,
   Saying, " Father, who makes it snow?"

Learn this rule: —

The first word of every direct quotation should begin with a capital letter.

SECTION 154

ORAL EXERCISE

Make sentences in which you report the exact words of another pupil.   Thus, —

John said, " I have lost my knife."
" I have found it," cried Robert.

SECTION 155

FOR STUDY

THE ANT AND THE GRASSHOPPER

One winter day a hungry grasshopper went to an ant to get something to eat.   She knew that the ant had worked all summer, and had stored away a good supply of food.
" Good morning, friend Ant," said the grasshopper.
" Good morning, neighbor Grasshopper," replied the ant.
" It is a cold morning," said the grasshopper.
" A very cold morning," answered the ant.
" I am very hungry," hinted the grasshopper.
" I am sorry," returned the ant.
Said the grasshopper, " I have no food."
" Why not ? " asked the ant.
" I had no time to get any," replied the grasshopper.
" What did you do all summer ? " the ant asked.
" I sang all summer," the grasshopper answered.
" Then you must dance all winter," said the ant.   " Those who will not work should not eat."

Read this fable; then close your book and tell it as well as you can.

SECTION 156

For Study

Study the fable in Section 155, and observe how the quotations are written.

First, every quotation in the fable begins with a **capital letter.**

Second, every quotation is included in **quotation marks.**

Third, every quotation is separated from the rest of the sentence by some **mark of punctuation.** Usually this mark is a **comma,** but when the quotation is a question, the **interrogation point** is used.

Study the fable until you can write every sentence correctly from dictation.

SECTION 157

Dictation Exercise

Write from dictation the conversation between the Ant and the Grasshopper from Section 155.

SECTION 158

Copy the story of " The Ant and the Grasshopper," omitting all marks of punctuation. Then close your book and see if you can insert the necessary punctuation marks in their proper places.

SECTION 159

WRITTEN EXERCISE

WHITEFACE, N. H.,
Aug. 7, 1910.

DEAR COUSIN WILL,

I came up here yesterday to stay a month. Uncle John likes boys. We always have a good time on the farm.

This morning Uncle John said, "Why didn't Will come with you?"

Of course I could n't say, "Because he was n't invited." But before I could speak, Aunt Jane said, "You 'd better write to Will. Ask him to come up to Whiteface and spend a month with you."

"That 's right," said Uncle John. "Two boys are better than one."

So come as fast as you can. Tell us when to meet you. Bring some good hooks and lines. There are trout in the brook. I can hardly wait to see you.

Your cousin,
FRED.

Read this letter, observing the quotations.
Copy the letter carefully.

SECTION 160

ORAL EXERCISE

Find in your reader some piece of poetry that contains quotation marks. Explain the use of capitals and quotation marks in it.

SECTIONS 161–163

ABBREVIATIONS

161. You have already learned how to use **abbreviations** like *Mr.*, *Mrs.*, *Dr.*, *Esq.*, *St.*, *Jan.*, and *Feb.* You have also learned the rule : —

Every abbreviation should be followed by a period.

Here are a few common abbreviations : —

Co. = Company, County	P.O. = Post-Office
ft. = foot, feet	R.R. = Railroad
in. = inch, inches	U.S. = United States
A.M. = forenoon	Eng. = England
P.M. = afternoon	Capt. = Captain
p. = page	Sr. = Senior
pp. = pages	Jr. = Junior

162. *Look up the abbreviations for the names of the states in your geography, and make a list of ten.*

Look up abbreviations in your arithmetic and make a list of ten.

163. Abbreviations should be sparingly used.

In the following sentences the italicized words (except *Mr.* and *Mrs.*) are correctly written in full; abbreviations would be improper.

1. The *captain* led his *company* forward.
2. *January* is the first month of the year.
3. My birthday comes in *February*.
4. The state is divided into *counties*.

5. *Mr.* and *Mrs.* Smith strolled up the *street* to the *post-office.*

6. Run for the *doctor.*

7. Washington was born in *Virginia.*

Mr., Mrs., and *Messrs.* are always written in the abbreviated form.   *Doctor* and *Esquire,* when used as titles, are commonly abbreviated.   Most titles, however, are better written in full: as, *President, Professor, General, Superintendent.*

If you receive a letter signed *Thos. A. Jackson,* it is proper to use the abbreviation *Thos.* in addressing your reply.   But if you do not know that Mr. Jackson is in the habit of abbreviating his first name, you should write *Thomas A. Jackson* in full.

The following is the safest rule : —

When in doubt, do not use an abbreviation.

SECTION 164

The Exclamation Point

When we speak suddenly and with strong feeling, — as when we are surprised, delighted, angry, or frightened, — we are said to **exclaim,** and what we say is called an **exclamation.***

In the following sentences you will find a number of **exclamations.**   Notice the mark of punctuation (!) that follows each of them.   It is called the **exclamation point.**

* To *exclaim* means really to *cry out.*

"Hurrah!" exclaimed Jamie. "My long problems are done!"

Jamie was pleased and excited, for he had wanted to get out to play, and the long problems had kept him in.

When he did begin to play ball, he played as well as he had worked.

"Three cheers for Jamie!" shouted the boys who saw him play.

When we speak in excitement, our voices show how we feel, but in writing we must use the **exclamation point.**

Copy the sentences and learn the rule: —

1. Oh! you hurt my hand!
2. Hurrah! Tom has found the ball.
3. Bravo! Mary is not afraid to tell the truth.
4. Three cheers! our boys have won!
5. Hurry up, Joe! the train is starting!
6. What a noise the cars make!
7. How sorry I am for the poor man!

The exclamation point is used after exclamations.

SECTION 165

ORAL EXERCISE

CAPITAL O

Study the sentences which follow.

Give a reason for the use of the exclamation point in each sentence.

Observe the word " O " which introduces the exclamations.

1. Sail on, O Ship of State!
   Sail on, O Union, strong and great!
2. Take, O boatman! thrice thy fee.
   Take! I give it willingly.
3. Give me of your bark, O Birch tree!
   Of your yellow bark, O Birch tree!
4. Break! break! break! on thy cold gray stones, O Sea!
5. O to be in England, now that April's there!
6. O boatman! row me o'er the stream.

Here is the rule for the word *O* : —

The word *O*, when consisting of a single letter, is always written as a capital.

SECTIONS 166–180

Miscellaneous Lessons

166. *Write ten sentences in which you use the names of places.*

Your sentences may be either questions or statements.

167. *Cut ten pieces of paper to represent envelopes and address each envelope as you choose.*

In each address you may use a title, and the abbreviation of the name of a state.

168. *Copy and read the following dates, using abbreviations when these are proper.*

January 1, 1899.	July 20, 1900.
February 15, 1876.	August 3, 1859.
March 9, 1759.	September 4, 1800.
April 13, 1756.	October 30, 1841.
May 30, 1890.	November 20, 1764.
June 24, 1365.	December 1, 1565.

169. *Write a note to your friend Mary Brooks, asking her to come to your house next Saturday afternoon to play.*

170. *Write all the rules that you can remember for the use of capital letters.*

171. *Write sentences illustrating some of these rules.*

172. *Write from memory some poem which you learned at home.*

173. *Write ten sentences beginning* You and I; *ten ending* you and me.

174. *Write to your cousin, Phebe Brown, and ask her to tell you how to make chocolate caramels like those she sent you last week.*

175. *Write Phebe's reply, explaining how she makes caramels.*

176. *You have a friend who lives in another state and has never seen your home. Write to him, telling him about your school and your city and asking him to tell you about his home and school.*

177. *Tell about the May Queen. Tell (1) how she is chosen; (2) how she is dressed; (3) what she does.*

178. *Fill the blanks with* I *or* me, *as the sentence may require:* —

1. Jane and —— are good friends.
2. Throw the ball to Jack or ——.
3. Charles and —— live in Schenectady.
4. Kate and —— have won prizes.
5. Mother made this cake for you and ——.

179. *Explain orally how to do some simple piece of work.*

180. *Write your explanation.*

PART TWO

SECTION 181

A Glance Backward

We are taking up our work again after a long vacation. Sports, games, and visits have made us ready for more study, but we have had time to forget. Happily, vacation is a good time to practise spoken language. We should speak more easily now than in June.

To make ready for our written work, let us recall some things that we learned last year in our language lessons.

Turn to Part One, and recall the rules for capital letters.

SECTION 182

A Look Forward

This year we are to write more letters, and longer ones; to tell stories and to write descriptions; to study characters; to draw up outlines; and to write clear explanations which others may understand.

119

All this we have practised before; but now we shall do better still, for " practice makes perfect." This year we are ready for rules and for " grown-up" names and definitions. We can work harder and more successfully than a year ago. This is our motto : —

> Without haste, without rest,
> Lifting better up to best.

Copy the motto in your notebook, and write what you think it means.

Tell how you believe you can improve your writing and speaking.

SECTION 183

Turn to the Selections, page 36, and read " Home, Sweet Home."

This is the home-song for England and America. It is plain that it was written by one who was travelling, away from home and friends. You may not know that the author had no home when he wrote the song.

The love of home is one of our strongest loves. Of all homes, our own should be dearest.

Can you tell why it is so dear, and why we are *homesick* when we leave it?

The last two lines of each stanza are alike. We call such repeated lines in a song the **refrain**.

Read the poem aloud slowly, clearly, and thoughtfully. Sing it until you know it by heart.

SECTION 184

Read these paragraphs from the diary of Robinson Crusoe. What is the subject, or topic, of each paragraph?

Nov. 13. This day it rained, which refreshed me exceedingly, and cooled the earth; but it was accompanied with terrible thunder and lightning, which frightened me dreadfully for fear of my powder. As soon as it was over, I resolved to separate my stock of powder into as many little parcels as possible, that it might not be in danger.

Nov. 14, 15, 16. These three days I spent in making little square chests or boxes, which might hold about a pound, or two pounds at most, of powder; and so, putting the powder in, I stowed it in places as secure and remote from one another as possible. On one of these three days I killed a large bird that was good to eat, but I know not what to call it.

Nov. 17. This day I began to dig behind my tent into the rock, to make room for my farther conveniency. *Note.*— Three things I wanted exceedingly for this work; namely, a pickaxe, a shovel, and a wheelbarrow or basket; so I desisted from my work, and began to consider how to supply that want, and make me some tools. As for a pickaxe, I made use of the iron crows, which were proper enough, though heavy; but the next thing was a shovel or spade. This was so absolutely necessary, that, indeed, I could do nothing without it; but what kind of one to make I knew not.

Nov. 18. The next day, in searching the woods, I found a tree of that wood, or like it, which in the Brazils they call the iron tree, for its exceeding hardness. Of this, with great labor and almost spoiling my axe, I cut a piece and brought it home too with difficulty enough, for it was exceeding heavy.

SECTION 185

A Diary

You have studied a part of Robinson Crusoe's diary.

Have you ever written a diary?

Write a diary of your own, telling what you did each day of the past week. See that your paragraphs are clear and complete.

SECTION 186

Fill the blanks in these sentences : —

1. Robinson Crusoe found an iron tree in the woods.
2. He did —— the tree.   He has —— the tree.
3. He made tools from the wood.
4. He did —— tools.   He has —— tools.
5. The next thing —— a shovel.
6. The next things —— a shovel and a spade.
7. He did not —— what to call the bird.
8. He has not —— what to call it.
9. He did —— three days in making boxes.
10. He —— three days.   He has —— three days.

SECTION 187

An Explanation

Write a short explanation called "How Robinson Crusoe Made a Shovel."

For Reading and Telling

STORY OF A SCULPTOR

Bertel Thorwaldsen was a famous sculptor. He was born in Copenhagen, Denmark, in 1770. His father was

a wood-carver, who made figure-heads for vessels, and little Bertel used to help him at his trade.

When the boy was eleven years old, his father sent him to a School of Fine Arts where he could receive free tuition. He learned very rapidly and at the end of six years won a prize.

The father was much pleased at his boy's success. "Now he can help me to make figure-heads," he said. But an artist, who saw that the boy's work was very promising, begged him to keep the lad in school. The wood-carver

consented, on condition that Bertel should help him whenever he could spare the time from his studies.

Bertel worked very hard and won medal after medal.
He not only helped his father in wood-carving, but he
began to carve figures in stone. At last he gained a prize
which allowed him to study abroad for three years. He
went to Rome to study the beautiful statues there. After

a few years, his statues became very famous. "Night"
and "Morning" are two celebrated bas-reliefs which he
modelled in 1813. Here are engravings which show you
something of their beauty.

In 1819 Thorwaldsen was asked to design a monument
to the memory of the Swiss Guards who were killed while
defending the Tuileries in Paris in 1792. This happened
during the French Revolution. The king, Louis XVI., had
taken refuge in the palace. The National Guards, who
should have protected him, joined the mob and took part

in the attack. But the gallant Swiss Guards remained
faithful to their trust, and were killed while defending the
king whose own soldiers had deserted him.

The Swiss people, proud of the valor and fidelity of
their countrymen, made a subscription for a memorial to

THE LION OF LUCERNE. BY THORWALDSEN

the Guards. Thorwaldsen modelled for the memorial "The
Lion of Lucerne," copied in the picture on this page. It
is cut out of the solid rock. The wounded lion protects
the French shield, even in the agony of death.

*Read "The Story of a Sculptor," first to get the
story. Then study each paragraph, to see what
its main sentence tells you.*

The chief sentence of a paragraph is sometimes
called the "topic sentence," because it shows the
subject or **topic** of the paragraph.

SECTIONS 189–190

DESCRIPTION

189. *Study the picture of the Lion of Lucerne.*

Try to see all that the artist meant to make the figure express.

Describe the picture in a written paragraph. First make notes for the paragraph.

190. *Look at the picture of " Night " ; " Morning."*

What do you find alike in both ? What is the difference between them ? Why did the sculptor put the owl in one ? the sleeping child ? Why did he put the flowers and the laughing child in the other ? Which seems more like night ? like morning ?

Write three paragraphs of description. In the first state what you are describing ; in the second describe one picture, and in the third the other.

SECTION 191

Find an anecdote that shows the character of Columbus, and copy it.

How does the anecdote show his character ? Was he courageous or timid ? patient or impatient ? persevering or easily discouraged ?

What kind of man do you think a discoverer or explorer ought to be ?

Tell the anecdote so as to bring out the character. Then write it.

SECTIONS 192–193

Names of Companies

192. Several persons may unite to form a **company** or **association** for business purposes, for charity, or even for the sake of amusement.

The Maryville Athletic Association is composed of boys who play football together.   The Enfield Charity Club was organized to take care of the poor of the village.

The **name** of such a **company** or **association** usually consists of several words.   Thus, —

> The Curtis Publishing Company.
> The Estabrook Steel Pen Company.
> Thompson Manufacturing Company.
> The Cambridge Iron Company.
> The Great American Tea Company.
> Merchants' and Manufacturers' Association.
> Mutual Benefit Association.

In these examples you will observe : —

1. That the first word of the name begins with a capital letter without regard to its importance.

2. That every important word in the name begins with a capital.

193. *Find in the newspapers or magazines the names of ten companies or associations.*

Copy these names in a column, and bring the list to the class with you.

Study your list, and observe how capital letters are used in the names which you have discovered.

SECTION 194

Titles of Books

The name or **title** of a poem, book, newspaper, or lecture is often composed of several words.

In School Days, Paul Revere's Ride, The Fringed Gentian, Old Ironsides, The Mountain and the Squirrel, October's Bright Blue Weather, Warren's Address to the American Soldiers — are names of poems.

Dombey and Son, The Pickwick Papers, The Voyage of the Sunbeam, The Children of the Poor, Tanglewood Tales, The Art of Living, Alice in Wonderland, Little Women, Under the Lilacs, The Fairyland of Science, How to Know the Wild Flowers, Madam How and Lady Why — are titles of books.

The New York Tribune, The Evening Post, The Boston Transcript, The Minneapolis Journal, The Springfield Republican — are names of newspapers.

The Atlantic Monthly, St. Nicholas, Harper's New Monthly Magazine, The American Monthly — are names of magazines.

In all these names or **titles,** the first word, as well as every important word that follows, begins with a **capital letter.**

Bring to school a list of titles of books, stories, papers, and magazines. Copy them carefully, and observe how the capitals are used.

Be ready to write the names from dictation.

SECTION 195

QUOTATION MARKS

When the **title** of a book, lecture, story, or the like is mentioned in writing, it is usually regarded as a **quotation** and is enclosed in **quotation marks.**

Study the following examples : —

Dickens wrote " Dombey and Son."

I have just read " The Country of the Pointed Firs."

Have you ever read Miss Alcott's " Little Women " ? It is a delightful book.

Rudyard Kipling's " Jungle Book " is in the library.

" Paradise Lost " was written by John Milton.

" The Vision of Sir Launfal " is an exquisite poem.

Hawthorne is the author of " Tanglewood Tales," a book which all boys and girls enjoy.

Write ten sentences in each of which you quote the title of some book or poem which you have read.

SECTION 196

Find some anecdote that shows the character of Sir Francis Drake or Sir Humphrey Gilbert.

If you have studied the life of Drake, you will know what is meant by " robbing the robber " and " singeing the beard of the King of Spain."

Write three paragraphs : — (1) Who was Drake (or Gilbert)? (2) What did he do? (3) What was his character ?

A Quotation within a Quotation

Study the quotation marks in the following passages : —

1. A wise man has remarked, " The person who is always saying ' Honesty is the best policy ' is not necessarily honest himself."

2. Said my uncle, " When the captain shouted ' Charge ! ' I was terribly frightened, but I was ashamed to run away."

3. The speaker began thus, " You have often heard the saying, ' Fine feathers do not make fine birds.' "

You notice that each passage contains a **quotation within a quotation.**

A quotation within a quotation is included within single quotation marks (' ').

SECTION 198

The picture on page 131 was painted by Julien Dupré, a French artist. You will find his name under the picture. Among his paintings are many scenes from country life.

Study the picture and find all that you can in it.

SECTIONS 199-200

199. *Write a description of the picture.*

200. *Write a simple story, or description, suggested by the picture.*

On the Prairie. By Dupré

SECTION 201

1. Every sentence should begin with a capital letter.

2. Every line of poetry should begin with a capital letter.

3. All names of persons, places, days, and months should begin with capital letters.

4. All initials should be written in capitals and should be followed by periods.

5. Every title attached to a person's name should begin with a capital letter.

6. Every word denoting the Deity should begin with a capital letter.

7. The words *I* and *O* should be written with capital letters.

8. The first word of every direct quotation should begin with a capital letter.

9. In titles of books and the like, the first word, as well as every important word that follows, should begin with a capital letter.

SECTION 202

Describe your school, writing a paragraph answering each of the following questions : —

1. Where is your school ?
2. Who is your teacher ?
3. What do you study ?
4. What school shall you attend after leaving this school ?

SECTION 203

Copy two paragraphs from your geography.

What does each paragraph tell about ?

Write three paragraphs about some city with which you are familiar. Write a topic for each paragraph, — for example, the situation of the city, the size of the city, the chief occupations of the inhabitants.

SECTION 204

WORD DRILL

Some words need close attention, for they are pronounced alike but spelled differently.[1]

Use the italicized words in sentences of your own.

1. *Two — too — to.*

I have *two* books. You have some books, *too*. Are you going *to* school ?

2. *There* are the lost pencils.

Mary and John called *their* father.

Come here ! Go *there* !

3. John *threw* the ball.

It went *through* the fence.

---

[1] Such words are called **homonyms**.

4. Who *won* the game ?
   You may have *one* dollar.
5. Do you *know* your lesson ?
   No, I have not learned it.
6. Are you a cobbler ? Is this *awl* yours ?
   Do you own this farm ? Is it *all* yours ?
7. The *hare* outran the hound.
   His *hair* is crisp and black and long.
8. Help me to *bury* this dead bird.
   What is the red *berry* you are picking ?

SECTION 205

STUDY OF A POEM

Copy " October's Bright Blue Weather " (Selections, page 32). Learn it by heart.

This song is as bright and joyous as the month of fruit, color, and sunshine of which it sings. It will make you love October even more than you do now.

Which of October's beauties, which the poem recites, do you know ? Do you *know* the loud hum of the bumblebee ? Why is he called " a vagrant " ? " belated " ? " thriftless " ? What are lanes ? Do *you* know where wild grapes grow ? Does their fragrance tell you ? What are the fringes of the gentian ? Who else has written about the gentian ? What are the " satin burrs " of the chestnut ? Are there stone walls in New York ? red apples growing ? and woodbines twining ? What " wayside things " did you see this morning ? And what " late aftermaths " do you know ? Have you seen the " idle golden freighting " on the still brooks ?

How is this poem like " September," which you have learned ? Which do you prefer ?

SECTION 206

Anecdote Showing Character

Find an anecdote about Captain John Smith.

Write two paragraphs, the first telling who Smith was, the second telling what kind of man he was.

If your teacher prefers, you may tell the story of Pocahontas.

SECTION 207

Letter Writing

Tom Brown writes a note to his friend Ernest Adams, asking him to join a party to go nutting next Saturday.

Ernest cannot go. He writes to Tom, telling why he cannot accept the invitation. Of course he is sorry that he cannot accept it.

Tom sends an invitation to Ralph Needham also. Ralph writes a reply, saying that he is glad to go, and asking some questions about the party.

Write Tom's note to Ralph or Ernest.

Write either Ralph's or Ernest's reply.

Be careful about capitals, punctuation, and paragraphs.

Do not forget to date and sign the notes.

Read your notes in the class, and compare them with those which the other pupils write.

SECTION 208

PATTERN SENTENCES

Use the italicized words in other sentences like the patterns : —

1. *You and I* must keep quiet.
2. *She and I* will try to draw the picture.
3. *He and I* both laughed at the joke.
4. This book is for *you and me.*
5. Give the picture *to her or to me.*
6. Send the letter *to him or to me.*
7. *George and I* tried a new game.
8. *He and I* are cousins.
9. *These* books are mine. Give *them* to me.
10. Are you sure that *they* are yours?

SECTION 209

AN EXPLANATION *

HOW THE IROQUOIS BUILT THEIR LOG FORTS

The French explorers in the land near Lake Champlain, and in what is now central New York, found many of the Iroquois villages protected by strong, well-built log forts.

They were built in this way. The Indians first found a place where there were many tall trees. These were set on fire near their roots, and stone axes were used to rub off the coals, so that they would burn faster. After the trees had fallen to the ground they were set on fire again, in places about three long steps apart. The fires burned through the logs in about half a day.

* Explanation is also called **exposition.**

As there were no horses, the logs were drawn by the Indians, and then put into place. Earth was heaped up on both sides of the logs to keep them from falling. The forts had two gates. The one in front for general use, the one in the rear was for use when getting water.

On the shores of the beautiful Seneca Lake, by the banks of the Mohawk and Genesee Rivers, in the forests of Oneida and Cayuga, and in many other parts of this fertile region, these strongholds of a savage people stood secure. Sometimes several acres of land were enclosed, with many homes well protected both day and night from wild animals and other foes.

MARY CATHARINE JUDD.*

Study this explanation : — (1) as a whole, to see what it tells ; (2) paragraph by paragraph.

What does each paragraph tell or explain?

Why do the sentences of each paragraph belong together?

SECTION 210

EXERCISE IN EXPLANATION

Mary has been taking lessons in housekeeping in a Saturday class. Yesterday she was asked to tell in writing how a bed should be made. You will find her explanation on the following page.

If you read it carefully, you will see that Mary arranged the explanation in the right order, so that it is perfectly clear.

* From "Wigwam Stories" (by permission of the author).

HOW I MAKE A BED

1. Before leaving my room in the morning, I open all the windows and hang the bedclothes over chairs in the fresh air.

2. After breakfast I turn the mattress and spread the mattress cover neatly over it, tucking it in firmly at the top and bottom.

3. Then I lay the under sheet evenly in place, and tuck it in firmly on all four sides.

4. Then I lay the upper sheet over the bed, evenly, leaving enough at the top to fold over the covers later, and I tuck it in smoothly at the bottom.

5. I next lay the blankets on, placing the upper edge about a foot from the head of the bed, and tucking them in evenly at the foot.

6. The thin blanket spread follows next. I fold it under the blankets at the top and tuck it in evenly at the foot.

7. Then I fold the upper sheet down over the covers, making it just even on both sides.

8. Now I cover the bed with the spread, letting the sides and the ends hang over the bed at equal distances from the floor.

9. Then I shake and smooth my pillows and lay them squarely at the head of the bed, side by side. The bed is made.

If you make your bed in a different way, you may explain your manner of making it. Or, if you prefer, you may explain how you make and care for a garden.

Try to explain clearly.

SECTION 211

THE SHEPHERDESS

THE SHEPHERDESS.   BY MILLET

Study the picture and talk about it in the class.

SECTION 212

"The Shepherdess" was painted by the great French artist, Jean François Millet (1814–1875).

Learn all that you can, from books or through friends, of the life and work of Millet.

You may arrange carefully all that you learn, and then write it out in paragraphs.

SECTION 213

Fill the blanks : —

1. The Indian threw his tomahawk.
   The —— threw their ——.
2. There is a fire in the woods.
   The forest —— have been dreadful.
3. Lucy Gray lived on a wide moor.
   There are wide —— in England.
4. Tennyson was an English poet.
   Can you name five American —— ?
5. The stream flows through the valley.
   —— flow through ——.
6. This board is too long by an inch.
   How many —— make a foot ?

Study the following sentences : —

1. Add 3 to 7.
   Count to 21 by 3's.
2. 4 and 4 make 8.
   How many 4's make 8 ?
3. That is a figure 5.
   What queer 5's you make !

Note that when you write of two or more *threes*, *fours*, *fives*, and so on, and use the **figure** instead of writing the word in full, you must add the **apostrophe** and **s** ('s). Thus, — 3's, 4's, 5's.

Fill the blanks : —

1. There are 4 —— in 20.
2. 6 —— make 36.
3. There are 9 —— in 63.
4. 7 —— are 77.

SECTION 214

ORAL EXERCISE

What do you know about any of the things mentioned in the list below?

leather	horses	stone	flowers
corn	rivers	gold	children
money	molasses	iron	books

Think about these things; then tell the class what you think.

While studying your lesson, make notes to help you recite readily. Thus, —

NOTES ON LEATHER

1. Hide of animal.
2. Tanned.
3. Tough, strong, flexible.
4. Used for shoes, bags, trunks, straps, etc.

You need not read your notes aloud. Let them suggest to you the framework of what you wish to tell.

SECTION 215

WRITTEN EXERCISE

Write three paragraphs about one of the subjects in the preceding Section. Make notes for each paragraph.

PARAGRAPHS

216. *Write three paragraphs about the games you like best.*

Begin the first paragraph: — The games I like best are —— and ——.

In the second paragraph, tell why you like the first game; in the last, tell why you like the other games.

217. *Explain orally how to play one of these games.*

SECTION 218

LETTER WRITING

Robert Mayhew lives in New Orleans. He has never seen snowdrifts or built snow forts.

Imagine that you live in Minnesota.

Write a letter to Robert, describing your winter games carefully.

Perhaps you will ask Robert to tell you about his home, his school, and his games in New Orleans.

SECTION 219

LETTER WRITING

John Gray and George Welch are cousins. John lives in Oldtown, Maine; George in Boston, Mass.

John writes to George, asking him to spend his summer vacation with him at Oldtown.

Write John's letter to George and George's reply.

SECTION 220

Write the addresses of the persons named below.

1. Miss Ernestine Robertson lives in Boston. Her home is in Springfield St., No. 1028.

2. Miss Kate R. Lewis lives in Madison, Jefferson County, Indiana.

3. Henry K. Reynolds is a physician. His office is at 1338 Erie St., Cleveland, Ohio.

4. Philip H. Barnes is with the Smith-Hall Elevator Co., 205 York St., Quincy, Illinois.

5. Miss Fannie Whitman lives in St. Paul, Minnesota, at 698 Dayton Avenue.

6. Mrs. Arthur Crocker lives in Minneapolis. Her address is 428 Pleasant Avenue, Sub-Station 5.

SECTION 221

Address make-believe envelopes to the persons named below.

1. Harry T. Atwood lives in Buffalo, New York, 1725 Amherst Street.

2. Mrs. John R. Fletcher lives at 54 North Clinton Street, Chicago, Illinois.

3. Miss Helen C. Mills has P. O. Box 1537, Denver, Colorado.

4. Orville H. Wood lives in Montreal, Province of Quebec, Dominion of Canada.

5. Mrs. Alfred E. Bartol may be addressed at the Windsor Hotel, Richmond, Virginia.

6. Henry O. Towne is the president of the Maryland Steel Company, Annapolis, Maryland.

Paragraphs in Exposition

Read this delightful description and explanation of an Indian ball game, which Miss Judd has written in "Wigwam Stories."

AN INDIAN GAME OF BALL

1. The Dakotas play their ball games in the hot moons of the summer and in the cold moons of the winter. The prairies give wide room for the games in summer, and the ice on the many lakes serves as winter ball grounds for them.

2. Large spaces are needed, for there are many players. There is only one ball, but there are as many bats as players. The bats are about thirty inches long, with a loop at the lower end. This is laced across with deer sinew, to make a pocket in which the ball is caught and thrown.

3. The centre of the ball ground is chosen. Stakes are set many feet away from the centre, on opposite sides, as the bounds for the game. Two parties of equal numbers are chosen. Each party chooses its own leader or chief.

4. The chief of one side drops his ball into the pocket of his bat and tosses it toward the centre ground between the stakes. Both sides rush toward the place where the ball may fall, each brave hoping he may be the lucky one to catch it. Whoever gets the ball tosses it with his bat into the air toward his side of the grounds. Then the screaming, howling mob of players tears across the field to the place where the ball may fall again. The ball is thrown and contended for until one side succeeds in throwing it beyond the bounds of the opposite party.

5. The prizes for the winning side have hung all this time on the prize pole. Dangling in the air, waiting the finish of the game, are the knives, tomahawks, blankets, moccasins, fine buffalo and deerskin robes which the winners will divide among themselves. Indian girls play the same game and with nearly as much vigor and skill as their brothers.

6. Always, at these games, the old men and squaws sit or stand at the outside of the ball ground, a mass of interested spectators.

7. The ball game in some form, it seems, has been the national game on American soil since before American history began.

MARY CATHARINE JUDD.

SECTION 223

STUDY OF PARAGRAPHS

Read "An Indian Game of Ball" again.
Study it paragraph by paragraph and sentence by sentence.

Are the paragraphs arranged in the right order, so that you can follow the explanation step by step?

Some of the paragraphs are much longer than others. Why is this?

What does each paragraph tell about?

Notice the order of the sentences in each paragraph. Could the order have been different?

SECTION 224

ORAL EXERCISE

OUTLINE FOR PARAGRAPHING

Study the following outline.

Compare it with the explanation of "An Indian Game of Ball." See if the outline agrees with the text.

The Dakotas play ball.

1. When and where.

2. Conditions of playing. { Large space.
   One ball.
   As many bats as players.

3. Description of ball ground.

   Choosing { places.
   parties.
   leaders.

4. Description of play.

5. Prizes. { Where.
   What.
   For girls as well as boys.

6. Spectators.

7. Ball game an old national game.

SECTION 225

Write a description or explanation of the Indian ball game.

SECTION 226

For Paragraph Study

Answer the following questions.

Write notes for your answers under the numbers of the several paragraphs, — 1, 2, 3, 4.

HOW PEOPLE TRAVEL

1. If you go from New York to Buffalo, how may you travel? What can you tell about the train? the engine? the cars? the engineer? the fireman? the conductor? the brakeman? How fast does the train go? How long will the journey be? What time will it take?

2. If you go by the Hudson River and the Erie Canal, will the journey be longer or shorter than by train? How long will it take? What can you tell about the boat on the river? about the canal boat?

3. Suppose you go in an automobile, what time will be required? What can you tell about the automobile? What provision will you make for your journey?

4. What kinds of travel have you tried? Which do you like best? Why?

SECTION 227

Paragraph Writing

Write four paragraphs on the subject of Section 226, "How People Travel." Use that lesson as a guide to your writing.

Be careful not to put into the same paragraph facts that do not belong together.

SECTION 228

DESCRIPTION

Copy these two paragraphs.   Be ready to tell what each paragraph contains.

Here I sit on the deck of our big ship, writing to you, dearest mother. We are in midocean, fifteen hundred miles from land. This morning the gray clouds hang low over a gray sea, with white-crested waves; north, east, south, west — just sky and sea.

The deck is clear, except for the empty chairs, set in careful rows for the passengers asleep in their berths. For I am up early, and have no companions except Mother Carey's chickens, flitting from wave to wave near the ship's stern. I am alone, yet you never seemed nearer, my mother.

SECTION 229

WRITTEN EXERCISE

Your friend Mary Baker is going to Germany with her aunt, to study music.   Write her a letter to read on the steamer.

You may tell her that you are glad she is to have the happy year abroad; that you know she will do well; that her friends will miss her and will welcome her back.

Then you may tell her about her friends and about events that will interest her.

Address the letter to her in care of the Steamship Teutonic, to sail from New York.

SECTIONS 230–234

OUTLINES FOR PARAGRAPHS

230. The Battle of Bunker Hill.
1. When fought, and where.
2. The cause of the battle.
3. The Americans.
4. The British.
5. The attack.
6. The result.

231. Peaches.
1. What they are.
2. Their appearance.
3. Their parts.
4. Their uses.

232. How to Build a Dam.
1. The place.
2. The material.
3. Putting the material in place.
4. The use of the dam.

233. How Shoes are Made.
1. Material used for shoes.
2. The parts of the shoe.
3. How put together.

234. Camping in the Woods.
1. The place.
2. The tent.
3. The fire.
4. The food.
5. The surroundings.
6. The nights and the mornings.

STUDY OF A POEM

Study Longfellow's poem, "The Builders" (Selections, page 34).

A poet sees in common things a picture of other things. He tells you what life is like.

Longfellow has been watching builders, — perhaps the carpenters next door. His thoughts travel to the great cathedrals, with massive walls and towering spires, which cost even centuries of toil. Then he thinks how we all are builders of a temple loftier yet and more enduring.

What likeness does the poet see between our building and the temple of stone?

SECTIONS 236–237

STUDY OF A CHARACTER

236. *If you have read "Little Lord Fauntleroy," try to answer the following questions :* —

1. How did Cedric look?
2. How did he feel toward Mr. Hobbs?
3. How did he feel toward Dick?
4. How did Mr. Havisham treat Cedric?
5. What did he think of Cedric?
6. Describe Cedric's first meeting with the Earl.
7. How did his behavior at this meeting show his character?
8. What do you think of Cedric as a manly boy?
9. Was he less manly because he was kind and gentle?
10. How did he show his manliness?

237. *Copy the first four paragraphs of Chapter III of "Little Lord Fauntleroy."*

Tell the story of "Cedric and the Apple Woman" in your own words.

SECTIONS 238-239

DESCRIPTION OF A PICTURE

238. On the next page you will find a picture of an Algerian, which was painted by Schreyer, the artist whose picture, called "The Emperor's Messenger," you have studied in Section 28.

Study the picture; then describe the horse, the rider, and their surroundings.

239. Compare the horse which the Algerian is riding with the horses pictured in Section 28; in Section 86. Which does he resemble more? Why?

Observe his harness or trappings; his movement; his style. What can you say of his spirit, judging from the picture?

How is the rider dressed? What does his dress tell you? How is he armed? Why is he armed, do you suppose? What does his attitude indicate?

What is there in the picture unlike any horse or rider whom you might see in your town?

Make up a story about the horseman.

AN ALGERIAN HORSEMAN.· BY SCHREYER

Ownership or Possession

Find, in the following selections, all the names which indicate ownership or possession.

1. My childhood's earliest thoughts are linked with thee.
   The sight of thee calls back the robin's song.

2. Rip's story was soon told, for the whole twenty years had been to him as one night.

3. He had played for his lordship's levee,
    He had played for her ladyship's whim,
   Till the poor little head was heavy,
    And the poor little brain would swim.

4. The sun does not shine for a few trees and flowers, but for the wide world's joy.

5. Till last by Philip's farm I flow,
    To join the brimming river.

6. Far in the Northern Land,
    By the wild Baltic's strand,
   I, with my childish hand,
    Tamed the gerfalcon.

7. Six spears' lengths from the entrance
    Halted that deep array.

8. O Tiber! Father Tiber!
    To whom the Romans pray,
   A Roman's life, a Roman's arms,
    Take thou in charge this day.

9. Children's voices should be dear to a mother's ear.

10. A boy's will is the wind's will.

11. The rich man's son inherits cares.
    What doth the poor man's son inherit?

12. Belgium's capital had gathered then
    Her beauty and her chivalry.
13. The unwearied Sun, from day to day,
    Does his Creator's power display.
14. Oh for boyhood's painless play,
    Sleep that wakes in laughing day,
    Health that mocks the doctor's rules,
    Knowledge never learned of schools,
    Of the wild bee's morning chase,
    Of the wild-flower's time and place,
    Flight of fowl and habitude
    Of the tenants of the wood.
15. The Mayor sent east, west, north, and south,
    To offer the piper by word of mouth,
    Wherever it was men's lot to find him,
    Silver and gold to his heart's content.
16. My friends' friends are my friends.
17. The Indians' weapons were bows, arrows, and tomahawks.

Ownership or **possession** is often shown in writing
by adding an **apostrophe** and **s** to the name of the
owner or owners.   If the name of the owners ends
in **s,** the **apostrophe only** is added.

SECTION 241

*Find in your reading book ten words which are
written with the apostrophe in order to indicate
ownership.*

*Copy the sentences in which you find such words,
noting the place of the apostrophe.*

SECTION 242

Ownership or Possession

In the following sentences point out all the words that express ownership or possession.

Write a list of these words.

1. This is my hat.
   The hat is mine.
2. Our horse is named Dobbin.
   This horse is ours.
3. Your book is on my desk.
   This reading book is yours.
4. John has lost his knife.
   Is this knife John's?
   I think it is his.
5. Anna has just had a present.
   Her aunt has given her a watch.
   The watch is hers.
6. That book is not very clean.
   Its covers are soiled.
7. The Indians paddled off in their canoe.
   The canoe was theirs.

SECTIONS 243–244

243. *Make ten sentences, using the words in your list (Section 242). Write your sentences.*

244. *Write ten sentences, using the words in the following list : —*

Anna's, boys, boy's, boys', horses, horse's, horses', our, ours, hers, yours, their, theirs, it, its.

SECTION 245

NAMES AND TITLES

You have already learned how to write **names and titles.** Thus, —

> Mr. John C. Brown.
> Mrs. Thomas Quincy.
> Miss Elinor Anderson.
> Dr. Malcolm Elson.

Copy the following sentences : —

1. Mrs. James Smith is the wife of Mr. James Smith.
   Mr. James Smith has a brother named Thomas.
   Mr. Thomas Smith's wife is Mrs. Thomas Smith.
   The Mrs. Smiths are warm friends.
2. Miss Jane Smith and Miss Emily Smith are sisters.
   The two Miss Smiths were at the party.
   The Misses Smith were at the party.

You notice that when you wish to speak of two or more persons named Mrs. Smith, you say *the Mrs. Smiths.* If the persons are named *Miss Smith,* you may say either *the Miss Smiths* or *the Misses Smith.*

Copy the following sentences : —

> Mr. Smith and Mr. Robinson are partners.
> We address them as Messrs. Smith and Robinson.

Messrs. is pronounced *Messers.* Like *Mr.,* it is always written as an abbreviation.

SECTIONS 246-247

Uses of the Comma

246. You have learned several uses of the comma. Each of these is shown in one of the following sentences : —

1. Hudson, Balboa, Cortez, and De Soto were explorers.
2. Longfellow says, " Life is real, life is earnest."
3. Yes, I am very late.
4. You look tired, Philip.

Give the reason for the comma in each sentence.

It is convenient to have a rule which includes all four of these uses of the comma : —

The comma is used (1) to separate words in a series, (2) before a direct quotation, (3) after *yes* and *no* when followed by other words in the sentence ; (4) to set off the name of the person addressed.

247. *Write twelve sentences to show that you understand this rule.*

SECTION 248

Repeat the rules that you have learned for the interrogation point and the exclamation point : —

Every direct question should be followed by an interrogation point.

The exclamation point is used after exclamations.

Write ten sentences, using after each either an interrogation point or an exclamation point.

ORAL EXERCISE

REVIEW OF PUNCTUATION

Explain every mark of punctuation in the following passages : —

1. Hurrah! the foes are moving.

2. Yes, that is the brave man who saved my brother Alfred from drowning.

3. No, Mary, that is not my pencil.

4. Mary, where are you going?

5. "Here's Martha, mother!" cried the two young Cratchits.

6. Hurry! There's such a goose, Martha!

7. "Rip Van Winkle!" exclaimed two or three. "To be sure! that's Rip Van Winkle yonder leaning against the tree."

8. A general shout burst from the bystanders, "A Tory! a Tory! a spy! a refugee! Hustle him! Away with him!"

9. Welcome home again, old neighbor! Where have you been these twenty long years?

10. But hark! a rap comes gently at the door.

11. Thrice welcome, darling of the Spring!

12. Toll for the brave! the brave that are no more!

13. Stand! the ground's your own, my braves.

14. Hats, caps, umbrellas, and cloaks were all blown away in a moment.

15. No, I cannot tell a lie.

16. Do you know where Lincoln was born?

17. My friends, you must not be sad.

SECTION 250

Read "The Ship of State" (Selections, page 34).

In the poem from which these lines are taken, Longfellow sees again, as in " The Builders," a picture of great
things. The ship which was built and launched in his
home town, moves him to think of *our* Ship of State,
which bears with it "our hearts, our hopes, our prayers."

You should read the whole poem, " The Building
of the Ship," that you may understand the selection. Then learn the lines by heart, and recite
them as a young patriot should.

SECTION 251

CHARACTER STUDY

*Find some anecdote that shows the character of
Governor Winthrop.*

Tell the anecdote.

*Write a short composition on Winthrop's charac-
ter, including the anecdote.*

SECTION 252

WORD DRILL

Study the following sentences.

*Write sentences of your own, using the italicized
words correctly. Bring your sentences to the class
and read them, asking others to spell these words.*

1. It is cold. Build a fire in the *grate*.
   He walked with *great* difficulty, for he was lame.
2. Mary can *sew* very well, *so* she made herself an apron.
   I am old, *so* old I can write a letter.
3. John owns this knife. Give it to *him*.
   Did you like the *hymn* we sang this morning?
4. Captain Jones has gone to *sea*.
   See me turn a handspring.
5. The *eye* was made for seeing.
   I will not tell a lie.

SECTION 253

The short words *I, me, we, us, he, him, she, her, they, them, who, whom,* are often used incorrectly.

The following sentences are correct. By taking them as patterns you will accustom yourself to the proper use of these troublesome words.

1. John and *I* are going to Buffalo.
2. I like *him*. *He* and *I* are good friends.
3. *We* boys went fishing. Uncle John went with *us*.
4. Kate and *I* won prizes.
5. *They* were very pretty prizes.
6. *She* and *I* both worked hard for *them*.
7. You and *I* are Americans.
8. He gave the books to you and *me*.
9. Throw the ball to John or *me*.
10. *Who* is Paul? *He* is my cousin.
11. *Whom* did you see? I saw *him*.
12. To *whom* did you give the letter?
13. The man *who* works will succeed.
14. The man *whom* we saw was an Arab.

SECTION 254

WRITTEN EXERCISE

THE HARE AND THE TORTOISE

A FABLE

A Hare one day met a Tortoise who was plodding slowly along. "Ho, ho!" laughed the Hare, "you are a slow and stupid fellow! What a long time it takes you to get anywhere!"

The Tortoise laughed, too. "You are as swift as the wind, and a fine fellow as well. But stupid as I am, I can beat you in a race."

"Impossible!" cried the Hare.

"Let us try," said the Tortoise.

"What shall be our goal?" asked the Hare.

"The old pine tree at the cross-roads," said the Tortoise.

"Agreed," said the Hare.

Away sped the Hare. The Tortoise plodded steadily along.

When the Hare had run awhile at the top of his speed, he stopped a moment to nibble some clover. It tasted so good that he ate more and more. Then, being tired, he lay down for a nap.

The Tortoise still plodded along, turning neither to the right nor to the left. When the lazy Hare awoke and remembered the race, he sped to the pine tree at the cross-roads, only to find the patient Tortoise there before him.

Some children are like the Hare, and some are like the Tortoise.

Read this fable; then write it in your own words.

SECTIONS 255-256

NOTES FOR COMPOSITIONS

255. What do you know about the hare? In what kind of places does it live? What do you know about its appearance? its size? its color? its ears? eyes? legs? tail?

What can you tell of its habits? What does it eat? What kind of teeth must the hare have in order to eat such food? What kind of home does it make for itself? Is it fearless or timid? fleet or slow? wild or tame?

A great many stories are told about the hare. You may have read the stories of "Uncle Remus" and know about "Brer Rabbit."

256. Have you ever seen a turtle or tortoise? Where did you find it? What was it doing? What covering had it? How did it move about? Describe its head; its legs; its tail. What did it do when touched? What does the turtle do when it is put into the water? Where does it like to stay? Is the turtle timid or fearless? slow or swift? wild or tame?

How is the turtle protected from its enemies?

SECTION 257

SUBJECTS FOR COMPOSITIONS

(1) The Story of Brer Rabbit and the Tar-Baby (from "Uncle Remus"); (2) Description of a Rabbit; (3) My Pet Rabbit; (4) The Habits of the Rabbit; (5) Mr. Terrapin Shows his Strength (story from "Uncle Remus"); (6) How I Caught a Snapping Turtle; (7) Description of a Turtle; (8) The Habits of the Turtle.

SECTION 258

For Reading and Writing

Charles Kingsley was an English clergyman. He loved children, and wrote stories and poems for them. Among these are " Water Babies," the story which he wrote for his own children, and " Madam How and Lady Why," a book which tells in a charming way about the wonderful world in which we live.

Mr. Kingsley used to take long walks with his children. He had much to tell them about all that they saw. One day a child asked him to write a song for her. This poem was his reply.

A FAREWELL

My fairest child, I have no song to give you;
No lark could pipe to skies so dull and gray;
Yet, ere we part, one lesson I can leave you
  For every day.

Be good, sweet maid, and let who will be clever;
Do noble things, not dream them, all day long:
And so make life, death, and that vast forever
  One grand, sweet song.

Tell of some historical character who " did noble things."

Clever means " quick-witted and skilful." This word is often used incorrectly with another meaning, which is not the true one.

SECTIONS 259–260

PARAGRAPH WRITING

259. *Write two paragraphs in a letter to your aunt.*

You may imagine that you are in a big hayfield, and have been helping to make hay, but are resting under a tree.

The first paragraph may describe the field; the second may tell about the haymakers and their work.

Do not forget to date your letter and to begin and end it properly.

260. *Explain how hay is made.   Write your explanation.*

Make three or four paragraphs.

SECTION 261

PARAGRAPH WRITING

Write four paragraphs, in which you tell three boys how to help you build a bonfire.

1. Call the boys by name, and tell them you want their help.
2. Choose one to gather the sticks.   Tell why.
3. Choose a second boy to lay the fire.   Tell why.
4. Choose a third boy to run for matches.   Tell why.

Add a fifth paragraph : —

5. When everything is ready, you will light the fire, and all will feed it and watch it. Of course you will not leave the fire until it has gone out.

SECTIONS 262–265

For Composition

262. A Jack o' Lantern. (1) What it is. (2) How it is made. (3) How it is used.

263. Stilts. (1) What they are. (2) How they are made. (3) How they are used.

264. About Pets. (1) Chickens. (2) Rabbits. (3) Dogs. (4) Cats.

265. A Sleigh-ride. (1) Getting ready. (2) The ride to grandmother's. (3) The dinner. (4) The ride home.

SECTION 266

Word Drill: Contractions

1. Have you seen Mary?
   No, I have not seen her to-day.
   I have n't seen her to-day.
2. Are you going to Buffalo?
   No, I am not going to Buffalo.

There is no contraction of *am not*. Never say *ain't*.

3. Are n't you going?
   Are you not going?
4. Did you go to Buffalo yesterday?
   Did n't you go to Buffalo yesterday?
   Did you not go yesterday?
5. Have you not been in Buffalo?
   Have n't you been in Buffalo?
   Have you been in Buffalo?

Play a game of question and answer, using names of other places, and answering in complete statements.

SECTIONS 267-269

Sentence-Making

267. *Tell one thing about* (1) Boston; (2) London; (3) Niagara; (4) Columbus; (5) Washington; (6) Lincoln; (7) Hiawatha; (8) Robinson Crusoe.

268. *Make sentences telling what is true about each of the following objects in spring:*— (1) flowers; (2) grass; (3) leaves; (4) air; (5) birds; (6) trees; (7) brooks; (8) child; (9) frogs; (10) rain.

269. *Ask a question about* (1) iron; (2) coal; (3) oil; (4) sugar; (5) clay; (6) lead; (7) lime; (8) salt; (9) gold; (10) copper.

SECTIONS 270-275

Letter Writing

270. You accepted an invitation to spend the afternoon of next Thursday with your friend Selma Van Buren, but you learn to-day that this would be impossible.

Write a note to Selma, explaining why you cannot keep your engagement.

271. *Write a note to your teacher telling her what you saw on your way to school this morning.*

272. *Write a letter describing a visit to a blacksmith's shop.*

273. *Describe some picture in your reading book in a letter to your teacher. Choose a picture that you like, and tell what pleases you in the picture.*

274. *Write a note to your father, asking him to visit your school next Friday afternoon.*

275. *Write to your friend, Margaret King, living in Scranton, Pennsylvania, asking her to visit you. Tell her what there is of interest in your city for her to see and enjoy.*

Broken Quotations

It often happens that a **quotation** is **broken** in two by the insertion of words which are not themselves quoted.

In the following selection from " Alice in Wonderland " you will find several **broken quotations.**

Read the selection, — first for the story, and again to find the broken quotations. Notice how these are written.

Find the quotations in each paragraph, and tell whether they are broken or entire.

THE MAD TEA PARTY

(Alice, the Hatter, the Dormouse, and the March Hare.)

1. " Suppose we change the subject," the March Hare interrupted. " I vote the young lady tells us a story."

2. " I 'm afraid I don't know one," said Alice, rather alarmed at the proposal.

3. " Then the Dormouse shall," they both cried. " Wake up, Dormouse ! " And they pinched it on both sides at once.

4. The Dormouse slowly opened his eyes. " I was n't asleep," he said in a hoarse, feeble voice. " I heard every word you were saying."

5. " Tell us a story," said the March Hare.

6. " Yes, please do," pleaded Alice.

7. "And be quick about it," added the Hatter, "or you'll be asleep again before it is done."

8. "Once upon a time there were three little sisters," the Dormouse began in a great hurry; "and their names were Elsie, Lucie, and Tillie; and they lived at the bottom of a well."

9. "What did they live on?" said Alice, who always took a great interest in questions of eating and drinking.

10. "They lived on treacle," said the Dormouse, after thinking a minute or two.

11. "They couldn't have done that, you know," Alice gently remarked, "for they would have been ill."

12. "So they were," said the Dormouse, "*very* ill."

13. Alice tried a little to fancy to herself what such an extraordinary way of living would be like, but it puzzled her too much, so she went on, "But why did they live at the bottom of a well?"

14. "Take some more tea," the March Hare said to Alice very earnestly.

15. "I've had nothing yet," Alice replied in an offended tone, "so I can't take *more*."

16. "You mean, you can't take less," said the Hatter; "for it's very easy to take more than nothing."

Make a rule for the use of quotation marks in writing each part of a broken quotation.

277. If you study "The Mad Tea Party" again, you will find that sometimes the quotation is broken into separate sentences, each of which begins (as always) with a capital letter. What happens when a sentence is broken in two? Does the second part begin with a capital? *Make a rule.*

SECTION 278

ANECDOTE SHOWING CHARACTER

MICHAEL ANGELO

A friend of Michael Angelo's watched the great artist at his work upon a statue which was nearly finished. Some time afterward he went again and found the sculptor still at work upon the same statue. The friend exclaimed, " You have been idle since I was here last! This figure was finished then."

" By no means," replied Michael Angelo. " I have softened this feature and brought out that muscle. I have given more expression to the lip and more energy to the eye."

" Well," said the friend, " but these are all trifles."

" It may be so," responded Angelo, " but trifles make perfection, and perfection is no trifle."

Tell the story orally ; then tell it in writing. Observe carefully the broken quotations.

SECTION 279

WRITTEN EXERCISE

Write a recipe for making bread.

You can learn at home what materials are needed and what rules should be followed.

Read your recipe in the class, and compare it with those which the other children write.

If you prefer, you may write directions for playing some game instead of the recipe for bread.

SECTIONS 280–282

A GAELIC LULLABY

Hush! the waves are rolling in,
 White with foam, white with foam;
Father toils amid the din;
 But baby sleeps at home.

Hush! the winds roar hoarse and deep, —
 On they come, on they come!
Brother seeks the wandering sheep;
 But baby sleeps at home.

Hush! the rain sweeps o'er the knowes,
 Where they roam, where they roam;
Sister goes to seek the cows;
 But baby sleeps at home.

A *lullaby* is a song which the mother sings to her baby as she rocks him to sleep. A *Gaelic* lullaby is one sung by a Gaelic mother, in the Scottish Highlands. The *knowes* are "knolls" or "low hills."

This lullaby contrasts the tumult of the storm with the quiet home where the baby is sheltered.

What scene is described in each stanza? What do the words make you see and hear?

281. *Commit to memory Shakspere's "Lullaby for Titania" (Selections, page 37).*

282. How does Shakspere's song differ from "A Gaelic Lullaby"? Titania was the Queen of the Fairies. You may review "Fairy Folk" (Selections, page 4).

SECTION 283

For Study

SENTENCES

A sentence is a group of words which expresses a complete thought.

Speech, oral or written, is always the **expression of thought,** for spoken or written **words** are only **signs** to indicate what one is thinking.

The only use of the **sentence** is to **express** some **thought** which one wishes to communicate to another.

Thought should always precede speech.

Write sentences expressing your thought about —

skating,	arithmetic,
firecrackers,	geography,
marbles,	fishing,
robins,	sweeping,
snakes,	tigers,
bees,	lions,
mice,	melons,
dolls,	grapes.

Remember that your sentence is to tell your thought about the things mentioned, not about yourself.

"Skating is fine sport" tells about *skating;* but "I like skating" tells about *you.*

SECTION 284

FOR STUDY AND WRITING

DECLARATIVE SENTENCES

Study the following sentence : —

Washington was born in Virginia.

You observe that this sentence states or **declares** something as a fact. For this reason it is called a **declarative sentence.**

A declarative sentence declares or asserts something as a fact.

The following are **declarative sentences :** —

1. Pizarro conquered Peru.
2. George MacDonald wrote " The Wind and the Moon."
3. Boston is the capital of Massachusetts.
4. New York is the largest city in the United States.
5. I have two blue pencils.
6. This coat belongs to Harry.
7. The happy children were playing in the field.

The following exercises will give you practice in writing declarative sentences. You will find that they are no new thing to you.

1. *Write one fact about each of the following objects.*

rose   bell   desk   umbrella   door
apple   vase   ball   picture   window

2. *Write one fact about* — Raleigh, Hudson, Roger Williams, Champlain, Penn, Franklin.

SECTION 285

Exercise in Making Sentences

Write a declarative sentence about each of the following objects, telling the material of which it is made.

chair	blackboard	window	spoon	shoe
curtain	schoolhouse	ring	pen	cup
crayon	wheelbarrow	hammer	knife	hat

After writing these declarative sentences, try to change them, in the class, to questions.

SECTION 286

Exercise in Making Sentences

1. *Make five oral sentences, each stating some fact which you have learned from your geography.*
2. *Write the sentences that you have made.*
3. *Make five oral sentences, each stating some fact of history.*
4. *Write the sentences.*

If you have written your sentences correctly, you have made ten declarative sentences.

Why are your sentences called **declarative**?

Recite the definition of a sentence.
Recite the definition of a declarative sentence.

SECTIONS 287-288

BEAUTIFUL THINGS

Beautiful faces are they that wear
The light of a pleasant spirit there, —
It matters little if dark or fair.

Beautiful hands are they that do
Work that is noble, good, and true,
Busy for others the long day through.

Beautiful feet are they that go
Swiftly to lighten another's woe,
Down darkest ways if God wills so.

Study these stanzas until you understand them.
Observe the capitals and punctuation marks and prepare to write the stanzas from dictation.

288. *Write the substance of the poem in three paragraphs of prose.*

What kinds of character have you described?

SECTION 289

EXERCISE IN MAKING SENTENCES

1. *State the use of each of the following :* —

cotton, wheat, sheep, cow, ship, wagon, mountain, river.

2. *Make sentences telling the color of* —

lemons, strawberries, leaves, the sky, the gentian, cherries, snow, grapes, lily, golden-rod, clover, aster, columbine.

SECTION 290

For Conversation

THE WISE FAIRY

Once in a rough, wild country,
On the other side of the sea,
There lived a dear little fairy,
And her home was in a tree,
A dear little, queer little fairy,
And as rich as she could be.

To northward and to southward,
She could overlook the land,
And that was why she had her house
In a tree, you understand,
For she was the friend of the friendless,
And her heart was in her hand.

And when she saw poor women
Patiently, day by day,
Spinning, spinning, and spinning
Their lonesome lives away,
She would hide in the flax of their distaffs
A lump of gold, they say.

And when she saw poor ditchers,
Knee-deep in some wet dyke,
Digging, digging, and digging
To their very graves, belike,
She would hide a shining lump of gold
Where their spades would be sure to strike.

And when she saw poor children
Their goats from the pastures take,
Or saw them milking and milking,
Till their arms were ready to break,
What a plashing in their milking-pails
Her gifts of gold would make!

Sometimes in the night, a fisher
Would hear her sweet low call,
And all at once a salmon of gold
Right out of his net would fall;
But what I have to tell you
Is the strangest thing of all.

If any ditcher, or fisher,
Or child, or spinner old,
Bought shoes for his feet, or bread to eat,
Or a coat to keep from the cold,
The gift of the good old fairy
Was always trusty gold.

But if a ditcher, or fisher,
Or spinner, or child so gay,
Bought jewels, or wine, or silks so fine,
Or staked his pleasure at play,
The fairy's gold in his very hold
Would turn to a lump of clay.

So, by and by the people
Got open their stupid eyes:
"We must learn to spend to some good end,"
They said, "if we are wise;
'T is not in the gold we waste or hold
That a golden blessing lies."

ALICE CARY.

SECTION 291

Tell the story of "The Wise Fairy" in prose, making a paragraph of each stanza.

First see clearly just what the stanza tells you.

SECTION 292

Tell the story of "The Wise Fairy" in four prose paragraphs.

In the first paragraph you may include all that the first two stanzas tell you. In the second paragraph you may tell what you find in stanzas 3, 4, 5, and 6; in the third paragraph, what you find in stanzas 7 and 8. In the fourth paragraph you may give the conclusion (stanza 9).

Think each paragraph out, just as if you were telling the story to your mother. Then be ready to tell each part in the class.

SECTION 293

The following words, in some form, are in "The Wise Fairy."

Use them in spoken sentences telling something about the fairy.

understand	understood	had understood
hide	hid	had hidden
dig	dug	had dug

strike	struck	had struck
see	saw	had seen
take	took	had taken
break	broke	had broken
make	made	had made
fall	fell	had fallen
tell	told	had told
buy	bought	had bought
eat	ate	had eaten
keep	kept	had kept
get	got	had got
spend	spent	had spent
hold	held	had held
lie	lay	had lain

SECTIONS 294–295

294. *Use in oral sentences of your own these words and groups of words from "The Wise Fairy":* —

1. The friend of the friendless.
2. Her heart was in her hand.
3. spinning
4. flax
5. distaff
6. dyke
7. belike
8. spade
9. goats
10. pasture
11. salmon
12. The fairy's gold in his very hold
    Would turn to a lump of clay.
13. 'T is not in the gold we waste or hold
    That a golden blessing lies.

295. *Write ten questions suggested by your conversation about "The Wise Fairy."*

SECTION 296

FOR CONVERSATION

THE GIANT

There came a Giant to my door,
A Giant fierce and strong;
His step was heavy on the floor,
His arms were ten yards long.
He scowled and frowned; he shook the ground;
I trembled through and through;
At length I looked him in the face
And cried, " Who cares for you ? "

The mighty Giant, as I spoke,
Grew pale and thin and small,
And through his body, as 'twere smoke,
I saw the sunshine fall.
His blood-red eyes turned blue as skies : —
" Is this," I cried, with growing pride,
" Is this the mighty foe ? "

He sank before my earnest face,
He vanished quite away,
And left no shadow in his place
Between me and the day.
Such giants come to strike us dumb,
But, weak in every part,
They melt before the strong man's eyes,
And fly the true of heart.
                                        CHARLES MACKAY.

*Read the poem, and tell the story in your own
words.*

SECTIONS 297-298

STUDY OF A POEM

297. *Describe the Giant (Section 296) as he first appeared.*

Describe the Giant as he appears in the second stanza.

What caused the change in the Giant's appearance?

298. Is this a true story? Why was it written?

A story which is told in order to teach some truth is called a **parable.**

The writer of this parable teaches his lesson in two ways: first by the story and then by the explanation. What is the truth that he tells?

Who are said to be able to conquer giants?

Name some giants that strong men have conquered.

SECTIONS 299-300

SENTENCES

299. *Write five sentences about the Giant as he looked and acted before the change in his appearance.*

Write five sentences about his appearance after the change.

300. *Write five sentences about strong men of history.*

Write five sentences about giants that they have conquered.

SECTION 301

MEMORY EXERCISE

Read the following poem : —

MARCH

The cock is crowing,
The stream is flowing,
The small birds twitter,
The lake doth glitter,
The green field sleeps in the sun ;
The oldest and youngest
Are at work with the strongest ;
The cattle are grazing,
Their heads never raising ;
There are forty feeding like one !

Like an army defeated
The snow hath retreated,
And now doth fare ill
On the top of the bare hill ;
The ploughboy is whooping — anon — anon : *
There 's joy in the mountains ;
There 's life in the fountains ;
Small clouds are sailing,
Blue sky prevailing ;
The rain is over and gone !

William Wordsworth was a poet who lived in the beautiful Lake Country in England. He loved

* *Anon* is an old word for " immediately." Here it indicates that the ploughboy will soon be in the field and ready for work.

out-of-door life, and one of his greatest pleasures was to walk in the fields and to climb the hills.

The poem on page 180 tells us what Wordsworth saw and heard as he walked near his home one March morning, after the long, cold winter.

Does the poem tell you anything about the poet's home?

Does it show you what he enjoyed? Does it reveal his character?

What does Wordsworth mean when he says: —

> "There's joy in the mountains;
> There's life in the fountains"?

SECTIONS 302-304

OUTLINES FOR COMPOSITIONS

302. The Snow Fort.

    1. Who planned it.

    2. How he made it.

    3. What we played there.

    4. What happened to the fort on a rainy Saturday?

303. The Fisherman.

    1. Where he lives.

    2. What he does.

    3. His boat.

    4. Dangers he must meet.

304. How Roger Won the Prize and Went to College.

    1. About Roger.

    2. About the prize.

    3. How Roger won it.

    4. Roger's character.

SECTION 305

FOR READING AND TELLING

ROSA BONHEUR

Rosa Bonheur was a French painter. She was born at Bordeaux, France, in 1822, and died in 1899.

Rosa was the eldest of four children. When she was only seven years old, her mother died. Her father, a poor drawing-master, went to live in Paris, where he worked hard for his family. He gave lessons in drawing and hired a woman to take care of the children.

Little Rosa ran wild. She gathered flowers in the wood and played in the fields. Her face was tanned, her hair was tangled, her clothing was odd and strange.

The father sent his motherless little girl to school that she might study writing and arithmetic. The well-dressed children teased her and laughed at her. Rosa did not dare to retort; but she drew comic pictures in which she made fun of her tormentors. Her pictures were discovered, and she was sent away from the school.

When Rosa returned from school she became her father's housekeeper. She took care of her brothers and sisters and learned to keep the little home in order. But what she liked best was to use her pencil. So she gathered the children about her and taught them to make sketches. She found some clay in a ditch, and with it she modelled beautiful figures.

The children made friends with the dogs and sheep in the fields near their home. They owned a goat which supplied them with milk. This goat they named Capricorn. They drew it again and again and modelled it in clay.

Rosa Bonheur became famous as a painter of animals. On page 184 you will find her portrait, copied from a painting by one of her friends. You may have seen some of her own pictures, — "Lions at Home," perhaps, or "The Horse Fair," or "Highland Cattle."

Even a child may learn from Rosa Bonheur's pictures that she loved animals, because her pictures help him to understand them and to love them better. You may be sure that she liked to be with them, that she knew their ways, and that she studied their life patiently as well as lovingly.

Read the story, and talk it over.

See what you can learn, at home or in the library, about Rosa Bonheur and her pictures.

SECTIONS 306–307

306. *Study the story of Rosa Bonheur.*
Write notes on each paragraph. Thus, —

1. Who she was.
   When she lived.
2. About her family.
   Eldest of four.
   Death of mother.   Rosa seven years old.
   Father drawing-master.
      Paris.   Hard work.   Lessons in drawing.
      Caretaker for children.

307. *Tell the story of Rosa Bonheur from the notes which you have written. See if you can also tell it from the notes of another pupil.*

Rosa Bonheur. By Dubufe

SECTION 308

Write from memory a paragraph about Rosa Bonheur, in your own words, as you would tell about her at home.

Let the paragraph tell who she was, where she lived, what she did, and what makes her pictures interesting.

SECTION 309

ORAL EXERCISE

Study the picture of Rosa Bonheur.

Is she alone ? What do you see beside her ?

Describe her face; her hair. How is she standing ? How is her right arm resting ? What has she in her right hand ? in her left ? What is the position of her left arm ? How is she dressed ?

Describe the animal : — color; horns; expression.

Why has the artist drawn her with this creature ? What does the painting really show us about her and her love for animals ?

SECTIONS 310–311

310. *Write a description of the picture, in three paragraphs. Make notes for each paragraph.*

311. Imagine that you are travelling in England. You visit the National Gallery and see a picture that you admire very much.

Write a letter to a classmate, telling how you came to visit the gallery, and describing the picture.

SECTION 312

LETTER WRITING

Write a reply to the following note.

21 DOVE ST.,
PHILADELPHIA,
Aug. 15, 1910.

MY DEAR JACK,

I have a holiday to-morrow afternoon. Can't you come and help me enjoy it? We will go to the Park, see the animals at the Zoo, and then take supper somewhere or other.

We shall manage to enjoy ourselves, I am sure. It will be great fun to have you with me.

We can start at one. Let me know where to meet you.

In haste,
UNCLE JACK.

SECTION 313

LETTER WRITING

Write a reply to the following note.

MAYWOOD, OHIO,
Sept. 10, 1910.

DEAR KATE,

Won't you come over this afternoon and take tea with us? Nellie White is here for a few days, and of course she wants to see you. Come as early as you can, so that we can have time to talk.

Your loving cousin,
ELSIE.

SECTION 314

FOR STUDY

WISHING

Ring-ting! I wish I were a primrose,
A bright yellow primrose blowing in the spring!
 The stooping bough above me,
 The wandering bee to love me,
The fern and moss to creep across,
 And the elm tree for our king!

Nay, — stay! I wish I were an elm tree,
A great lofty elm tree, with green leaves gay!
 The winds would set them dancing,
 The sun and moonshine glance in,
And birds would house among the boughs,
 And sweetly sing.

Oh, no! I wish I were a robin, —
A robin, or a little wren, everywhere to go,
 Through forest, field, or garden,
 And ask no leave or pardon,
Till winter comes with icy thumbs
 To ruffle up our wing!

Well, — tell! where should I fly to,
Where go sleep in the dark wood or dell?
 Before the day was over,
 Home must come the rover,
For mother's kiss, — sweeter this
 Than any other thing.

WILLIAM ALLINGHAM.

For Conversation

WISHING

This poem was written by an English poet. Primroses are fragrant blossoms that grow wild in the woods of England.

The poet represents the child as wishing. The rhymes which you find at the beginning of the poem are put in to make a pleasant jingle.

The first stanza makes a pretty picture of the pleasant things in the life of the primroses. The child fancies that the primroses must have a happy time, and he wishes that he might be a primrose, too.

The second stanza shows that he changes his mind. Now what does he wish to be? What are the pleasant things that he describes in the life of an elm tree?

In the third stanza we find the child changing his mind again. He wishes he were a robin. The English robin is a much smaller bird than our robin redbreast. It has a much brighter breast. The English children know and love it dearly.

Study carefully the last two lines of this stanza. Should you have thought to say the same thing in the same way? The sound of this stanza is very pleasing. Read it aloud to yourself and see if it pleases you.

In the last stanza the child remembers something better yet, and now wishes to be what? Where now would he like to go? What is the sweetest thing after all for him?

Read this poem a great many times to yourself until you can read it well aloud. It is a musical poem, and it will sing itself to you after you know it well.

SECTIONS 316–319

316. *Write a paragraph describing the primrose. Take a hint from the picture which the poet makes for you in the first stanza.*

317. "I wish I *were*" is correct, in prose as well as in poetry.

Use the expression in three written sentences.

Use the following words or expressions in sentences : —

wandering, lofty, glance, house (as it is used in the poem), ask leave, dell, rover.

318. *Read " The Brook "* (*Selections, page 26*).

What do you know about brooks? Where have you seen one?

Tell in what ways Tennyson's brook is like your brook.

What are "skimming swallows"? Why are they so called? What is the "netted sunbeam"? What are "sandy shallows"?

Learn the poem by heart.

319. *Read the letter on page 191. Study the paragraphs.*

You note that each paragraph tells of a single topic (or subject) and only one. What does each tell?

For Reading and Study

SUCCESSION OF THE FOUR SWEET MONTHS

> First, April, she with mellow showers,
> Opens the way for early flowers;
> Then after her comes smiling May,
> In a more rich and sweet array;
> Next enters June, and brings us more
> Gems, than those two that went before;
> Then, lastly, July comes, and she
> More wealth brings in than all those three.
>   HERRICK.

Read these lines carefully and think what every line means.

1. Which are the " four sweet months " ?

2. How does the poet describe each of them ?

3. Why are April showers called mellow showers? Why is May said to be smiling? What is her " rich and sweet array " ? What gems does June bring us ? What wealth is brought us by July ?

Written Exercise

Imagine that you are one of the months. Tell what you bring with you, what you do, and how you are liked.

SECTION 322

LETTER WRITING

Answer the following letter.

HERKIMER, N. Y.,
Oct. 11, 1910.

DEAR COUSIN ROBERT,

Of course you want to hear from me and to know how I like my new school.

It seems very odd to be away from home in a strange place. I miss the boys and girls I have always played with, and I am not used to the new ways.

Uncle George is very good to me and treats me as if I were his own boy, and Aunt Kate makes cookies and pies without end, because she knows that boys like such things.

Percy Brown lives next door and happens to be in my class; so we are together a good deal. Sometimes we study together in the evening, either here or at his house. Saturdays we go off for fun — sometimes nutting, sometimes fishing, and sometimes just for a walk.

I have begun to study Latin and algebra. I am not very quick, but I do the best I can, and Uncle George says that's all he wants.

My last letter from father and mother was written at London. They are enjoying themselves hugely. They say they miss me, and I know I miss them. I shall be glad when I can go to England, too.

Now write me a good long letter. Tell me what you are doing at school and at home, and all about the boys and girls that I know. Do not forget that I miss you, and that every word you write will give me pleasure.

Your old friend,

FRANK.

SECTION 323

LETTER WRITING

Helen Winter, living in Detroit, Michigan, writes to her friend Esther Copeland, who lives in Buffalo, New York, inviting her to visit Detroit as her guest.

Helen tells Esther to take an Anchor Line steamer at Buffalo any Tuesday noon. She will then have a pleasant trip of two days on Lake Erie, reaching Detroit at noon, Thursday. She will be met by Helen's older brother, who will escort her to the house.

Helen promises her friend to take her to the beautiful park, Belle Isle, in the Detroit River, and to many other places that she will enjoy.

She warns her to take warm wraps, as it may be very cool on the lake, and closes her letter by saying that she hopes soon to hear that Esther can come.

Imagine that you are Helen Winter. Write the letter to Esther.

SECTION 324

You have been collecting stamps and wish to secure certain stamps in exchange for duplicates which you do not care to keep.

Write to your cousin Jack and describe your collection.

Ask him if he can send you some of the stamps which you wish to get, in exchange for yours.

SECTION 325

THE WORK OF THE PARTS OF A SENTENCE

Examine the following short sentences : —

1. Plants grow.
2. Fishes swim.
3. Hailstones fall.
4. Winds blow.
5. Ships sail.
6. Rivers flow.
7. Balls roll.
8. Lead sinks.

Study the first sentence : Plants grow.

The word *plants* shows you **what** grows. It **names** the things that you think about as growing. *Grow* **tells** what plants **do**.

Divide the other sentences into parts in the same way.

Find in every sentence the word which tells what something does.

You have divided each sentence into **two parts.** One part **names the thing** which you are thinking about, the other part **tells something** about that **thing.**

In these sentences, then, you find two distinct sets of words, that is, two sets of workers. You have already begun to learn something about **the work which words do.**

SECTION 326

THE SUBJECT OF THE SENTENCE

Write a sentence about —

Thomas Jefferson, pine trees, schoolhouse, horses, Africa, Cuba, Germany.

Example : — Thomas Jefferson | was a great statesman.

Divide your sentences like the model, so that the name of the person or thing you have written about shall stand by itself.

This part of the sentence is the **subject.**

Find the subjects of all your sentences.

The subject of a sentence designates the person, place, or thing that is spoken of.

SECTION 327

Divide the following sentences as in Section 326. Then name the subject of each sentence.

1. The maples are red.
2. The asters hang over the brook.
3. Mount Tacoma is in the State of Washington.
4. A boy's whistle was a happy invention.
5. Chestnuts ripen in the fall.
6. The lizard sleeps through the winter.
7. Bees carry pollen from flower to flower.
8. Indians used arrows as weapons.
9. Potatoes were first found in America.

SECTION 328

THE PREDICATE OF THE SENTENCE

Study the following sentences.

1. *Find the subject of each.*
2. *Find what is said about the subject.*

1. The orioles build hanging nests.
2. Shepherds watched their flocks by night.
3. The lark sings at heaven's gate.
4. Longfellow wrote "The Village Blacksmith."
5. The clock strikes one.
6. Dinner comes at one o'clock.
7. The steed flew along the drawbridge.
8. The great gates swung upon their hinges.
9. The lights streamed through the western windows.
10. The general rode upon a black horse.

The predicate is that which is said of the subject.

SECTION 329

Write sentences in which you tell something about each object named in the following list.

football	chestnuts	lions	oranges
rivers	wheat	tigers	butterflies
children	roses	books	iron
gold	violets	silver	camels

Read the predicate of each sentence.

SECTION 330

Find and name the subjects and the predicates in the sentences which follow : —

1. Primroses peeped from beneath the thorn tree.
2. The steamer glided away from the pier.
3. The child carried flowers in her hand.
4. The clerk worked at his desk.
5. The king gathered brave knights about him.
6. The hero forgot his own danger.
7. The rain beat against the window.
8. The bucket hung in the well.
9. The coral builds the islands of the sea.
10. The ships suddenly dashed against the rocks.
11. Every boy prizes his jackknife.
12. The great fire roared up the chimney.
13. The forests of the Adirondacks are extensive.
14. Much fruit is raised in New York.
15. Henry Hudson was a famous explorer.
16. Mexico was conquered by Cortez.
17. Captain John Smith was saved by Pocahontas.

SECTION 331

Use each of the following words, or groups of words, as either the subject or the predicate of a sentence : —

The River Nile, the Indian Ocean, large trees, a heavy rain, grew by the river, are found in California, fell into a snowbank, ran past, discovered America, Longfellow, Mexico, is a weed.

SECTION 332

In the following sentences the vertical lines separate the **subjects** from the **predicates**.

Read each sentence and select the subject and the predicate, remembering the definition of each.

1. Congress | presented a sword to Admiral Dewey.
2. The children | are let loose from school.
3. A Newfoundland dog | is an intelligent animal.
4. The windows | looked out upon the playground.
5. The children of the village | shouted with joy at the sight of Rip Van Winkle.
6. The muscles of his brawny arms | are strong.
7. The flock of wild geese | sailed high above our heads.
8. Down came | the storm.
9. Down the street ran | the merry children.
10. Quickly passed | the hours of that sunny day.

SECTION 333

Divide each of the following sentences into the two groups of words called subject and predicate : —

1. The fleecy clouds sail slowly across the sky.
2. The quiet sheep nibble the grass in the pasture.
3. The runaway horse threw his rider.
4. Every word has a work to do.
5. The schoolroom door opens at nine o'clock.
6. The cottage has a thatched roof.
7. The cows stand knee-deep in the water.
8. Edgar Allan Poe wrote " The Raven."
9. Frank has written his composition.

Exercise in Giving Directions *

One of the members of your class is a stranger in your town or city.

Tell him how to find his way from the schoolhouse to the post-office.

Your directions should be short and plain, and should say just what you mean.

Write the directions which you have given to your classmate.

Study this story, and write about Landseer as you did about Rosa Bonheur.

SIR EDWIN LANDSEER

Edwin Landseer was one of the most famous artists of modern times. He lived from 1802 to 1873.

He was born in London. His father was an engraver whose work was much admired. His brother was also a famous engraver.

The lad learned to draw at a very early age. He loved to go out into the fields with his paper and pencil, and draw the trees and the animals he saw there. He drew so well that his friends soon began to be surprised at his work. If you ever go to England and visit the great museum at South Kensington, in London, you may still see some

---

* This exercise may be extended or varied. Such practice should help to cultivate accuracy in speech.

of the drawings which he made before he was eight years old.

Whenever the boy went to walk, he took his sketch-book with him and told with his pencil what he saw. He liked best to sketch animals, and he went wherever he could find animals to sketch.

Young Landseer became the pupil of a famous English painter, Benjamin Hayden. Hayden taught him to study the structure of the animals he painted, so that he might know the place and shape of every bone and muscle. But Landseer was not contented with studying merely the bodies of the animals; he watched them as they moved about in the fields, played with one another, slept, or sought for food. He was their friend, and he understood them almost as if they could have spoken to him.

When Landseer was fifteen years old, he painted a picture of dogs fighting. Every one who saw it admired it, and it was sold at a good price. He painted dogs, sheep, and deer so that every one who studied his pictures went away with a real liking for the animals themselves. In the picture on page 166 Landseer represents himself as sketching, and his two dogs as looking over his shoulder at the sketch, as if they were judging whether it is good or bad. One hardly knows which to like more in the picture, the frank, open face of the artist with its clear eyes and noble brow, or the earnest, intelligent faces of the dogs who look over his shoulder.

You have doubtless seen other pictures by this same artist. In a later lesson you will study one of them. Perhaps you can bring others to the class.

You may sometimes see the artist's name written "Sir Edwin Landseer." Queen Victoria made him a knight with the title "Sir," because his work had been so well done.

The Connoisseurs.   By Landseer

SECTION 336

STUDY OF A PICTURE

"The Connoisseurs" was painted by Landseer.

Look up the word in your dictionary.

Who are the connoisseurs? Do they appear to be intelligent, or not? What do you suppose was the artist's thought in painting the picture?

Why are the dogs so deeply interested?

What does the picture tell you about the artist? about the dogs?

Write a description of the picture.

SECTION 337

Study Holmes's "Old Ironsides" (Selections, page 31).

Find in your history, or at the library, the story of "Old Ironsides." Then you will know why these verses were poured out in scorn when it was proposed to destroy the old ship that had served her country so well.

Read the poem for the first time to share the poet's loyalty and devotion to the heroes who fought on the ship. Then read it again, to understand why he says, "The harpies of the shore shall pluck the eagle of the sea," and "Give her to the god of storms, the lightning, and the gale."

Read the poem again, to see how great are the things which it makes you remember. The poet's indignation was kindled because others had forgotten. His words made them remember, and saved the ship.

SECTION 338

Modifiers

Study the thought expressed in each of the following pairs of sentences : —

1. { The child fears the fire.
2. { The *burnt* child fears the fire.

3. { The tree is covered with blossoms.
4. { The tree *in your yard* is covered with blossoms.

5. { The fox catches no poultry.
6. { The *sleeping* fox catches no poultry.

7. { Make hay.
8. { Make hay *while the sun shines.*

9. { Strike.
10. { Strike *while the iron is hot.*

11. { The dog will carry a bone.
12. { The dog *that will fetch a bone* will carry a bone.

13. { The sunflower stood.
14. { The *yellow* sunflower *by the brook in autumn beauty* stood.

In the first sentence the word *child* may refer to any child in the world, — "The child fears the fire." But when the word *burnt* is added, the meaning of the word *child* is **changed** or **modified**. It is now the "*burnt* child" that fears the fire; the thought applies only to the burnt child, and all other children are excluded.

In the same way, examine the third and fourth sentences.

Tree may mean any tree of which it is possible for you to think, — an apple tree or a cherry tree, a tree in Cuba or a tree in Japan. But when you add to the word *tree* the phrase *in your yard*, the thought and the statement apply only to the tree which is growing in your yard. All others are excluded.

Examine the remaining sentences, and observe the work of the italicized words and groups of words.

See if you can tell how the thought is changed by the addition of these words.

SECTION 339

Study the six pairs of sentences below, and observe the work which is done by the italicized words : —

1. A man fears no foe.
2. A *brave* man fears no foe.
3. Rivers are swift and turbulent.
4. Rivers *in mountainous regions* are swift and turbulent.
5. A cannon ball is a harmless thing.
6. A cannon ball is a harmless thing *when it is piled with others on the ground.*
7. A watch is useless.
8. A watch *without hands* is useless.
9. The wheels make no noise on the pavement.
10. The wheels *with rubber tires* make no noise on the pavement.
11. The air is fragrant.
12. The air is fragrant *when apple trees are in blossom.*

SECTION 340

MODIFIERS

In the examples which you have just studied you find that the meaning of the sentences is changed by the addition of the italicized words or groups of words.

Thus, *brave* describes *man* and **changes** or **modifies** the meaning of the first sentence. *In mountainous regions* describes *rivers* and **changes** or **modifies** the meaning of the third sentence, so that *rivers* is made to apply only to those in mountainous regions. It is not true that all rivers are " swift and turbulent," but it is true that " rivers in mountainous regions " are " swift and turbulent."

You have already learned to find the **subject** and the **predicate** of a sentence. Your study of the examples in Section 339 has shown you that many sentences contain words or groups of words which **modify** the meaning of other words in the sentence.

Such words or groups of words are called **modifiers.** They make it possible for us to say exactly what we mean.

Thus, nobody intends to say that a watch is useless. That is untrue. But the added **modifier,** *without hands,* makes the sentence true, — " A watch without hands is useless."

Some sentences contain words or groups of words which are joined to other words to limit or modify their meaning. Such parts of the sentence are called modifiers.

SECTION 341

Study the following sentences.

1. *Find the subject.*
2. *Find the predicate.*
3. *Find the words or groups of words which modify either the subject or the predicate.*

Tell the use of each modifier. Thus,—

" Fragrant roses grow by the roadside." *Roses* is the subject of the sentence. *Grow* is the predicate. The subject, *roses,* is modified by the word *fragrant,* which describes the roses. The predicate, *grow,* is modified by the phrase *by the roadside,* which tells where the roses grow. *Fragrant roses* is the complete subject, *grow by the roadside* is the complete predicate.

~~~~~~~~~~~~~

1. The babbling brook runs through the meadow.
2. The fields are watered by the April showers.
3. The old horse stumbled over a stone.
4. The merry-hearted child went happily on her way.
5. The careless bobolinks sing in the meadows.
6. Three bears lived in the woods.
7. The oaken floor was covered with a rich carpet.
8. The old house stood near a beautiful grove.
9. The little streams were swollen by the rain.
10. A stately stranger came to the tent.
11. The river was crossed by a bridge.
12. The Mississippi River was discovered by De Soto.

Find the subject, the predicate, and the modifiers in the sentences which follow.

Describe them as in Section 341.

1. A bright fire burned cheerily in the fireplace.
2. The old squire sat contentedly in his armchair.
3. The great dog was stretched by the fire.
4. The unlucky Rip was filled with despair.
5. The old stagecoach was crowded with passengers.
6. A huge roll of colored handkerchief was knotted about his neck.
7. An admiring throng of boys hung round the hand organ.
8. The shouts of children at play came to us through the window.
9. A group of village idlers sat on the porch of the tavern.
10. The little fellows leaped with joy around the Christmas tree.

Modifiers may be single words or groups of words.

Study the following examples : —

1. *Yellow* dandelions dot the lawn.
2. *Merry* children surround the teacher.
3. *Gentle* rains refresh the fields.
4. The captain *of the steamer* is a man *of great power.*
5. Washington was first *in war,* first *in peace,* and first *in the hearts of his countrymen.*

Compare the italicized modifiers in the first three sentences with those in the last two sentences.

In the first three sentences the modifiers which are italicized are **single words.** In the last two, each modifier is a **group of words.** Such a group of words is often called a **phrase.** You will understand the word *phrase* if it is used hereafter.

Study the sentences in the two preceding sections. Select all the modifiers of the subjects. Tell whether each modifier is a single word or a phrase.

SECTION 344

Expand the following sentences by adding modifiers to the subject and the predicate.

Enclose the separate modifiers in curved lines, and be ready to tell what word is modified in each case.

1. Cows graze.
2. Clouds gather.
3. Bells ring.
4. Sparks fly.
5. Clover blooms.
6. The bobolink sings.
7. The mountain is grand.
8. The sailors landed.
9. The waves dance.
10. The miner digs.

SECTION 345

DICTATION EXERCISE

When President Garfield was a young boy, a friend asked him what he meant to be when he grew up.

"I shall make a man first of all," he replied. "If I do not succeed in that, I can succeed in nothing."

SECTION 346

THE SEMICOLON

You have already studied words in a **series,** as in the following sentence : —

Boxes, crates, barrels, and *parcels* were tumbled about in confusion.

In the following passage you have another kind of series, — namely, a series of sentences all put together to make one longer sentence : —

You should write plainly ; you should spell correctly ; you should be careful about capital letters ; you should use marks of punctuation in the right places.

Observe the mark of punctuation (;) which separates the parts of the series. It is a **semicolon.** Its use is something like that of a comma and something like that of a period.

A semicolon is often used to separate parts of a sentence when a comma would not separate them enough.

Observe the semicolons in the following passage : —

Be not false, unkind, or cruel ;
Banish evil words and strife ;
Keep thy heart a temple holy ;
Love the lovely, aid the lowly ;
Thus shall each day be a jewel
Strung upon thy thread of life.

SECTION 347

CHARACTER STUDY

If you have read "The Dragon's Teeth" in Hawthorne's "Tanglewood Tales," you have certainly noticed the differences of character among the four boys.

Which of the four gave up the search first? What did he say? What did he do? Why did the people choose him for their king? What was his "very first decree of state"? What did this show?

Which of the four gave up next? Was he sorry? What did he say to the queen at parting? What was one of his first acts after he became king? Compare his character with that of Phœnix.

Which of the four gave up next? Why? Were his reasons different from those of the first and second? Why was he chosen king? What did he do then? How do his acts show his character?

What can you say of the character of Cadmus?

What did the queen say on parting with Phœnix? with Cilix? with Thasus? How does the difference in what she said to each show their characters?

What did the queen say to Cadmus when she died?

SECTION 348

If you have a copy of "Tanglewood Tales," copy the last paragraph of "The Pomegranate Seeds."

How does what Proserpina says show her character? Do other passages give you the same idea of her?

SECTION 349

BUSINESS LETTERS

Business letters should be plainly written, so that the message may be easily read ; and carefully expressed and punctuated, so that the meaning may be perfectly clear. They should contain no unnecessary matter and no roundabout phrases to steal the time of the person to whom they are sent.

A business man is busy. His time is usually filled with work, and the letter which you send to him is doubtless one of many thousands which he receives. Always remember this in writing a **business letter.** Ask your questions so clearly, make your business so plain, write so legibly, punctuate so carefully, that there can be no doubt of your meaning and no difficulty in getting at it.

Be courteous in letter writing. Consider the feelings of the person who is to receive your letter. Say what you have to say as politely as you can. Be sincere, honest, and kind, and write sincerely, honestly, and kindly. Never write a rude or unkind letter. You will be sure to regret it even more than you will regret an unkind speech.

In a **friendly letter** you may write of all the trifles which happen at home or in school, or of anything that interests you. You know that your friends are glad to learn about the little incidents of your everyday life. A **business letter,** however, should contain nothing but business, and should be as concise as possible.

The **full address** of the writer should appear in every business letter. It is often inserted at the end.

If the writer is a lady, the address should include the title *Miss* or *Mrs.*, in order that the reply may be correctly addressed.

For closing a business letter " Yours respectfully," " Yours truly," " Very truly yours," " Sincerely yours," are appropriate forms.

SECTION 350

Answer the following business letter : —

WATERTOWN, N. Y.,
Jan. 10, 1910.

MESSRS. E. M. BLAKE & CO.,
      209 Washington St.,
         Buffalo, N. Y.

GENTLEMEN : —

The picture which I bought on Friday arrived promptly Saturday afternoon, as you had promised.

I find upon removing it from the case that the frame is seriously marred. This may have happened on the way here, but that seems hardly possible.

I am sorry to trouble you, but I am sure you expected the picture to arrive in good condition. If you will kindly advise me what to do in the matter, you will oblige

      Yours very truly,

           ALICE T. ATWOOD.

(MRS. E. M. ATWOOD.)

SECTION 351

Answer the following business letter : —

ASHTABULA, OHIO,
May 16, 1910.

MY DEAR MISS EARLE,

I have long been in search of a good home-school for my niece, a girl of thirteen years.   My friend Mrs. J. L. Jenks has advised me to write to you on the subject.

May I ask you to send me a catalogue of your school, with such further particulars as occur to you ?

Sincerely yours,

(MISS) ELLA S. MEADE.

MISS MARY N. EARLE,
Saratoga Springs, N. Y.

SECTION 352

Copy this letter, observing its arrangement : —

EASTON, VERMONT,
January 25, 1910.

MRS. CHARLES W. KEENE,
427 Locust St.,
Harrisburg, Pa.

DEAR MADAM : —

Your letter was received this evening.

I shall be careful to follow your instructions in securing the farm, and will write to you as soon as the business is concluded.

Very truly yours,

ELMER A. CUTTING.

SECTIONS 353-357

NOTE TO TEACHER. — The following exercises in letter writing are to be used as the needs of the pupils suggest. Each exercise will be more valuable if it is first discussed by the class so that the conditions under which the letter is assumed to be written may be definitely understood.

353. Write a note to one of your school friends, inviting him or her to go with you to hear a lecture on Friday evening. Tell your friend where the lecture is to be given and at what hour. Tell him the subject of the lecture and add that it will be illustrated by stereopticon pictures.

354. Imagine that you are a young man named George Holt. You have graduated from the Grammar School and want to find work for the summer in the country. Write to your Uncle John, who lives in Mason City, Iowa, and ask him to tell you whether you could find employment in that neighborhood.

355. Imagine that you are a graduate of a High School and desire a position as bookkeeper. Write to Eliot Smith, Esq., a lawyer, who lives in Troy, N. Y., and who knows your family. Tell him what you desire, and ask him to give you the names of persons in Troy to whom you may apply for a position.

356. You wish to buy a boat. Write to Capt. Ethan Stone of Truro, Mass. Ask him to tell you whether you can obtain in Truro the kind of boat which you desire.

If you do not know anything about boats, ask your schoolmates to describe one for you.

357. Write to the owner of a wood-yard and order three cords of wood to be delivered at your house.

SECTION 358

STUDY OF A PICTURE

THE CARAVAN. BY L. D. ELDRED

THE CARAVAN

Write a description of the picture, in careful paragraphs. First make an outline.

What is a caravan? Of what is this caravan composed? Through what kind of country is it travelling? What do you know about the desert? What does the picture tell you about the riders? Describe them. How is the first rider distinguished from the rest?

SECTION 359

REVIEW OF RULES AND DEFINITIONS

I. CAPITAL LETTERS

1. Every sentence should begin with a capital letter.

2. Every line of poetry should begin with a capital letter.

3. All names of persons, places, days, and months should begin with capital letters.

4. All initials should be written in capitals and should be followed by periods.

5. Every title attached to a person's name should begin with a capital letter.

6. Every word denoting the Deity should begin with a capital letter.

7. The words *I* and *O* should be written with capital letters.

8. The first word of every direct quotation should begin with a capital letter.

9. In titles of books and the like, the first word, as well as every important word that follows, should begin with a capital letter.

II. MARKS OF PUNCTUATION

1. Every written statement should end with a period.

2. Every direct question should be followed by the interrogation point.

3. An exclamation is followed by an exclamation point.

4. Every abbreviation should be followed by a period.

5. The comma is used (1) to separate words in a series, (2) before a direct quotation, (3) after *yes* and *no* when followed by other words in the sentence ; (4) to set off the name of the person addressed.

6. The apostrophe must be used in contractions to denote the omission of a letter or letters.

7. Ownership or possession is often shown by adding the apostrophe and *s* to the name of the owner or owners.

If the name of the owners ends in *s*, the apostrophe only is added.

8. Quotation marks are used to enclose every direct quotation, and each part of a broken quotation.

A quotation within a quotation is enclosed in single quotation marks.

9. The title of a poem, book, lecture, or story is usually regarded as a quotation and enclosed in quotation marks.

10. The hyphen is used to separate the syllables of a word. When a word is divided at the end of a line, that part of the word which remains on the line must be followed by a hyphen.

III. SENTENCES

1. A sentence is a group of words which expresses a complete thought.

2. A declarative sentence declares or asserts something as a fact.

3. Every sentence consists of a subject and a predicate.

4. The subject of a sentence designates the person, place, or thing that is spoken of.

5. The predicate is that which is said of the subject.

6. A word or group of words that changes or modifies the meaning of another word is called a modifier.

PART THREE

INTRODUCTION

A family follows certain customs of its own, and is governed by certain rules. Our language, too, obeys definite rules, and follows certain customs, which change in the course of time, just as family customs change.

Our **language** is like a family. The **words** are the members, every one of which has a definite work to do. **Each word does its work,** just as each player takes his part in a game and each child performs his duties in the household.

If you study the **sentences** which express your thought, you will discover the kind of work which is done by the various words that you use.

Such study will help you to choose words wisely, to use them correctly, and to enjoy and appreciate good literature.

In the lessons which follow, we shall study

THE WORK WHICH WORDS DO.

SECTION 361

The Work of Words in a Sentence

You have already learned that each **word** in a sentence **has its own work** to do in the expression of thought.

The exercise that follows will make this important truth clearer to you.

Read the following sentence, then ask and answer the questions : —

Sue saw six slender saplings.

Who saw ?	*Sue.*
What did Sue do ?	*Saw.*
What did Sue see ?	*Saplings.*
How many saplings did Sue see ?	*Six.*
What kind of saplings did Sue see ?	*Slender.*

What word tells you who saw ?	*Sue.*
What word tells you what Sue did ?	*Saw.*
What word tells you what Sue saw ?	*Saplings.*
What word tells you how many saplings Sue saw ?	*Six.*
What word tells you what kind of saplings Sue saw ?	*Slender.*

What have you learned in asking and answering these questions ?

SECTION 362

Copy and number these sentences : —

1. Ill news travels fast.
2. Money is a good servant.
3. A small spark makes a great fire.
4. A barking dog seldom bites.
5. Tall oaks from little acorns grow.

Enclose in curved lines the words, or groups of words, which answer the following questions : —

1. What word **names** that which you tell something about? What word tells what news **does**? What word tells **what kind of** news it is that travels fast? What word tells **how** ill news travels?

2. What word names what your thought is about? What word tells what money is? What word tells what kind of servant?

3. What word names that which you tell something about? What word tells what a spark does? What word describes spark? What word names what the spark makes? What word describes fire?

4. What are you talking about in this sentence? What word describes dog? What word tells what the dog does? What word tells when he does it?

5. What word names that which grows? What word tells what oaks do? What words tell from what tall oaks grow? What word describes oaks? acorns?

Using the papers which you have written, tell what work each of the marked words has to do in the sentence.

SECTION 363

Study the following sentences.
Try to tell what work is done by every word in each sentence.

1. Little leaks sink great ships.
2. I know three happy children.
3. Jack found your tin whistle.
4. Mary wears blue ribbons.
5. Miss Meade teaches arithmetic.
6. Fortune favors the brave.
7. Ella sings sweetly.
8. Carl runs fast.
9. Edith found a woodpecker's nest.
10. Washington crossed the Delaware.
11. George found a gold locket.
12. Mr. Ames makes ploughs.
13. The big balloon floated lightly away.
14. The warm sunshine melted the snowbanks.
15. Joseph writes a good letter.
16. The flood destroyed the town.

SECTION 364

WORDS USED AS NAMES (NOUNS)

In other lessons you have written your own names and the names of your classmates. Have you thought that **everything** which you know has **a name,** just as every person has? These names are very convenient. We should find it hard to

talk without them.   Try it.   You will not succeed,
but the attempt will teach you an important fact : —

**When we express our thoughts in language we must
use words to name things.**

Copy and learn : —

Some words are used as the names of objects.
All names of persons, places, or things are nouns.
A noun is the name of a person, place, or thing.

SECTIONS 365–368

365. *Make lists of words which are used as names,
— that is, as nouns.*

    1. Names of things in the room.
    2. Names of articles of food.
    3. Names of toys.
    4. Names of fruits.
    5. Names of flowers.
    6. Names of trees.
    7. Names of animals.
    8. Names of articles of furniture.

366. *Name something* —

1. That unlocks a door.	7. That we live in.
2. That draws a wagon.	8. That we ride in.
3. That gives out heat.	9. That tells time.
4. That gives shade.	10. That keeps off rain.
5. That we eat or drink.	11. That we wear.
6. That keeps us warm.	12. That we write.

367. *Name something that grows —*

in a garden,	in a forest,
in a field,	in an orchard,
in a lake,	in the sea,
in a swamp,	by the roadside,
on tree trunks,	over old stone walls.

368. *Write the names which you have used in this exercise. Use them as subjects of sentences.*

SECTIONS 369–370

369. *Copy this riddle. Note the apostrophes : —*

A BOOK

I 'm a strange contradiction.　I 'm new and I 'm old;
I 'm often in tatters, and oft decked with gold.
I 'm always in black, and I 'm always in white;
I 'm grave and I 'm gay, I am heavy and light.
In form, too, I differ, — I 'm thick and I 'm thin;
I 've no flesh and no bone, yet I 'm covered with skin.
I 've more points than the compass, more stops than the flute;
I sing without voice, without speaking confute.
I 'm English, I 'm German, I 'm French, and I 'm Dutch.
Some love me too fondly, some slight me too much.
I often die soon, though I sometimes live ages,
And no monarch alive has so many pages.

HANNAH MORE.

370. *Explain every contrast in the riddle.*

How are books new and old, grave and gay, — and so on ?

Many of the words in the rhyme are used with a double meaning.　Can you find some of these words and explain their meanings ?

SECTION 371

WORDS WHICH ASSERT: VERBS

You have learned (pages 193–195) that every **sentence** contains a **subject** and a **predicate**.

You have also learned that the **subject** is that part of the sentence which **names** that of which we think, speak, or write, and that the **predicate** is that part of the sentence which **tells something** about the subject.

Study the sentences which follow : —

1. Kings reign.
2. Boys play.
3. The blackbirds chatter.
4. Children romp.
5. Leaves rustle.
6. Birds sing.
7. Balls roll.
8. Gulls scream.

In these sentences the **predicate** consists of a single word. This word **tells something** about the **subject**.

If you omit *reign* in reading the first sentence, your hearers may say, " Why did you not complete your sentence ? What did you wish to say about kings ? " The word *kings* does not **tell** anything.

We have described the work of such words as *reign* by saying that they **tell** something. It would be more exact to say that they **state**, or **assert** something. The sentence " Kings reign " may be called a **statement** or **assertion**.

In every assertion there must be a **word which asserts**. Such words are called **verbs**.

A verb is a word which asserts.

SECTION 372

Find, in the following sentences, words which you think are verbs : —

1. I slip, I slide, I gloom, I glance,
    Among my skimming swallows;
   I make the netted sunbeam dance
    Against my sandy shallows.
2. Good actions ennoble us.
3. Man beholds the face, but God looks upon the heart. Man considers the actions, but God weighs the intentions.
4. She learned the luxury of doing good.
5. The wind blew freshly, and drove the chest away from the shore, and the uneasy billows tossed it up and down.
6. Midas paused and thought awhile.
7. Meanwhile Hercules travelled constantly onward, over hill and dale, and through the solitary woods.
8. The young man looked down into the dimpling mirror of the fountain.
9. Mrs. Cratchit made the gravy hissing hot. Master Peter mashed the potatoes with incredible vigor. Miss Belinda sweetened up the apple-sauce. Martha dusted the plates. Bob took Tiny Tim beside him in a tiny corner at the table. The two young Cratchits set chairs for everybody, and, while they mounted guard at their own posts, crammed spoons into their mouths lest they should shriek for goose before their turn came to be helped.

SECTION 373

VERBS EXPRESSING ACTION

Most **verbs** express **action,** as in the following
sentences : —

1. Horses *run.*
2. Birds *fly.*
3. The train *moves.*
4. The boat *touched* the pier.
5. The boy *found* his book.
6. The child *thanked* his father.

*In the selections on page 224 find all the verbs
which seem to you to express action.*

In looking for such verbs, you should remember that
actions are performed by the mind as well as by the body.
When you think, judge, consider, reason, love, fear, succeed, and fail, as well as when you are running, jumping,
or playing, you are acting.

**In making your lists, give careful attention to the
meaning of the word.   Get the sense of every sentence.**

SECTION 374

Write from dictation : —

THE COURAGEOUS TRAVELLERS

A gentleman who had travelled in Africa told his friends
that he and his servant once made fifty Arabs run.   All
who heard the story were amazed.

"How did you manage it ? " asked one.

"O, it was nothing very wonderful," replied the traveller.   "We ran, and they ran after us."

SECTION 375

FOR READING AND TELLING

Dean Stanley tells this story about Sir William Napier, an English officer.

Sir William Napier once met a little girl, five years old, who was sobbing over a pitcher which she had broken. When he tried to comfort her, she asked him to mend the pitcher. He told her that he could not mend it, but that he would give her sixpence to buy a new one.

On looking in his purse, he found that he had no money to give the child. "I will bring you the sixpence to-morrow," he said. "Meet me here at this same hour." The child was comforted, and the officer went on his way.

When Sir William reached home, he found awaiting him an invitation from a friend which he greatly desired to accept, but his acceptance would have prevented him from meeting the little girl. He therefore declined the invitation, writing to his friend, "I could not disappoint the child, because she trusted in me."

SECTION 376

WRITTEN EXERCISE

Write the anecdote of Sir William Napier.

Try to tell the story so as to make the meaning clear.

Take care to use the punctuation marks correctly.

Arrange your story in paragraphs.

How does the story show Sir William's character?

SECTION 377

FOR READING AND TELLING

THE BELL OF JUSTICE

In a village of Italy, years ago, a good king hung a bell in the market-place and covered it with a sheltering roof. Then, calling his people together, he told them what he had done. " This is the Bell of Justice," he said. " Whenever a wrong is done to any man, I will call the judges to make it right, — if he but rings the great bell in the square."

With so good and just a king the people of the village lived happily. The bell called the judge, whenever wrong was done, and he heard all complaints. After many years the bell-rope was worn away by use. It hung out of reach until some one, passing by, mended it with a wild vine.

Now it happened that a famous knight dwelt in the village. When he was young, he had many hounds and horses and spent his time in hunting and feasting, but when he became an old man he had no love for anything but gold. So he sold his hounds, gave up his rich gardens, and kept but one horse, that starved in the stable. At length he became so greedy and selfish that he grudged the poor horse his scanty food and turned him out to feed in the streets. The poor creature wandered about, — uncared for, unfed, and forsaken.

One summer afternoon, as the people dozed in their houses they heard the sound of the Bell of Justice. The judge hastened to the market-place, where the great bell was ringing. " Who hath been wronged ? " he asked. But, reaching the belfry, he saw only the starving horse struggling to reach the vine which had been tied to the bell-rope.

"Ah!" said the judge, "the steed pleads his cause well. He has been forsaken by the master whom he served, and he asks for justice."

The people had gathered in the market-place, and among them the knight. The judge spoke gravely.

"Here came the steed who served his master well, yet who was abandoned and forgotten. He pleads for justice, and the law decrees that the man whom he served shall provide him with food and shelter, that he may abide in comfort.

The knight, ashamed, led home his faithful horse. The king approved the righteous judgment, — saying, "My bell indeed may be called the Bell of Justice. It pleads the cause even of the dumb, who cannot speak for themselves."

The story of "The Bell of Justice" is beautifully told by Longfellow in the poem called "The Bell of Atri." If you have a copy, read the poem for yourself. If you do not own the book, get it from the library.

Read the story. Make an outline, and tell the story from your outline.

SECTIONS 378–379

378. What does "The Bell of Justice" tell you about the character (1) of the knight; (2) of the judge?

Write your answer in two paragraphs.

379. *Use, in oral sentences of your own, the following words from "The Bell of Justice" : —*

village, just, feasting, selfish, steed, gravely, abandoned, righteous, market-place, complaints, dwelt, forsaken, pleads, served, provide, approved, sheltering, famous, grudged, belfry, cause, justice, decrees, abide.

SECTION 380

The following paragraphs are taken from an interesting story of life in Norway, called "Lisbeth Longfrock": —

Kjersti Hall, the mistress of Hall Farm, was in *her* kitchen, over by the white wall of the big open fireplace, grinding coffee. *She* looked up when *she* heard the door open.

Lisbeth Longfrock stood still for a moment, then made a deep courtesy under her long frock, and said, in a grown-up way, just as *she* had heard *her* mother say, "Good day, and God bless *your* work."

Kjersti Hall had to smile when *she* saw the little rolypoly bundle over by the door, talking in such a grown-up fashion. But *she* answered as soberly as if *she* also were talking to a grown-up person, "Good day. Is this a young stranger out for a walk?"

"Yes."

"Then what is the stranger's name, and where is *she* from? *I* see that *I* do not know *her*."

"No, *you* could not be expected to know *me*. *My* mother and Jacob call *me* Lisbeth Longfrock, and *I* am from Peerout Castle. Mother sent *me* here with the woolen yarn *she* has spun for *you*. *She* told *me* to say that *she* could not come with *it* before, for *she* did not get the last spool wound until late last night."

Read the paragraphs, giving attention to each italicized word. For what does each italicized word stand?

If you try to use other words in place of the italicized words on page 229, your sentences will be both awkward and confusing.

The italicized words, then, are of great importance to us in expressing our thoughts. They enable us to avoid the awkward and puzzling repetition of nouns, and thus they make our speech both clearer and more direct. Such words **stand for nouns.** They **point out** or **designate** objects, though they do not name them as nouns do.

Some words stand for nouns.

A pronoun is a word used instead of a noun. It designates a person, place, or thing without naming it.

SECTION 381

Find the pronouns in the following passages: —

1. The flying spider climbs upon a post or tree and spins a little thread which floats off upon the air. As soon as he makes enough of it to carry him, he floats off with it on the breeze, and in that way he travels over the landscape by wings of his own making.

2. I have a squirrel that lives in my study wall. He is on the lookout for the apples which I put for the little rabbit that lives under the floor, and he often gets them.

3. Dear little blossoms down under the snow,
   You must be weary of winter, I know.

4. "Will you walk into my parlor?"
   Said the spider to the fly.

5. A squirrel's tail not only aids him in flying, but it also serves as a cloak.

382. *Find the pronouns in the following passages, and tell the noun for which each pronoun stands :* —

1. A great elm spread its broad branches over the house.
2. He spoke not a word, but went straight to his work.
3. The frugal snail, with forecast of repose,
   Carries his house with him where'er he goes.
4. The blossoms drifted at our feet,
   The orchard birds sang clear.
5. Sleep, baby, sleep!
   Thy father's watching the sheep,
   Thy mother's shaking the dreamland tree,
   And down drops a little dream for thee,
           Sleep, baby, sleep!
6. Little Bell sat down beneath the rocks,
   Tossed aside her gleaming golden locks.
7. The wind, wife, the wind! how it blows, how it blows!
   It grips the latch, it shakes the house, it whistles, it
       screams, it crows,
   It dashes on the window-pane, then rushes off with
       a cry, —
   You scarce can hear your own loud voice, it clatters
       so loud and high.
8. One day my dog and I were sitting beside a small water-
course in the woods when I saw a mink coming up the stream.

383. *Make a list of all the pronouns which you have found in Sections 380–383.*

Make a list of pronouns which you find used as subjects of sentences.

Do you ever find me, us, him, her, them *so used?*

SECTION 384

STUDY OF A POEM

Read the " Lullaby of an Infant Chief."

This poem was written by Sir Walter Scott, some of
whose stories you have doubtless read and enjoyed.

1. What does it tell you about the life of the people
whom it describes?

2. What does it show you about the feeling of the
singer?

3. Compare it with " A Gaelic Lullaby " (page 169),
and with Shakspere's " Lullaby for Titania " (Selections, page 37).

LULLABY OF AN INFANT CHIEF

O, hush thee, my baby, thy sire was a knight,
Thy mother a lady both lovely and bright;
The woods and the glens from the tower which we see,
They all are belonging, dear baby, to thee.

O, fear not the bugle, though loudly it blows,
It calls but the warders that guard thy repose;
Their bows would be bended, their blades would be red,
Ere the step of a foeman draws near to thy bed.

O, hush thee, my baby, the time will soon come
When thy sleep shall be broken by trumpet and drum;
Then hush thee, my darling, take rest while you may,
For strife comes with manhood, and waking with day.

SIR WALTER SCOTT.

SECTION 385

ADJECTIVES

Copy these sentences. Then read them, omitting the italicized words.

1. I have a *red* box.
2. Mary wears *blue* ribbons.
3. Philadelphia is a *large* city.
4. A *merry* heart doeth good like a medicine.
5. An *honest* man is the *noblest* work of God.
6. A *wise* son maketh a *glad* father.

Tell how omission of the word changes the meaning of the sentence.

What change is made in each sentence?
What is the use of *red* in the first sentence?
What is the use of *blue* in the second sentence?
What is the use of *large* in the third sentence? of *merry* in the fourth? of *honest* in the fifth? of *noblest*? of *wise*? of *glad*?

In the sentences above, what does *red* describe? *blue*? *merry*? *honest*? *noblest*? *glad*? *wise*?

Red, blue, large, merry, honest, noblest, wise, and *glad* help us to **describe** persons, places, and things. Such words are called **adjectives.**

Adjectives help us to describe persons, places, or things.

Find the adjectives on page 231 and use them in sentences of your own.

SECTIONS 386-392

386. *These words are adjectives.   Use them orally in sentences.*

keen	high	playful	airy
sad	quiet	studious	careless
weary	mild	beautiful	glassy
droll	sly	curious	brittle
gentle	brave	pleasant	tough
dull	bright	faithful	starry
easy	funny	glorious	shrewd

387. *Use these adjectives in written sentences.*

ripe	strong	graceful	saucy
silent	weak	awkward	neat
kindly	rough	courteous	feeble
difficult	smooth	talkative	stern
large	rainy	merciful	old
sunny	polite	graceful	dirty
saucy	young	friendly	frail

388. *Use the following adjectives in sentences.*

industrious	hasty	loyal
hospitable	slow	boyish
splendid	manly	juicy
wonderful	joyous	fleecy
porous	awful	poor
fertile	grand	stony
grateful	lovely	cozy
drowsy	true	fiery
wealthy	pale	rich

If you do not understand the meaning of all the words in the lists, you should use your dictionary.

389. *Write fifteen sentences, each containing one of the adjectives in the preceding list.*

Let some of your sentences be statements, some questions, and some commands or requests.

390. *Make a list of adjectives which you can use in describing —*

a dandelion, an apple, an orange, a horse, a cent, a chair, your desk, your ball, your book.

391. *Find, in the following sentences, words which you think are adjectives : —*

1. Ring out, wild bells, to the wild sky,
   The flying cloud, the frosty light.
2. An old, bent man, worn out and frail,
   He came back from seeking the Holy Grail.
3. Brutus is noble, wise, valiant, and honest.
   Cæsar was mighty, bold, royal, and loving.
4. "Come in," the Mayor cried, looking bigger,
   And in did come the strangest figure!
   His queer long coat from heel to head
   Was half of yellow and half of red;
   And he himself was tall and thin,
   With sharp blue eyes each like a pin,
   And light loose hair, yet swarthy skin,
   No tuft on cheek, nor beard on chin,
   But lips where smiles went out and in.

392. *Write ten sentences containing adjectives that you have found in the preceding Section.*

SECTION 393

The adjectives which you have studied have **described** objects by indicating some quality.

Some adjectives do not really describe objects, but they **point out** or **number** persons or things.

> *Many* men attended the meeting.
> This is the *fifth* book that I have read this month.
> A *few* cherries are left on the tree.
> *Three* crows sat on the oak.

An adjective is a word which describes or limits a noun or pronoun.

In some poem or story in your reading book, find words which seem to you to be adjectives. Do they describe, or number, or point out (designate) objects?

SECTION 394

Compare the following sentences : —

> A *wooden* club ⎫
> A club *of wood* ⎬ was the savage's weapon.

In the first sentence, *wooden* is an **adjective** describing *club*. In the second, *of wood* is a **phrase** which does the same work as the adjective *wooden*.

A group of connected words, not containing a subject and a predicate, is called a phrase.

Of wood in the second sentence is called an **adjective phrase,** because it does the work of an adjective.

SECTION 395

Bring to school a blossoming plant.
Observe the plant carefully, and talk about it in the class.

EXAMPLE. — STUDY OF A GERANIUM

1. Where does it grow? What care does it require? How does it change from month to month? What is its use? Where is the geranium a wild flower?

2. Observe the stem, the leaves, the blossoms. Observe the size, shape, position, color, arrangement.

3. Of what use are the leaves to the plant? the blossoms? the seed? Is there any reason for the bright color of the blossom? Which remains longer upon the plant, the blossom or the seed? Why? If you turn the geranium away from the window, so that its leaves and blossoms look toward you and look away from the sun, what will happen? Do you know why?

4. After talking about the geranium, find in books anything which will help you to answer the questions which have arisen in your conversation.

NOTE TO THE TEACHER. — Use, in similar exercises, different plants which are available in your neighborhood.

SECTION 396

Draw the plant which you have just studied.

SECTION 397

Write a description of the same plant.

SECTIONS 398–401

398. *Make a list of the adjectives used in your description of the plant (Section 397).*

Compare your list, in the class, with those which the other pupils have made.

399. 1. *Write a description of your teacher's desk.*
2. *What is a desk? Write your reply.*

In the first exercise you make a **description**; in the second, a **definition**. Compare the description and the definition. What must a definition tell? Both the definition and the description are often necessary to an **explanation**.

400. *Find in your dictionary the definitions of ten common objects :* as, —

chair, table, street, house, knife, shell, cat, toy.

401. *Write a description of one of the objects which you defined in the preceding section.*

Of course your description must apply to a particular chair, shell, toy, etc.

SECTIONS 402–403

DICTATION EXERCISES

THE FAINT-HEARTED MOUSE

1. A timid little mouse lived in the house of a great magician. The poor creature was in constant fear of the cat and had not a moment's peace.

2. The magician, taking pity on the mouse, turned it into a cat. Then it suffered for fear of the dog. To cure this fear, the magician turned it into a dog. Then it

trembled for fear of the tiger. The magician changed it into a tiger, but it at once began to tremble for fear of the hunters.

3. " Be a mouse again ! " cried the magician in disgust. " You have the heart of a mouse, and cannot be helped by wearing the body of a nobler animal."

Study the story, and prepare to write it from dictation.

Note every mark of punctuation.

403. The story in Section 402 is a fable. It is told for the sake of teaching a lesson about human life and character. What is the lesson ?

Are some children timid by nature and others naturally courageous ? Could the mouse be expected to change its nature ? Can we change or improve our natural character by taking pains ?

Tell a story about a faint-hearted boy who over-came his timid nature.

SECTIONS 404-410*

LETTER WRITING

404. Rachel Foster is making a collection of postal cards. Her friend Helen Wright has sent her a number of cards to add to her collection.

Imagine that you are Rachel Foster, and write to Helen to thank her.

* Sections 404–410 are meant to furnish additional practice in letter writing. Teachers who do not care for such practice at this point may go on with Section 411 at once, omitting Sections 404–410.

405. Write to your friend, Harry Eastman, and ask him to spend next Saturday with you. Tell him that there is fine skating on Crystal Lake, near your home. The snow has been scraped off the ice, and sheds, in which skaters can warm themselves, have been built near the shore.

406. You have had five dollars given you to use in buying books.

Write to your teacher and ask her to suggest some good books for you to buy. Tell her what kind of books you like best.

407. *Write a letter to a friend, telling him how you spent an October day in the woods.*

408. Vacation is drawing near. Write to your cousin, Enoch Bryant, who is fitting for college at an academy, and ask him to spend the vacation with you. Tell him what you will do to make his stay a pleasant one.

409. You have received an invitation from a friend staying at Atlantic City to spend two weeks with her at the seashore.

Write accepting the invitation.

410. Your father has just given you a new camera.

Write to a friend, making an appointment to go with him next Saturday to photograph the Library Building.

SECTION 411

An Explanation or Exposition

Write a composition on the Stamp Act.

Explain (1) who passed the act, and when; (2) what it was; (3) why the Americans objected to it.

SECTION 412

ARTICLES

There are three little adjectives that are hard-worked members of the word-family. They appear in almost every sentence which is spoken or written. These adjectives are **a, an,** and **the.** They are called **articles.**

A and *an* are really two different forms of the same word, which means *one.*

A is used before a word beginning with a consonant sound ; *an* before a word beginning with a vowel sound.

Thus we say "*a* lemon," but "*an* orange"; "*a* book," but "*an* arithmetic"; "*a* man," but "*an* old man."

If you try to use *a* in the examples where *an* appears, or *an* in the place of *a*, your phrases will be very awkward.

SECTION 413

Use the following words in sentences, placing before them a, an, or the.

valley	picture	carriage
corn	star	elephant
eagle	tree	amethyst
child	animal	Indian
key	robin	ox
apple	library	yellow
orange	kitten	large

SECTION 414

Read this song and describe the singer : —

A SEA SONG

A wet sheet and a flowing sea,
 A wind that follows fast,
And fills the white and rustling sail
 And bends the gallant mast;
And bends the gallant mast, my boys,
 While, like the eagle free,
Away the good ship flies, and leaves
 Old England on the lee.

"O for a soft and gentle wind!"
 I heard a fair one cry;
But give to me the snoring breeze
 And white waves heaving high;
And white waves heaving high, my lads,
 The good ship tight and free, —
The world of waters is our home,
 And merry men are we.

There's tempest in yon hornèd moon,
 And lightning in yon cloud;
But hark the music, mariners!
 The wind is piping loud;
The wind is piping loud, my boys,
 The lightning flashes free,
While the hollow oak our palace is,
 Our heritage the sea.

ALLAN CUNNINGHAM.

SECTIONS 415–417

415. *Use in written sentences of your own the following nouns, adjectives, and verbs, from the song in the preceding section : —*

Eagle, old England, gentle wind, white waves, follows, bends, flashes, lightning, hollow oak, waters, merry men, yon cloud.

416. *Tell a story suggested by "A Sea Song."*

If you cannot make up a sea story, find one in some book that you have read.

417. *Find and copy an anecdote showing the character of John Paul Jones or some other naval hero.*

Tell the story so as to bring out the hero's character.

Write the story.

SECTION 418

Copy Emerson's "Concord Hymn" (Selections, page 42), and learn it by heart.

The first stanza of this poem is famous. The third and fourth lines are oftenest quoted. You well know why the shot was "heard round the world" and has echoed through all the years since. What was the spirit that "made those heroes dare to die and leave their children free"?

The movement of the hymn is quiet and even, and its temper is serene. Contrast the poem with "Warren's Address" (Selections, page 36) and "The Burial of Sir John Moore" (Selections, page 51). Do you see the reason for the difference?

SECTION 419

REVIEW OF THE WORK WHICH WORDS DO

Study this selection; then read it aloud. Tell in your own words the contents of each paragraph, as you read.

TREASURE–BOXES

1. We all have our treasure-boxes. *Misers* have *strong iron-bound* chests full of gold; *stately ladies*, pearl inlaid *caskets* for their jewels; and even *you* and *I*, dear child, have our own. Your *little* box with lock and key, that *Aunt Lucy* gave *you*, where you *have kept* for a *long* time your choicest *paper* doll, the *peacock* with spun-glass tail, and the *robin's* egg that we *picked* up in the path under the *great* trees that *windy* day *last* spring, — that is your treasure-box. *I* no less have *mine;* and, if you will look with *me*, I *will show* you how the *trees* and *flowers* have theirs, and what is packed away in *them*.

2. Come out into the *orchard* this *September* day, under the low-bowed *peach trees*, where *great downy-cheeked* peaches almost *drop* into *our hands*. Sit on the *grassy* bank with *me*, and I *will show* you the peach tree's *treasure-box*.

3. What does the peach tree regard as most precious? If *it* could speak in words, it would tell you *its seed* is the one thing for which it cares most; for which it *has worked* ever since spring, storing *food*, and drinking in *sunshine*. And it is so dear and valued, because, when the peach tree itself dies, this seed, its child, may still live on, growing into a *beautiful* and *fruitful* tree; therefore the mother tree *cherishes* her *seed* as her *greatest* treasure, and has

made for it a *casket* more beautiful than *Mrs. Williams's* sandalwood jewel-box.

4. See the great crack where this *peach broke* from the *bough*. We *will pull it* open; this is opening the *cover* of the *outside* casket. See how rich is the outside color, and how wonderfully beautiful the deep *crimson* fibres which *cling* about the hard shell inside! For this seed cannot be trusted in a *single* covering; moreover, the *inner* box is locked *securely*, and, I am sorry to say, we have n't the key; so, if I would show you the inside, we must break the *pretty* box, with its *strong, ribbed* walls, and then at last we shall see what the *peach tree's* treasure-box holds.

5. The *tall* milkweed that *grew* so fast all summer, and *threatened* to overrun the garden, now pays well for its lodging by the exquisite treasure which its *rough-covered, pale-green* bag *holds.* Press your thumb on its closed edges; for *this casket opens* with a spring, and, if it is ripe and ready, it will unclose with a touch, and show you a *little fish*, with *silver* scales laid over a covering of *long, silken* threads, *finer* and more *delicate* than any of the sewing silk in your mother's workbox. *This* silk is really a wing-like float for *each scale ;* and the *scales* are seeds, which will not stay upon the *little* fish, but long to float away with their *silken* trails, and, alighting here and there, *cling* and *seek* for a good place to plant *themselves.*

6. Autumn is the time to open these treasures. It takes all the spring and summer to prepare them, and some even need all of September too, before they are ready *to open* the little *covers.* But go into the *garden* and *orchard*, into the *meadows* and *woods*, and you have not far to look before finding enough to prove that the *plants*, no less than the children, *have treasures* to keep, and *often* most *charming* boxes to keep them in.   JANE ANDREWS.

SECTION 420

FOR CONVERSATION

Read " Treasure-Boxes " (pages 244, 245), and tell what work is done by each of the italicized words.

If you are not sure about the work of any word, you may pass it by.

First think what the sentence *tells you, and then think what the* word *tells you.*

Examples : —

Misers names the persons who have the chests of gold.
The sentence tells us about misers.
Strong describes the chests of gold.
Caskets names what stately ladies have for their jewels.
Will show tells us what *I* will do.

SECTION 421

Write an explanation called " How Nature Protects Seeds."

Use the following topics, and find material partly in " Treasure-Boxes " and partly with your own eyes.

1. Seeds are very important. (*Show this.*) Therefore they must be protected.
2. How the peach tree protects its seeds.
3. How the milkweed protects and plants its seeds.
4. How the seed of the oak is protected and planted.
5. Nature, like ourselves, has treasure-boxes.

SECTION 422

Study the poem according to the following plan: —

Read the poem once to get the story.

Read it again and imagine the scenes that it describes.

After reading the first three stanzas, describe the school-house in your own words.

Describe the scene pictured in the next four stanzas.

Tell the story which is told in the next two stanzas.

What do the last two stanzas tell you?

Read the poem again, and imagine yourself an old man relating this experience of your childhood.

Try to see the schoolhouse, the winter sunset, and the children.

IN SCHOOL DAYS

Still sits the schoolhouse by the road,
  A ragged beggar sunning;
Around it still the sumachs grow,
  And blackberry vines are running.

Within, the master's desk is seen,
  Deep scarred by raps official,
The warping floor, the battered seats,
  The jack-knife's carved initial;

The charcoal frescoes on its wall;
  Its door's worn sill, betraying
The feet that, creeping slow to school,
  Went storming out to playing!

Long years ago a winter sun
  Shone over it at setting;
Lit up its western window panes,
  And low eaves' icy fretting.

It touched the tangled golden curls,
    And brown eyes full of grieving,
Of one who still her steps delayed
    When all the school were leaving.

For near her stood the little boy
    Her childish favor singled,
His cap pulled low upon a face
    Where pride and shame were mingled.

Pushing with restless feet the snow
    To right and left, he lingered;
As restlessly her tiny hands
    The blue-checked apron fingered.

He saw her lift her eyes; he felt
    The soft hand's light caressing,
And heard the tremble of her voice,
    As if a fault confessing.

"I'm sorry that I spelt the word;
    I hate to go above you,
Because," — the brown eyes lower fell, —
    "Because, you see, I love you!"

Still memory to a gray-haired man
    That sweet child-face is showing.
Dear girl! the grasses on her grave
    Have forty years been growing!

He lives to learn, in life's hard school,
    How few who pass above him
Lament their triumph and his loss,
    Like her, — because they love him.

WHITTIER.

SECTION 423

ADVERBS

Study the following sentences, observing the work of the italicized words : —

1. The boy runs.
2. The boy runs *swiftly*.
3. The girls laughed.
4. The girls laughed *heartily*.

Note the difference in meaning between 1 and 2.

What word causes this difference or change in meaning ? What does *swiftly* modify ?

Note the difference in meaning between 3 and 4.

What causes this difference or change ? What does *heartily* modify ?

In sentences 2 and 4 we find words which modify verbs. *Swiftly* modifies the verb *runs*. *Heartily* modifies the verb *laughed*.

Swiftly and *heartily* are **adverbs,** — so called because they are **added to verbs.**

Some words are used to modify the meaning of verbs. Such words are called adverbs.

SECTION 424

The following words are adverbs : —

Easily, soon, carefully, nearly, thoughtfully, thoroughly, tenderly, hurriedly, slowly, eagerly.

Use these adverbs in sentences.

SECTIONS 425-428

425. *Find adverbs in the following sentences :* —

1. The children play merrily.
2. The boy ran hastily from the room.
3. The river flows rapidly.
4. That bird sings sweetly.
5. George never lies.
6. Arthur studies faithfully.

426. *Expand the following sentences and modify their meaning by adding adverbs to the verbs. Thus,* —

The boy ran.   The boy ran swiftly.

1. The bird sang.
2. Flowers bloom.
3. The soldier fought.
4. The boat sailed.
5. The horse ran.

6. The dog barked.
7. The river flows.
8. Rain falls.
9. The wind blows.
10. The sun shines.

427. *Make ten sentences, each containing a verb modified by an adverb.*

428. *Complete these sentences orally by adding adverbs which answer the question "How?" Insert each adverb in place of a blank.*

1. Jack Frost does his work ——.
2. The stockings were —— hung by the chimney.
3. The kitchen clock ticks ——.
4. The mother-bird sits —— at home in her nest.
5. Robert of Lincoln is —— dressed.
6. The little sandpiper skims —— along the beach.

SECTION 429

ADVERBS

Adverbs do not always modify **verbs.** In the following sentences the italicized words are adverbs. What does each adverb modify?

> The child saw a *very* large dog.
> Your apron is *too* long.
> This pen is *not* good.

In the first sentence *very* (an adverb) modifies *large* (an adjective). In the second sentence *too* (an adverb) modifies *long* (an adjective). In the third sentence *not* (an adverb) modifies *good* (an adjective).

Some adverbs modify adjectives.

Make or find ten sentences in each of which an adverb modifies an adjective.

SECTION 430

ADVERBS

Study the following sentences.

The italicized words are **adverbs.** What do they modify?

> James, you write *too* rapidly.
> Mary walked *very* slowly.
> He skates *quite* easily.
> You write *rather* badly.
> Speak *more* plainly.

In the first sentence *too* (an adverb) modifies *rapidly* (an adverb). In the second sentence *very* (an adverb) modifies *slowly* (an adverb). In the third sentence *quite* (an adverb) modifies *easily* (an adverb). Compare the work of the italicized words in the other sentences.

Your study of these sentences shows you that adverbs sometimes modify other adverbs.

Adverbs are always used as **modifiers.** They usually modify **verbs,** but sometimes limit or modify **adjectives** or other **adverbs.**

An adverb is a word which modifies a verb, an adjective, or another adverb.

SECTIONS 431–432

431. *Make ten sentences in each of which an adverb modifies an adverb.*

432. *Expand the following sentences by adding one or more modifiers. Thus,—*

> The boy ran.
> The boy ran swiftly.
> The boy ran swiftly across the field.
> The older boy ran swiftly across the field.

1. The cock is crowing.
2. The streamlet is flowing.
3. The birds twitter.
4. The lake glitters.
5. The cattle are grazing.
6. The snow hath retreated.
7. The ploughboy is whooping.

In the fourth example, the **phrase** *across the field* is called an **adverbial phrase,** because it modifies the verb (*ran*) as an adverb would do.

Yes and No

433. *Yes* and *no* are two very important words which have a peculiar work to do. Either of them may express the thought of a whole sentence : —

"Is this your ball, John?" "Yes." "Is this your bat, too?" "No."

John's reply, "Yes," is equivalent to saying, "That is my ball." His second reply, "No," is the same as the sentence, "It is not my bat."

John might have replied, "Yes, that is my ball." "No, that is not my bat." In that case the meaning would have been the same as when he said merely "yes" and "no," for he would simply have repeated the assent and the denial.

You will observe in these sentences, as you have before learned, that *yes* and *no* are separated from the rest of the sentence by a **comma**. You will now state the rule in this form : —

Yes and *no*, expressing assent or denial, are separated from the rest of the sentence by a comma.

434. *Write ten sentences in reply to written questions. Use* yes *or* no *in each reply. Thus,* —

> Do you know how to swim, John?
> No, but I should like to learn.

435. *Prepare a dictation exercise, using sentences which contain* yes *or* no.

SECTION 436

For Conversation and Composition

1. *Learn all you can about some noted person: as, — Patrick Henry, Philip Schuyler, John Paul Jones, Daniel Boone, Robert Fulton, Grant, Farragut.*

2. *Talk about the person whose life you have studied, answering the following questions : —*

When did he live ?
Where did he live ?
For what is he noted ?
What was his character ?
What particular work makes us remember him ?
What anecdotes do you know that illustrate his character ?
What else can you say about him ?

3. *After reading what you can find in books, and talking together in the class, write the answers to the questions. Arrange your answers in paragraphs.*

Note to Teacher. — This exercise may be repeated indefinitely, according to the needs of the pupils. It may be varied by discussing a place instead of a person.

SECTION 437

Write an account of some well-known person, without using his name.

Your account may be read to the class and the name guessed by the other pupils.

SECTION 438

WORDS WHICH SHOW RELATION

Study the following sentences, observing the work of the italicized words : —

1. Henry sat *beside* the boat.
2. Henry sat *behind* the boat.
3. Henry sat *upon* the boat.
4. Henry sat *in* the boat.

If you read the sentences, omitting the italicized words, you will discover that the sense is incomplete. You have an idea of Henry and of the boat. You know that Henry sat somewhere, but your thought and your statement are unfinished. You have no notion of the **relation** of the boat to the other ideas suggested by the sentence. But when the italicized word is supplied, you see this **relation** or **connection**: "Henry sat *in* the boat." The missing link is supplied, and the words make sense.

SECTION 439

Use the following words in sentences to show relation, as in the examples just studied.

in	by	before
through	over	behind
toward	under	for
upon	into	against
with	after	above

SECTION 440

PREPOSITIONS

The words *beside, behind, upon, in, for, toward, by, under,* which we have just studied (p. 255), with many other similar words, are **prepositions**.

They are so called because they are **placed before** a noun or pronoun. As we have seen, they **show the relation** between a noun or pronoun and some other part of the sentence.

Study the following sentences, and change each preposition so that a different relation shall be expressed.

For example, in the fifth sentence, you might use *from* or *at* or *after* in the place of *toward.* How would the relation be changed?

1. The book lies upon the table.
2. The child stands behind the table.
3. Jack ran to his father.
4. Leave the flower in the vase.
5. The dog saw his master and ran toward him.

SECTION 441

Find the preposition in each example above.

Find the noun or pronoun which follows the preposition.

A preposition is a word placed before a noun or pronoun, to show its relation to some other word in the sentence.

SECTION 442

Complete the following sentences orally by inserting appropriate prepositions.

What noun or pronoun follows each preposition?

Can you insert other prepositions in the same sentences, so as to show different relations?

1. The girl put the hammer —— the box.
2. The picture hangs —— the window.
3. The rug lies —— the table.
4. The boy threw his ball —— me.
5. The teacher said, " Lay your pencils —— your desks."
6. The railroad runs —— the hill.
7. The sparrow flew —— him.
8. Some plants grow —— the water.
9. Place your paper —— your books.

SECTION 443

Name objects in the schoolroom and tell their relation to other objects.

What **preposition** do you use in each sentence to express this relation?

Examples : —

> The bell is *on* the desk.
> The fern is *near* the window.
> James sits *beside* me.
> A picture hangs *over* the door.

SECTIONS 444–445

444. *Read this poem until you think you understand its meaning.   Then tell what you think the
poet wishes us to learn from the poem.*

ABOU BEN ADHEM

Abou Ben Adhem (may his tribe increase!)
Awoke one night from a deep dream of peace,
And saw within the moonlight of his room,
Making it rich, and like a lily in bloom,
An angel, writing in a book of gold.
Exceeding peace had made Ben Adhem bold,
And to the presence in the room he said,
"What writest thou?" The vision raised its head,
And, with a look made all of sweet accord,
Answered, "The names of those who love the Lord!"
"And is mine one?" said Abou. "Nay, not so,"
Replied the angel. Abou spoke more low,
But cheerly still, and said, "I pray thee, then,
Write me as one who loves his fellow men."
The angel wrote and vanished. The next night
It came again, with a great wakening light,
And showed the names whom love of God had blest;
And lo! Ben Adhem's name led all the rest!

Leigh Hunt.

445. *Copy Shakspere's " Mercy " (Selections, page
49), and learn it by heart.*

Is the lesson that it teaches like that in " Abou
Ben Adhem " ?

SECTION 446

CONJUNCTIONS

1. Mary went to Boston yesterday.
2. Kate went to Boston yesterday.
3. Mary and Kate went to Boston yesterday.

1. Speech is silver.
2. Silence is golden.
3. Speech is silver, but silence is golden.

1. Men have fought for their country.
2. Men have bled for their country.
3. Men have died for their country.
4. Men have fought and bled and died for their country.

If you study the first group of sentences in the examples, you will see that the third sentence contains the thought of the other two. It is possible to express the two thoughts in one sentence because we have the help of the little word *and*. In the third example *and* connects *Mary* and *Kate* and thus enables us to express the thought in a single sentence.

And is called a **conjunction** because it **joins** or **connects** words. This is its work in the sentence.

Find in the second group of sentences the word which joins or connects the parts of the sentence.

Find the conjunction in the third set of sentences and show its use.

Learn the definition : —

A conjunction connects words or groups of words.

SECTION 447

Find conjunctions in the following sentences, and tell what parts of the sentence are connected by them.

1. He rode all unarmed and he rode all alone.

2. O, come ye in peace here, or come ye in war,
   Or to dance at our bridal, young Lord Lochinvar?

3. Vessels large may venture more,
   But little boats keep near the shore.

4. He spoke not a word but went straight to his work.

5. The rain is over and gone.

6. It was midnight on the waters
   And a storm was on the deep.

7. Catch me if you can.

8. Brag is a good dog, but Holdfast is a better.

9. Help the weak if you are strong.
   Love the old if you are young.
   Own a fault if you are wrong.
   If you are angry, hold your tongue.

10. We never know the worth of water until the well is dry.

11. Keep thy shop and thy shop will keep thee.

12. Fools make feasts and wise men eat them.

13. Silks and satins, scarlet and velvets, put out the kitchen fire.

14. It is easier to build two chimneys than to keep one in fuel.

15. Sloth makes all things difficult, but industry makes all things easy.

SECTION 448

Copy "The Burial of Sir John Moore" (Selections, page 51).

This is a famous poem, which not only keeps a hero in memory, but also tells us something of the awfulness of the soldier's experience.

The words are simple; you are used to them all. The rhythm is slow, even, and steady, like a solemn march. The feeling is sad but heroic, as if the words were spoken by men whose comrades had shed their blood for their country.

Read the poem slowly, and learn it by heart.

Try to find out something about Sir John Moore.

SECTION 449

OUTLINE FOR EXPOSITION

Study the outline, and make notes for each topic.

The Horse and the Automobile.

1. What work can a horse do?
2. How is he fitted for this work?
3. How is he trained to do it?
4. What care does he require?
5. How does an automobile take the place of a horse?
6. What can each do that the other cannot?
7. Which do you prefer, and why?

Make an oral explanation of the subject, using your notes.

Interjections

In the examples below you will find words which stand apart from the rest of the sentence. Some of these words simply represent sounds which express strong or sudden feeling. They are called **interjections,** because they are "thrown into" the sentence and often have no share in it.

In speaking, the **voice** naturally expresses feeling or emotion; but in writing, the interjection is followed by an **exclamation point,** which is a sign to the reader.

Study the following sentences. Find the words which you think are interjections.

1. Hark! how the music leaps out from his throat!
   Hark! was there ever so merry a note?
2. Hush! the bear will hear thee!
3. "It snows!" cried the schoolboy.   "Hurrah!"
4. Alas! alas for Hamelin!
5. And lo! Ben Adhem's name led all the rest.
6. There goes Friday running for his life to the little creek!   Halloo! whoop! halloo!
7. And lo! as he looks, on the belfry's height,
   A glimmer and then a gleam of light!
8. "Bah!" said Scrooge.
9. "Caw! caw!" the rooks are calling.
10. "Ho! ho!" the breakers roared.

An interjection is a cry or other exclamatory sound expressing surprise, anger, pleasure, or some other emotion or feeling.

SECTION 451

*Study the following sentences, and point out all
the words which you think are interjections.*

Can you tell what feeling is expressed by each
interjection?

1. Hurrah! the procession is coming.
2. O velvet bee! you 're a dusty fellow,
   You 've powdered your legs with gold!
3. Hurrah! what fun we shall have!
4. Ho there! ship ahoy! What ship's that?
5. Alas! the wretched scene that opened on their view!
6. O joy! the travellers gaze on each other with hope-
brightened eyes.
7. O, whither sail you, brave Sir John?
8. "O, haste thee, haste!" the lady cries.
   "The tempests round us gather."
9. Pshaw! what a nuisance it is!
10. Ah! how can I tell you?

SECTION 452

*Copy the sentences in Section 451, observing the
use of the exclamation point.*

Be ready to write the sentences from dictation.

*Remember the rule to which you have been accus-
tomed : —*

**The interjection *O* is always written with a capital
letter.**

In previous lessons you have studied the **kinds of work** which words have to do in sentences.

Let us now gather together the principal facts which you have learned.

The Work which Words Do

1. Some words **name** persons, places, or things. Such words are called **nouns**.

2. Some words **stand for** persons, places, or things, without actually naming them. Such words are called **pronouns**.

3. Some words **describe** persons, places, or things. Such words are called **adjectives**.

4. Some words **assert** something concerning a person, place, or thing. Such words are called **verbs**.

5. Some words **modify** the **meaning** of verbs or adjectives. Such words are called **adverbs**.

6. Some words **show** the **relation** of nouns or pronouns to other words in the sentence. Such words are called **prepositions**.

7. Some words **join** other words or groups of words. Such words are called **conjunctions**.

8. Some words, like *oh! ah! ow!* are mere cries or **exclamatory sounds** expressing sudden emotion, — as surprise, anger, or fear. Such words are called **interjections**.

Every word in the dictionary belongs to some one of these eight groups, which are called **parts of speech.**

The work which a word has to do determines its place among the parts of speech.

If the word *names* something, it is a noun. If it *stands for* a noun, it must be a pronoun. If it *asserts* something, it is a verb — and so on.

You have already discovered something about these parts of speech. Now you are ready to learn more about them.

SECTION 454

Rule a sheet of paper like the model.

Write in the proper column, so far as you can, each word of the sentences on page 260.

You should make a separate list of all words which you cannot classify with certainty, and should not write any word in any column unless you are sure where it belongs.

Nouns.	Pronouns.	Adjectives.	Verbs.	Adverbs.	Prepositions.	Conjunctions.	Interjections.

NOTE FOR TEACHER. — Exercises of this nature may be continued indefinitely, but should *not* be absolutely exhaustive at this stage. It is well to use selections from the reading book at this point, but only on condition that doubtful words be passed by for the time being.

SECTION 455

REVIEW OF RULES AND DEFINITIONS

A sentence is a group of words which expresses a complete thought.

Every sentence consists of a subject and a predicate.

The subject of a sentence designates the person, place, or thing that is spoken of; the predicate is that which is said of the subject.

A declarative sentence asserts or declares something as a fact.

A word or group of words that changes or modifies the meaning of another word is called a modifier.

Every word has its own work to do in the expression of thought.

In accordance with their use in the sentence, words are divided into classes called parts of speech.

There are eight parts of speech, — nouns, pronouns, adjectives, verbs, adverbs, prepositions, conjunctions, and interjections.

The work which a word has to do determines its place among the parts of speech.

1. A noun is the name of a person, place, or thing.

2. A pronoun is a word used instead of a noun. It designates a person, place, or thing without naming it.

3. An adjective is a word which describes or limits a noun or pronoun.

4. A verb is a word which asserts.

5. An adverb is a word which modifies a verb, an adjective, or another adverb.

6. A preposition is a word placed before a noun or pronoun to show its relation to some other word in the sentence.

7. A conjunction connects words or groups of words.

8. An interjection is a cry or other exclamatory sound expressing surprise, anger, pleasure, or some other emotion or feeling.

SECTION 456

LESSON TO SHOW THAT THE SAME WORD MAY HAVE DIFFERENT USES IN DIFFERENT SENTENCES

Remember that a word is always classified according to its use in the sentence. If the word is used to modify a noun in one sentence, and to modify a verb in another, it is an adjective in the first sentence and an adverb in the second.

    1. The *fast* horse ran in the race.
    2. The horse ran *fast*.

In the first sentence *fast* modifies the noun *horse*, and is an adjective. In the second sentence *fast* modifies *ran*, and is an adverb.

    1. Our *walk* was a pleasant one.
    2. We *walk* to school.

In the first sentence *walk* is a noun. Why?
In the second sentence *walk* is a verb. Why?

Ask yourselves this question, " What work does this word do in this sentence?" Then you can readily decide to what part of speech it belongs.

Learn to use your own judgment, to weigh the words in the sentence, to get their meaning, and to think how they are used. Then name them.

Find in your dictionary ten words each of which may be used in more than one way.

SECTIONS 457–459

VERB-PHRASES

457. Sometimes a verb consists of two or more words.

1. I *study* geography.
2. I *shall study* geography.
3. I *have studied* geography.
4. I *may study* geography.
5. I *am studying* geography.
6. I *shall be studying* geography soon.

In the first example, the verb consists of one word, *study*. The assertion is made by that single word. In the second sentence, two words (*shall study*) are needed, and in the sixth we find three.

Shall study, *have studied*, *may study*, *am studying*, *shall be studying*, and other similar **phrases** which do the work of verbs, are called **verb-phrases**.

458. *Mention the verb or verb-phrase in each sentence:* —

1. The town-crier has rung his bell at a distant corner.
2. Little Annie stands on her father's doorsteps.
3. The crier is telling the people about a menagerie.
4. Strange beasts from foreign lands have come to town.
5. Perhaps little Annie would like to see them.
6. She shall take a ramble with me.
7. We turn the corner. The crowds are moving slowly.

459. *Use each of these verbs and verb-phrases in a sentence:* — may go, is trying, am working, walk, was driven, speaks, has seen, is flying, has been running, has been studying, strike, may be reading, had taken, were rushing, shall go, has done.

SECTION 460

EXPLANATION OR EXPOSITION

Study the following explanation (or exposition) from Mrs. Gulick's book on "Emergencies":—

CRAMPS

Cramps seize one most frequently when in the water. Many deaths from drowning are due to cramps. Even good swimmers are sometimes unable to escape them. If you have ever had cramps, never swim far from shore or out of reach of prompt help of some kind. It is not safe. No matter how good a swimmer you are, remember that being in the water a long time makes you more liable to have cramps.

People in general are learning to be more careful about running risks of this kind. It is recognized as foolhardy to go long distances from shore without having some one near by with a boat. It is more and more the custom for boys and girls and even grown-up people, when taking long-distance swimming tests, to have a boat alongside for each swimmer.

A cramp in the leg is about as painful as anything of which I know. The muscle becomes contracted and forms a bunch or knot. It makes one helpless and faint. Brisk rubbing will take the cramp out better than anything else. When cramps come in the leg a good remedy is to stretch the heel out and away as far as possible. A friend who is subject to cramps has found this method always successful. I have had muscles sore for days after having a cramp.

This is a good example of clear and simple explanation. There are three paragraphs arranged as in the outline below: —

1. Cramps often attack swimmers.
2. They are very dangerous to swimmers.
3. The pain from cramps and its relief.

Study each paragraph and observe how the sentences refer to the topic in the outline. Observe also that the sentences are arranged so as to make the meaning of the paragraph clear.

SECTIONS 461-462

461. *Make an oral explanation like that in Section 460.*

462. *Write your explanation in three paragraphs. Compare your composition with the original, and see if your paragraphs are good.*

SECTIONS 463-464

463. *Tell a story about a swimming match or some swimming adventure. Or, if you prefer, explain how you learned to swim.*

464. *Write three paragraphs about swimming. In the first tell of swimming as a pleasure or a sport; in the second, as a benefit to the health; in the third, as a means of saving life.*

SECTIONS 465-467

THE STUDY OF NOUNS

465. A noun is the name of a person, place, or thing.

Everything which we can think about has a **name.** It is easy to recognize some names as **nouns,** because they name objects or persons that we see, or hear, or read about, every day. But it is sometimes difficult to realize that the names of thought-objects are as truly nouns. Thus, —

Where there's a will, there's a way.

Here are two **nouns,** *will* and *way.* They **name things,** but not things which you can see, or hear, or touch, or taste, or smell. You can simply think about them, name them, and say or assert something about them.

In the following sentences you will find such nouns.

Point them out. Use each noun in a sentence of your own.

1. Temperance is a virtue.
2. Haste makes waste.
3. Sloth consumes like rust.
4. Truth is stranger than fiction.
5. I value his friendship.
6. Youth is the time for sowing, age for reaping.
7. Flattery encourages deceit.

466. *Write the names of ten actions : as,* — rowing, leaping, swimming, throwing, battle, deed, struggle.

Write the names of ten things which you know by hearing : as, — music, a song, a voice, a chirp.

Use the nouns in sentences of your own.

467. *Write the names of ten things which you can think about, but cannot see with your eyes, or hear with your ears : as,* — goodness, trust, mercy, truth, courage, wisdom.

COMMON AND PROPER NOUNS

1. That *person* lives in the *city*.
2. You know that *James Ryder* lives in *Chicago*.
3. The *steamship* crossed the *ocean* in safety.
4. The *Etruria* crossed the *Atlantic* in eight days.
5. We made a *camp* on the side of the *mountain*.
6. We visited *Camp Worth*, on *Mount Ossipee*.

Compare the pairs of nouns in the following columns.

person	James Ryder
city	Chicago
steamship	Etruria
ocean	Atlantic
camp	Camp Worth
mountain	Mount Ossipee

James Ryder is the name of a particular *person*.
Chicago is the name of a particular *city*.
Etruria is the name of a particular *steamship*.
Atlantic is the name of a certain or particular *ocean*.
Camp Worth is the name of a particular *camp*.
Mount Ossipee is the name of a particular *mountain*.

These names, *person, city, steamship, ocean, camp, mountain,* are names which may be applied to **any** object of their class, — any person, any city, any steamship, any ocean, any camp, any mountain. They are therefore called **common nouns,** because they are *common* to all objects in the class which they name.

James Ryder is the name of a particular person, and can be applied to that person only. *Chicago* is the name of a particular city, and the name cannot be applied to all cities. *Etruria* is the name of a particular steamship of the Cunard Line.

Such names are called **proper names** or **proper nouns.** If you look in the dictionary, you will find that **proper** is derived from a word which means "one's own." One's own name, then, is a "proper" name.

Learn : —

Nouns are either proper nouns or common nouns.

A proper noun is the name of a particular person, place, or thing.

A common noun is a name which may be applied to any one of a class of persons, places, or things.

A proper noun should always begin with a capital letter.

SECTION 469

1. *Write the names of ten of your schoolmates.*

2. *Write the names of ten towns or cities.*

3. *Write the names of ten birds that you know.*

4. *Write the names of two trees, flowers, vegetables, fruits, days, kinds of cloth, dishes, months, holidays.*

SECTION 470

Use in oral sentences the names in the lists which you have made in studying the preceding section.

PERSONIFICATION

It often happens in literature that an animal is referred to as if it were a person. This is common in fables. So also a thing without life, or a quality of mind or character (like goodness, truth), may be spoken of as living and acting. Thus, in the poem "Lady Moon" (page 107), the moon holds a conversation with a child. Compare "The Wind and the Moon" (Selections, page 14). In proverbs and in poetry, we find examples of traits of character represented as acting. Thus, —

1. Foolhardiness comes swaggering up, and pretends that he is Courage.

2. Truth crushed to earth shall rise again,
    Th' eternal years of God are hers.

This practice of treating things and animals as if they were **persons** is called **personification.** The noun which names the thing personified is written with a capital letter.

Here are examples of **personification.**

Find the nouns which name the thing personified.

Put into plain words the thought which is expressed through personification.

1. Said the Mouse to the Lion, " You spared my life, and now I have saved yours."

2. Laziness travels so slowly that Poverty soon overtakes him.

3. The Frost looked forth one clear cold night.

4. Pride breakfasted with Plenty, dined with Poverty, and supped with Infamy.

5. Laziness is a dangerous comrade.

EXPLANATION OR EXPOSITION

Study the following three paragraphs of explanation : —

HOW ROCK CHANGED INTO SOIL

Learned men believe that at first the surface of the earth was solid rock. How were these rocks changed into workable soil? Occasionally a curious boy picks up a rotten stone, squeezes it, and finds his hands filled with dirt, or soil. Now, just as the boy crumbled with his fingers this single stone, the great forces of nature with boundless patience crumbled the early rock mass. These simple but giant-strong agents that beat the rocks into powder with a club-like force a million fold more powerful than the club force of Hercules were chiefly : (1) heat and cold; (2) water, frost, and ice; (3) a very low form of vegetable life; and (4) tiny animals, if such minute bodies can be called animals. In some cases these forces acted singly; in others, all acted together to rend and crumble the unbroken stretch of rock. Let us glance at two of the methods used by these skilled world-makers.

Heat and cold are working partners. You remember that most hot bodies shrink, or contract, on cooling. These early rocks were hot. As the outside shell of rock cooled from exposure to air and moisture, it contracted. This shrinkage of the rigid rim, of course, broke many of the rocks, and here and there left cracks, or fissures. In these fissures water collected, froze, and, as freezing water expands with irresistible power, the expansion still further broke the rocks to pieces. The smaller pieces again, in the same way, were acted upon by frost and ice, and again crumbled. This process has continued more or less until this day.

Running water was another giant soil-former. If you would understand its action, observe some usually sparkling stream just after a washing rain. The clear waters are discolored by mud washed in from the surrounding hills. As though disliking their muddy burden, the waters strive to throw it off. Here, as low banks offer a chance, they run out into shallows and drop some of it. Here, as they pass some quiet pool, they deposit more. At last they reach the still water at the mouth. There they shake off the last of their mud load, and often form of it little islands, or deltas. In the same way, bearing acres of soil in their waters, mighty rivers like the Amazon, the Mississippi, and the Hudson, when they are swollen by rain, sweep to the seas. Some soil they scatter over the lowlands as they whirl seaward; the rest they deposit in deltas at their mouths. It is estimated that the Mississippi carries to the ocean each year enough soil to cover a square mile of surface to a depth of two hundred and sixty-eight feet.*

Study each paragraph, and make notes.

Copy the first two sentences of the first paragraph, the first sentence of the second, and the first sentence of the third.

These four sentences give a good idea of the plan of the whole explanation.

With the teacher's help, make an outline of the explanation, using your notes.

* From " Agriculture for Beginners."

Paragraph Study

473. If you wish to improve in writing English, you should often examine your sentences and paragraphs, and see if they obey the rules which you have learned, or are like the patterns which have been shown you.

In examining your paragraphs, these test questions may help you. Sometimes the class may answer them for you, for others can often see our mistakes, as well as our successes, better than we can.

1. What is the **topic** or subject of my paragraph?

2. Does the paragraph clearly show this topic?

3. Do the sentences of the paragraph refer to the topic or relate closely to it (explaining it, or adding to it)?

4. Are the sentences arranged in good order? For example, is the arrangement good as to the **time of events?** as to **consequences** or **results** of events? Do the sentences march in an orderly file, or are they scattered and mixed?

5. Are the sentences clear, so that the thought is clear?

6. Is the thought of the paragraph complete, so that my reader will understand the whole of what I wished to say?

474. *Study the selection in Section 472.*

Test each paragraph by the questions in Section 473.

475. *Describe Beth in "Little Women."*

First, tell who she was; second, describe her appearance; and third, describe her character. Test your paragraphs.

SECTION 476

GENDER OF NOUNS AND PRONOUNS

Observe the italicized words in this sentence : —

Robert and his *sister* have sailed for Europe.

Each of these italicized nouns indicates the **sex** of the person named. We know at once that *Robert* is a man or a boy, and that his *sister* is a woman or a girl. Accordingly, the noun *Robert* is said to be of the **masculine gender,** and the noun *sister* is said to be of the **feminine gender.**

The pronoun *he* stands for a **masculine** noun, *she* for a **feminine** noun, *it* for a **neuter** noun.

Gender is distinction according to sex.

A noun or pronoun denoting a male being is of the masculine gender.

EXAMPLES : — man, boy, brother, gentleman, carpenter.

A noun or pronoun denoting a female being is of the feminine gender.

EXAMPLES : — woman, girl, sister, lady, sempstress.

A noun or pronoun denoting a thing without animal life is of the neuter gender. *

EXAMPLES : — tree, book, apple, house, brick, glass.

* *Neuter* means "neither" (that is, "*neither* masculine nor feminine").

SECTIONS 477-478

477. *In the following pairs of words, tell which nouns are of the masculine gender and which are of the feminine.*

man	woman	gander	goose
boy	girl	drake	duck
father	mother	horse	mare
brother	sister	ram	ewe
uncle	aunt	buck	doe
nephew	niece	hart	hind
father-in-law	mother-in-law	deacon	deaconess
king	queen	actor	actress
duke	duchess	lion	lioness
count, earl	countess	tiger	tigress
man-servant	maid-servant	hero	heroine

478. The gender of nouns is usually shown by their meaning only: as, — uncle (*masculine*), aunt (*feminine*), animal (*masculine or feminine*), rock (*neuter*).

Sometimes the gender of nouns is shown by their form.

1. Many nouns ending in *or* or *er* are masculine: as, — sailor, actor, carpenter, bricklayer. Others are either masculine or feminine: as, — teacher, worker, basket-maker.

2. Some feminine nouns are formed with the ending *ess*: as, — lioness (from *lion*), heiress (from *heir*), actress (from *actor*), empress (from *emperor*).

3. The nouns *man* and *woman* (or *maid*) are sometimes added or prefixed to other nouns to show gender: as, — (1) workman, workwoman; salesman, saleswoman; (2) man-servant, woman-servant or maid-servant.

4. The pronouns *he* and *she* are sometimes prefixed: as, — he-goat, she-goat.

SECTIONS 479–481

479. *Use the following nouns in oral sentences. Tell whether each is masculine, feminine, or neuter:* — king, Martha, lioness, cow, arrow, child, duke, robin, empress, mason, cowboy, washerwoman, postman, miller, doe, velvet, explorer, engineer, conductor, hatchet, poem.

480. *Tell the corresponding masculine or feminine:* — actress, uncle, heir, duchess, ram, she-goat, saleswoman, gentleman, drake, sister-in-law, grandfather, hero.

481. *Find the pronouns in the extracts on page 231. Tell the noun for which each pronoun stands. Tell the gender of each noun and of each pronoun.*

SECTION 482

Read "Puck and the Fairy" (Selections, page 48).
Learn, from Shakspere's play, who Puck was.
Learn more about the fairy. Then read the selection carefully aloud, to get the measure of the lines.

What words in the lines are new to you? *Thorough* is an old form of *through*. (When do you think this poem was written?) *Pale* stands for the word you know as *paling* in connection with fences. Who but a fairy could wander where this fairy roams? Where is the court of the Fairy Queen? When is it held? What are pensioners? Have *you* seen the freckles of the cowslip? Can you fancy them as rubies?

The lines are light and joyous, fit for fairies and flowers.

Learn the selection by heart.

SECTION 483

Singular and Plural Number

Arrange the italicized nouns in two columns.

In the first column write the nouns which name one object, and in the second column those which name more than one object.

1. A *farmer* was working in the *field*.
2. *Farmers* were working in the *fields*.
3. The *boy* has a new *kite*.
4. *Boys* like to fly *kites*.
5. The *dog* ran mad.
6. Let *dogs* delight to bark and bite.
7. That *girl* is my sister.
8. The two *girls* are sisters.
9. The *church* stands by the side of the *road*.
10. You will see the *churches* at the meeting of the *roads*.
11. The *soldier* slept at his post.
12. The *soldiers* were led by General Schuyler.
13. The *tree* was blown down.
14. Many *trees* were felled.
15. Our guide led us through the *pass*.
16. There are many *passes* in these mountains.

Nouns denote one object or more than one.

Nouns which denote a single object are said to be in the singular number.

Nouns which denote two or more objects are said to be in the plural number.

Farmer, field, boy, kite, dog, are in the **singular number**.
Farmers, fields, boys, kites, dogs, are in the **plural number**.

SECTION 484

Change the following sentences so as to make the statement about more than one object : as, —

The *boys* were playing in the yard.

1. The *boy* is playing in the yard.
2. The *dog* barked noisily.
3. The *brook* leaps over the stones.
4. The *bush* grows by the wall.
5. The *horse* is fearless and fleet.
6. The *apple* is red.
7. The *hen* cackles.
8. The *plate* is broken.
9. An *elm* shades the house.
10. The *ditch* is broad.

Write the italicized words in a column and complete the pairs.   Thus, —

One (SINGULAR)	TWO OR MORE (PLURAL)
boy	boys
dog	dogs

What is the difference in *form* between the singular and the plural of each noun in your list ?

Most nouns form the plural number by adding *s* or *es* to the singular.

Such plurals are said to be regular, that is, according to rule.

When a plural is formed in any other way, it is said to be irregular.

SECTION 485

Write a list of nouns which form their plural by adding s *or* es *to the singular.*

See how long a list you can make.

If you think of any nouns which do not follow the rule, write them in a separate list, giving both singular and plural.

Use the nouns in your lists in oral sentences.

SECTIONS 486–488

RULES FOR SPELLING THE PLÚRAL

486. *Study the italicized words :* —

> The *berry* is red. [SINGULAR.]
> The *berries* are red. [PLURAL.]

You notice that *berry* ends in **y** preceded by a consonant, and that in *berries* this **y** is changed to **i** before the plural ending **es**. Here are other examples : —

SINGULAR	PLURAL	SINGULAR	PLURAL
fly	flies	lady	ladies
cry	cries	cherry	cherries
baby	babies	lily	lilies
dolly	dollies	story	stories

Write sentences containing these nouns in the singular; in the plural.

Nouns ending in *y* preceded by a consonant change *y* to *i* and add *es* in the plural.

487. *Study the italicized words : —*

A *loaf* of bread lies on the table.   [Singular.]
Two *loaves* of bread lie on the table.   [Plural.]

Write the singular and the plural of loaf, leaf, calf, half, wolf, shelf, knife, wife, life.

A few nouns change *f* to *v* before the plural ending.

488. *Write the singular and the plural of the following nouns.   Then use the nouns in sentences.*

Bud, ship, robin, spider, jay, tree, crocus, orange, leaf, fly, brush, oriole, burr, chickadee, ditch, knife, house, echo, carriage, dish, inch, lass, stitch, judge, cry, potato, tomato, study, daisy, valley, journey, mile, country, city, library, colony, bay, sea, rat, salary, calf, delay, speech, slave, dress, chief, victory, pupil.

SECTIONS 489–491

Irregular Plurals

489. You can easily make a definition for an **irregular plural,** — that is, for one which is not formed according to rule.

An irregular plural is one which is not formed by adding *s* or *es* to the singular.

Here are some **irregular plurals : —**

Singular	Plural	Singular	Plural
man	men	goose	geese
woman	women	mouse	mice
foot	feet	ox	oxen
tooth	teeth	child	children

490. 1. A few nouns are alike in singular and plural : as, — deer, sheep, Japanese.

> The *sheep* is nibbling the grass.   [SINGULAR.]
> The *sheep* are nibbling the grass.   [PLURAL.]

2. A few nouns have two plurals : as, — fish, penny, brother.

> 1. Here are three *fishes*.
>   The *fish* do not bite.
> 2. I see two *pennies* on the floor.
> 3. English money is counted in pounds, shillings, and
>   *pence*.

3. Foreign words often keep their foreign plurals : as, — stratum, *plural* strata ; crisis, *plural* crises ; alumnus, *plural* alumni.

491. When a **letter,** a **figure,** or a **sign** is used as a name it becomes a noun.   Thus, —

> You do not write plainly. I cannot tell your *a* from your *o*.
> The alphabet begins with *a* and ends with *z*.

Letters of the alphabet, figures indicating number, and other signs add '*s* in the plural.

 1. Mind your *p's* and *q's*.
 2. Count all the *3's* in the column.
 3. Now add by *5's* to sixty.
 4. You make your +'s and your ×'s too much alike.

When words are spoken of as **things,** their plural is written like the plural of letters or signs.   Thus, —

> Children use too many *and's* in composition.
> Write the *Sarah's* with h's.

Make ten sentences in which you apply these rules.

SECTION 492

SPECIAL RULES FOR PROPER NOUNS

1. The plural of *Mr.* is *Messrs.* (pronounced *Messers.*). Thus, —

   1. *Mr.* John *Smith* and *Mr.* Thomas *Smith* were present.
   Messrs. John and Thomas *Smith* were present.
   The Messrs. Smith were present.

   2. John Jones and his cousins, George Brown and Peter Smith, are forming a company. It will be called *Brown, Jones & Smith.* When writing to them, you will address them as *Messrs. Brown, Jones & Smith.*

2. You may say —

   Miss Smith and her sister are coming to dinner.
   The Misses Smith are coming to dinner.
   The Miss Smiths are coming to dinner.

All three ways are correct. The second is more formal than the others.

3. When the title is *Mrs.*, the plural sign is attached to the family name.

   1. Have you seen the other *Mrs. Baker?*
   Are there two *Mrs. Bakers?*
   2. I saw *Mrs. King* with her son's wife.
   So we have two *Mrs. Kings* with us.

Make ten sentences in which you use the forms that you have just been studying.

SECTION 493

Compound Nouns and their Plurals

Some nouns are made up of two or more words united into one.

Examples of such **compound nouns** are : — playfellow, wheelbarrow, father-in-law, man-of-war, window-pane, fisherman.

Make a list of compound nouns which you have used.

A compound noun usually forms its plural regularly.   Thus, —

eyebrow, eyebrows ; bookcase, bookcases ; candlestick, candlesticks ; workbench, workbenches.

Sometimes the first part of the compound noun is made plural; sometimes both parts are changed.

The plurals *mothers-in-law*, *men-of-war*, show the first part changed; in *men-servants* both parts are changed.

SECTIONS 494–495

494. *Write the plural of each of the following nouns and use the plural in an oral sentence :* —

fireman, ox, carpenter, fly, blackberry, echo, motto, jack-knife, brother-in-law, washerwoman, penny, scratch, man-of-war, man-servant, dish, tax, mass.

495. *Tell the gender and number of* —

duchesses, drake, mares, sister-in-law, bakers, arrow, clerk, bookkeeper, generals, admiral, doe, hens, calves, millers, weaver, actress, tigresses, emperor.

SECTIONS 496–499

FOR ORAL AND WRITTEN COMPOSITION

496. Many of you have read " Squirrels and Other Fur-Bearers," by Mr. John Burroughs. What do you know about squirrels, either from the book or from your own observation ?

Make notes of what facts you remember, and make an outline for three or four paragraphs about squirrels.

497. *Describe some squirrel that you have seen.*

498. *Read the following extract : —*

One reason, doubtless, why squirrels are so bold and reckless in leaping through trees is that, if they miss their hold and fall, they sustain no injury. Every species of tree-squirrel seems to be capable of a sort of rudimentary flying, — at least of making itself into a parachute, so as to ease or break a fall or a leap from a great height.

What is a parachute ? How are parachutes used with balloons ? Describe a parachute if you have ever seen one. What does "rudimentary" mean ? Find a word of similar meaning.

499. How does a squirrel make himself into a kind of parachute ? If you look in Mr. Burroughs's book, you will find this question answered by two stories.

*Tell one of these stories in your own words.**

* For other subjects from " Squirrels and Other Fur-Bearers" see page 334.

SECTIONS 500-501

Gender and Number of Pronouns

500. *Study the following sentences :* —

The *gentleman* took *his* umbrella with *him*.

Mary has torn *her* dress.   *She* is crying.

John has an aching *tooth*.   *He* pretends that *it* does not hurt.

The *lion* leaves the *lioness* to care for *her* cubs.

Men must bear hard things as best *they* may.

Men and *women* must bear hard things as best *they* may.

Which pronouns refer to persons ?   Which refer to things ?   Which refer to a man or boy ?   Which refer to a woman or girl ?   Which noun names the male lion ? the female lion ?   Which pronoun refers to the female lion?   Which pronoun refers to men (*plural*) ?

This study has taught you that **pronouns,** like **nouns,** may be of the **masculine,** the **feminine,** or the **neuter** gender, and of the **singular** or the **plural** number.

Learn the following rule : —

A pronoun must be in the same gender and number as the noun for which it stands or to which it refers.

501. *Review the definitions on page 278.*

Copy the definitions.   Observe that they apply to pronouns as well as to nouns.

Make a list of pronouns which may be used in speaking of a boy or boys ; of a girl or girls ; of a book or books.

Write each list in a separate column.

502. *He, his, him* are always **masculine singular.**

She, her, hers are always **feminine singular.**

It, its are always **neuter singular.**

They, their, them may be **masculine, feminine,** or **neuter plural.**

 1. Where are the *boys?* Have you seen *them?*

 2. There are the *girls.* Who is with *them?*

 3. The *boys* and *girls* are playing. Hear *them.*

 4. Here are twelve *oranges.* Count *them.*

In the first sentence, *them* is **masculine ;** in the second, **feminine ;** in the third, **masculine** or **feminine ;** in the fourth, **neuter.** Why ?

Make five sentences like the examples, using the pronouns my, our, they, their.

Tell the gender of each noun and pronoun in your sentences.

503. *Tell the gender of each italicized pronoun on pages 229 and 244. Give your reasons.*

504. *If you have read Aldrich's " Story of a Bad Boy," find a description of Pepper Whitcomb.*

Repeat the description in your own words.

505. *If you have read " The Birds' Christmas Carol," describe Carol's character, or tell a story which shall explain why her father called her " an angel of the house " (Chapter II).*

For Conversation and Writing

506. Lincoln once wrote a letter to a young man in which he said : —

The way for a young man to rise is to improve himself in every way he can, never suspecting that anybody wishes to hinder him. Suspicion and jealousy never helped any man in any situation.

Read this passage until you understand it.

Why do you suppose Lincoln wrote in this way ? What had the young man probably written to him ? What were the young man's feelings about other people ? Did he think they were eager to help him ? What did he suspect ?

Tell some story of Lincoln which shows that he tried "to improve himself in every way."

507. *Study the following passages until you understand the meaning of each. Explain them.*

1. The reward of one duty fulfilled is the power to fulfil another.
2. No endeavor is in vain,
   Its reward is in the doing,
   And the rapture of pursuing
   Is the prize the vanquished gain.

Can you give an example of some task which makes you able to perform another?

To whom is the "reward of the doing" given?

Can you give examples which you have observed ?

SECTIONS 508–509

ORAL EXERCISE

KINDS OF SENTENCES

508. *Observe the sentences which follow:* —

    1. Peanuts grow in the ground.
    2. Where do peanuts grow?
    3. Give me some peanuts.

The first sentence **states** or **declares** a fact; the second **asks a question**; the third is either a **command** or a **request**.

Learn the definitions: —

1. A declarative sentence declares or asserts something as a fact.

2. An interrogative sentence asks a question.

3. An imperative sentence expresses a command or a request.

These are the three main kinds of sentences, as defined according to their use in expressing thought.

509. 1. *Make five declarative sentences which state some fact of history or geography.*

2. *Make five interrogative sentences which ask questions about your geography lesson.*

3. *Make five sentences which ask questions in arithmetic.*

4. *Make five sentences which ask questions about your last reading lesson.*

5. *Make five sentences which express a command or a request. These will be imperative sentences.*

SECTION 510

DECLARATIVE SENTENCES

1. *Write one fact about each of the following persons, places, or things.*

Jefferson	Jackson	Chicago	mason	city
Hamilton	Fulton	Baltimore	miller	fire

2. *Change each of your declarative sentences to a question (or interrogative sentence).*

SECTIONS 511–512

INTERROGATIVE SENTENCES

511. *Write a question about each of the following : —*

shepherd, carpenter, mason, merchant, banker, lawyer, doctor, postman, grocer, baker.

512. *Ask ten questions about things in the schoolroom. Write the questions, using the proper marks of punctuation.*

SECTION 513

IMPERATIVE SENTENCES

Find in your reading book ten sentences which express a command or a request.
Copy them to read to the class.

Imperative sentences are usually followed by a period.
Do you find any exceptions?

SECTION 514

Oral Exercise

KINDS OF SENTENCES

Read the following sentences and tell whether they are declarative, interrogative, or imperative.

Give your reasons.

Observe the mark of punctuation after each sentence.

1. Primroses grow wild in England.
2. Have you ever seen a primrose?
3. March on to victory!
4. Repeat the rule for the interrogation point.
5. A noble deed is a step toward God.
6. There's many a slip 'twixt the cup and the lip.
7. Do not make your *a*'s so carelessly.
8. How are canoes made?
9. Shine like the sun in every corner.
10. Schuyler was a general in the Revolution.
11. Where was he born?
12. The sea is a jovial comrade.
13. Who wrote "Old Ironsides"?
14. Did Daniel Defoe write "Robinson Crusoe"?
15. Kind hearts are more than coronets.
16. Heaven is not reached at a single bound.
17. There's a song in the air! There's a star in the sky!
18. I met a little cottage girl.
19. Alexander sighed for more worlds to conquer.
20. Why does a rolling stone gather no moss?
21. Emma has a fine canoe.
22. Who gave it to her?

SECTION 515

REVIEW OF SUBJECT, PREDICATE, AND MODIFIERS

You know how to divide a sentence into the **complete subject** and the **complete predicate.** You have also learned the definitions : —

The subject of a sentence designates the person, place, or thing that is spoken of.
The predicate is that which is said of the subject.

Each of the following sentences is divided into the **complete subject** and the **complete predicate** by a vertical line : —

1. *Thomas* | *ran.*
2. Young *Thomas* | *ran* swiftly.
3. *He* | *travelled.*
4. The old *queen* | *sent* for her son.
5. *She* | *wept* bitterly.
6. The *voice* of the captain | *rang* through the air.
7. *It* | *called* us to the fight.
8. Two great *owls* | *roosted* on the branch.
9. *They* | *hooted* dismally.

In the first sentence, the subject is the noun *Thomas ;* the predicate is the verb *ran.*

In the second, the subject noun (*Thomas*) is modified by the adjective *young,* and the predicate verb (*ran*) is modified by the adverb *swiftly.*

In the third, the subject is the pronoun *he.*

In the seventh, the subject is the pronoun *it.*

You have found that the chief word of the complete subject is always a **noun** or a **pronoun,** and that the chief word of the complete predicate is a **verb.** You know also that both the complete subject and the complete predicate may contain one or more **modifiers.**

Mention the complete subject and the complete predicate of each of the sentences in the list.

Mention the subject word of each, and tell whether it is a noun or a pronoun.

Mention the predicate verb of each sentence.

Mention the modifiers, and tell whether each modifies the subject word or the predicate verb.

The subject word (noun or pronoun) is called the **simple subject.**

The predicate verb is called the **simple predicate.**

SECTIONS 516–518

CASE: THE NOMINATIVE CASE

516. *Study the following pairs of sentences :* —

1. $\{$ *John* | swims well.
2. $\{$ *He* | swims well.
3. $\{$ *John's* knife | fell into the river.
4. $\{$ *His* knife | fell into the river.

What is the subject of the first sentence ? of the second ?

What does *John's* show in the third sentence ? What does *his* show in the fourth ?

You have seen that nouns and pronouns may **change their form.** Thus in the first sentence *John* is the form of the noun; in the third, *John* is changed to *John's*. In the second sentence *he* is the form of the pronoun; in the fourth, *he* is changed to *his*.

These changes **show the relation** of the noun or pronoun to some other word or words in the sentence.

Thus in the first sentence *John* is the **subject**; in the third the form *John's* shows ownership, and is a **possessive** form.

Such changes are called changes in **case**.

When a noun or pronoun is the **subject word** of a sentence, it is said to be in the **nominative case**; when it has the form that shows **ownership** or **possession,** it is said to be in the **possessive case**.

The subject of a sentence is in the nominative case.

517. *Point out all the nouns and pronouns in the nominative case that you can find in these sentences; also all the predicate verbs.*

1. Squirrels make their nests in hollow trees.
2. The brown buds burst their coats in the spring.
3. The great ship sails proudly out to sea.
4. Roland sent you a letter last week.
5. He wrote it in his very best hand.
6. It told about his work at school.
7. My nearest relatives live in Indiana.
8. They expect to come to Albany soon.
9. I long for a visit from them.
10. The nimble little monkey climbed the mast in a twinkling.

518. The following pronouns can be used in the nominative case only : — *I, we, he, she, they*.

Use these pronouns as subjects in ten sentences of your own.

Turn to some page of your reading book and point out all the nouns and pronouns that you can find in the nominative case. Tell why you think they are nominatives.

SECTIONS 519-520

NOMINATIVE IN DIRECT ADDRESS AND IN EXCLAMATIONS

519. A noun used in **direct address** or as an **exclamation** is in the **nominative case.**

I. In direct address : —

> *William*, you are very careless.
> See, *Kate*, here is the first violet.
> Your coat needs brushing, *Herbert*.
> My *child*, you look tired.

II. As an exclamation : —

> Poor *William !* he has a hard life.
> *Thieves ! thieves !*　Run for the police !
> *Nonsense !*　I don't believe it.
> Fresh *fish !* fresh *fish !*

520. *Write five sentences, each containing a nominative of direct address.*

Write five sentences, each containing a nominative of exclamation.

SECTIONS 521-523

PREDICATE ADJECTIVES AND PREDICATE
NOMINATIVES

521. There are a few little **verbs** which appear in
our sentences oftener than any other verbs. These
are : *is, am, was, were, has been, have been, shall be,
will be,* and a few others like them. They do not
express action, like *walk, run,* or *go,* but they have
a special work of their own. Thus, —

> The robin *is* cheery.
> The boy *was* tardy.
> He *has been* ill.
> Kate *will be* sorry.

Here we find an adjective standing in the **predicate,** yet describing the **subject.** This is called a
predicate adjective.

The verb makes an assertion, not simply by
expressing meaning of its own, but by tying the
subject and the predicate adjective together. A verb
which has this use is called a **copula,** or " coupler."

522. *Change the following phrases to sentences by
inserting the copula. Thus,* —

> The merry boy.   The boy is merry.

The rosy-cheeked girls,   the merry children,   the
juicy apple,   the heavy load,   the gentle horse,   the
difficult lesson,   the fleecy cloud,   the turbulent river,
the old house,   the yellow paper.

523. The **copula** often ties together the **subject** and another **noun** or **pronoun** which describes or explains the subject : —

> John is my *brother*.
> You are *he*.

The noun or pronoun following the copula in the predicate is called a **predicate noun** or **pronoun**. Like the subject, it is in the **nominative case**.

The predicate nominative is also common after *is called, is named, is chosen,* and similar expressions. Thus, —

> This bird is called an *owl*.
> My cousin is named *William*.
> Jack was chosen *captain*.

Find the predicate nominative in each of the following sentences : —

1. Those ships are warships.
2. That mountain is Mount Shasta.
3. Madrid is the capital of Spain.
4. His speech was the event of the evening.
5. Fruit is an important export of California.
6. Samuel Adams was a statesman.
7. The golden-rod is a wayside flower.
8. The name of that famous inventor is Edison.
9. You are a patriot, sir.
10. The Marseillaise is the French battle hymn.
11. Which of these boys is named John ?
12. That is he.
13. Lincoln was a native of Kentucky.

SECTION 524

NOMINATIVE IN APPOSITION

Study the following sentence : —

Tom, the newsboy, | found a watch in the street.

The simple subject is the noun *Tom*. The second noun, *newsboy*, is added to define the first; it explains to us who Tom was.

In such sentences the second noun is said to be **in apposition** with the first.

A noun added to another noun to explain it, and signifying the same person or thing, is called an appositive and is said to be in apposition.

A noun in apposition with the subject is in the nominative case.

Find the subject of each of these sentences, and point out the noun in apposition with the subject : —

1. Washington, our first President, was born in 1732.
2. Tennyson, a great English poet, wrote " The Brook."
3. Jefferson, a Virginian, founded a university.
4. Daniel Boone, the pioneer, had little education.
5. Toby, my dog, barked furiously.
6. Albany, the capital of New York, is on the Hudson.
7. The chief, a tall savage, hurled his tomahawk.
8. My friend Andrew has just arrived.
9. Your sister Mary draws beautifully.
10. The elm, a stately tree, was struck by lightning.

SECTION 525

NOMINATIVE ABSOLUTE

Examine this sentence : —

The hour arriving, the ship sailed.

The subject noun is *ship ;* the predicate verb is *sailed.* The noun *hour*, with its modifier *arriving*, shows the time or circumstances of the ship's sailing.

A noun or pronoun followed by its modifier may express the cause, time, or circumstances of an action.

This is called the absolute construction.

The noun or pronoun is in the nominative case and is called a nominative absolute.

SECTION 526

REVIEW OF RULES AND DEFINITIONS

Nouns and pronouns may change their form to show some of their relations to other words in the sentence.

Such changes of form are called changes in case.

1. The subject of a sentence is in the nominative case.

2. A noun or pronoun used in direct address or as an exclamation is in the nominative case.

3. A noun or pronoun in the predicate describing or explaining the subject is called a predicate nominative and is in the nominative case.

4. A noun or pronoun in apposition with the subject is in the nominative case.

5. A noun or pronoun in the absolute construction is in the nominative case.

SECTION 527

STORY WITH DESCRIPTION

THE OTTER

I was sitting very still in the bushes on the bank, one day in spring, watching for a wood duck. Wood duck lived there, but the cover was so thick that I could never surprise them. They always heard me coming and were off, giving me only vanishing glimpses among the trees, or else quietly hiding until I went by. So the only way to see them was to sit still in hiding, for hours if need be, until they came gliding by, all unconscious of the watcher.

As I waited, a large animal came swiftly up stream, just his head visible, with a long tail trailing behind. He was swimming powerfully, steadily, straight as a string; but, as I noted with wonder, he made no ripple whatever, sliding through the water as if greased from nose to tail. Just above me he dived, and I did not see him again, though I watched up and down stream breathlessly for him to reappear.

I had never seen such an animal before, but I knew somehow that it was an otter, and I drew back into better hiding with the hope of seeing the rare creature again. Presently another otter appeared, coming up stream and disappearing in exactly the same way as the first. But though I stayed all the afternoon, I saw nothing more.*

WILLIAM J. LONG.

Make an outline, and tell the story.
Describe the scene.

* From " Secrets of the Woods " (by permission).

The Possessive Case

528. The possessive case denotes ownership or possession.

Find examples of nouns and pronouns in the possessive case in the following sentences.

Tell whether each noun or pronoun is in the singular or the plural number.

Tell the gender of each.

1. Webster's great gift was oratory.
2. The bird's note came clearly through the frosty air.
3. The boys were called to the Doctor's study.
4. Their steps were slow.
5. Tom's room was on the east side.
6. His desk stood near a window.
7. The blacksmith's work is done.
8. The pen was made from an eagle's feather.
9. The soldier's march was long and weary.
10. We heard the robin's song.
11. The robins' songs filled the orchard.
12. This is the king's highway.
13. The elephant's tusks furnished much ivory.
14. The elephants' tusks furnished much ivory.
15. The children's laughter was pleasant to hear.
16. The old man understood the boy's motive.
17. The ship's guns sounded through the fog.
18. Women's hats were displayed in the shop window.
19. Our boat sank under us.
20. Her cries alarmed the family.
21. The firemen's ladders were too short.

529. You have had much practice in writing nouns in the possessive case. These are the rules : —

1. **The possessive case of most nouns has, in the singular number, the ending 's:** as, — the *lion's* head.

2. **Plural nouns ending in s add the apostrophe alone in the possessive :** as, — the *lions'* heads.

3. **Plural nouns not ending in s take 's in the possessive :** as, — the *men's* shoes.

Write sentences containing the possessive singular and plural of —

boy, man, child, mouse, ox, oriole, pirate, woman, sheep, deer, horse, carpenter, tailor, goat, girl, Indian, pupil, boatman, sailor, tigress.

NOTE. — A proper noun of more than one syllable, ending in *s*, may add *'s* or *'* alone to form the possessive. Thus, —

> Jonas's book is a history.
> Jonas' book is a history.
> Mr. Douglas's horse is a roan.
> Mr. Douglas' horse is a roan.

A possessive phrase beginning with *of* is often substituted for the possessive case of a noun. Thus, —

1. The life *of* a *soldier* is hard.
2. The danger *of* the *soldiers* was great.
3. The noise *of* the *train* drowned our voices.
4. The color *of* the *paper* was blue.
5. The population *of Chicago* has increased rapidly.

We should generally use the *of*-phrase when speaking of places or of things without life. Such expressions as "the *train's* noise," "*Chicago's* population," "the *house's* front" are not correct.

SECTIONS 530-532

530. *Write a letter to a friend who lives in a country where no apples grow.*

You wish to tell him all that you know about apple trees and apples. Use these notes in preparing the paragraphs of your letter.

NOTES

1. Appearance of an apple tree as compared with other trees.
2. Appearance of orchards in spring.
3. Time of apple gathering.
4. Description of apples.
5. Uses of apples.

531. You have a friend who is studying geography. He lives in a town where he has no chance to observe the action of running water in forming soil. You live near a small river, and have often seen for yourself the process described in the explanation on page 276.

Your friend has written to you, asking you to tell him about your river.

Read the paragraph on page 276 carefully. Then prepare an outline for a letter of four or five paragraphs. The letter is to describe the river and explain how it acts "after a washing rain."

532. *Write the letter, using your outline.*

The Object: Objective Case

533. Some verbs which express action are followed by a noun or pronoun which denotes the **receiver of the action** or **the result of the action.** This is called the **direct object** of the verb. Thus, —

Receiver of the action.	1. The child broke his *plaything*.
	2. The hunter killed the *bear*.
	3. The Indian bent his *bow*.
	4. The woman cut the *pie*.
Result or product of the action.	5. The man built the *wall*.
	6. The dressmaker made the *dress*.
	7. The mouse gnawed a *hole* in the cheese.
	8. The child wrote a *letter*.

The first four sentences contain nouns which name the **receiver** of the action expressed by the verb. Thus, in (1) the child **performs** the action (breaking) and the plaything **receives** it. In (2) the hunter performs the action (killing) and the bear receives it. In (3) the Indian performs the action (bending) and the bow receives it. In (4) the woman performs the action (cutting) and the pie receives it.

Each of the nouns (*plaything, bear, bow, pie*) names the **receiver** of the action expressed by the verb.

In (5) the man *builds*, and the *wall* is the **result** or **product** of his building. In (6) the dressmaker makes, and the dress is the result or product of her making. In (7) the mouse gnaws, and the hole is the result of its gnawing. In (8) the child writes, and the letter is the result of his writing.

Learn the rules and definitions : —

Some verbs may be followed by a noun or pronoun denoting that which receives the action or is produced by it.

Such a noun or pronoun is called the object of the verb.

A noun or pronoun used as the object of a verb is said to be in the objective case.

In **nouns** the form of the objective is like that of the nominative.

In **pronouns,** however, the objective case often has a special form. Thus, —

Nominative Singular	I	thou	he	she	it
Objective Singular	me	thee	him	her	it
Nominative Plural	we	you		they	
Objective Plural	us	you		them	

534. *In the following sentences point out (1) the subject noun or pronoun, (2) the predicate verb, (3) the object of the verb.*

In preparing for the exercise, you should rule your paper as in the following example.

SUBJECT	VERB	OBJECT
James	found	(a) pearl
(The) Spaniards	burned	(their) ships
Columbus	discovered	America
I	see	him
Artists	paint	pictures

1. The soldier began his story.
2. I heard a loud noise.
3. The story surprised me.

4. The noise frightened the horse.
5. I have described Tom's school days.
6. Tom followed his guide.
7. The Indian tossed the tomahawk into the canoe.
8. The crew understood the situation.
9. The pilot gave the command distinctly.
10. Ichabod wore a small wool hat.
11. The party had now reached the road.
12. They found the horse next morning.

SECTION 535

The Indirect Object

Examine the following sentence : —

Thomas sent a book.

Here the verb *sent* is followed by its direct object, *book*. If we wish, however, to mention the **person to whom** Thomas sent the book, we may put a noun or pronoun immediately after the verb. Thus, —

Thomas sent $\left\{ \begin{array}{c} Mary \\ her \end{array} \right\}$ a book.

The verb will then have two objects : —

(1) its direct object, *book ;*

(2) an indirect object, *Mary* (or *her*), denoting the *person to whom* John sent the book.

Some verbs may take two objects, a direct object and an indirect object.

The indirect object denotes the person or thing toward whom or toward which is directed the action expressed by the rest of the predicate.

SECTIONS 536–538

The Object of a Preposition

536. In the following sentences you recognize the italicized words as prepositions : —

> Tom threw the ball *to* Jack.
> Jack threw the ball *to* me.
> The train *from* Buffalo has arrived.
> You heard the story *from* him.

The noun or pronoun which follows a preposition is called its object, and is in the objective case.

Thus in the first sentence above, the noun *Jack* is the object of the preposition *to ;* in the second, the pronoun *me* is the object of *to*, and so on.

You notice that the pronouns *me* and *him* are clearly in the objective case. They have the same forms that they would have if they were the objects of some verb (as in, — Jack struck *me*).

You are now ready for the complete rule for the objective case : —

The object of a verb or preposition is in the objective case.

537. *Review the exercises on page 257. Tell the object of each preposition.*

538. *Write sentences containing the following prepositions, each followed by its object :* — on, in, upon, from, until, about, through, with, toward.

SECTION 539

DAFFODILS

I wandered lonely as a cloud
That floats on high o'er vales and hills,
When all at once I saw a crowd,
A host, of golden daffodils,
Beside the lake, beneath the trees,
Fluttering and dancing in the breeze.

Continuous as the stars that shine
And twinkle on the milky way,
They stretched in never-ending line
Along the margin of a bay :
Ten thousand saw I at a glance,
Tossing their heads in sprightly dance.

The waves beside them danced; but they
Outdid the sparkling waves in glee :
A poet could not but be gay
In such a jocund company.
I gazed, and gazed, but little thought
What wealth the show to me had brought.

For oft, when on my couch I lie
In vacant or in pensive mood,
They flash upon that inward eye
Which is the bliss of solitude;
And then my heart with pleasure fills,
And dances with the daffodils.

WORDSWORTH.

SECTION 540

Read to yourself the poem on page 311 two or three times, or until the lines become familiar to you.

What is the subject of the poem?

How does the poet describe himself in the first stanza?

Wordsworth loved to spend his days in wandering over the hills. When he says that he is "lonely," does he mean simply that he is alone, or is he describing his mood? Does his mood change during the walk? What words indicate the change? What was the cause of the change? How does he describe the daffodils?

What words or phrases, in the description of the daffodils, show the joyousness of the poet's feelings? What kind of "company" has he now?

SECTION 541

Mr. Charles E. Alton, a friend of your father's, wishes to hire a man to take care of his place in the country. A young man who lives in your neighborhood has asked you to recommend him to Mr. Alton. You know the young man well, and think well of him.

1. Write a short note to Mr. Alton, recommending the young man and saying that you will gladly give further particulars.

2. Write Mr. Alton's reply, asking for a description of the man and an account of his character. (Is he careful, industrious, good-natured, intelligent? What experience has he had? Is he a trained gardener?)

3. Reply to Mr. Alton in a letter of five or six paragraphs.

SECTIONS 542-544

PERSON: PERSONAL PRONOUNS

542. *Pick out all the pronouns that you can find in the following sentences. Write them in a column.*

1. I, Tom Jones, live at Plymouth with my father, and my cousin George lives near me.

2. You, Tom Jones, live at Plymouth with your father, and your cousin George lives near you.

3. He, Tom Jones, lives at Plymouth with his father, and his cousin George lives near him.

4. It (Tom's book) is kept in its place on the shelf, where Tom can easily reach it.

In sentences 1, 2, and 3 all the **pronouns** refer to Tom Jones. Every one of them is necessary, because each has its own special work to do.

In sentence 1, Tom is speaking, and the pronouns which represent him as the **speaker** are *I*, *my*, and *me*.

In sentence 2, Tom is spoken to, and the pronouns which represent him as **spoken to** are *you* and *your*.

In sentence 3, Tom is spoken of, and the pronouns which represent him as **spoken of** are *he*, *his*, and *him*.

In sentence 4, the book is spoken of, and the pronouns which represent it as **spoken of** are *it* and *its*.

Such pronouns are called **personal pronouns**, because they all (except *it*, *its*) stand for **persons**.

The personal pronouns serve to distinguish (1) the speaker, (2) the person spoken to, (3) the person or thing spoken of.

The pronouns which represent the person as the **speaker** are said to be in the **first person**.

The pronouns which represent the person as **spoken to** are said to be in the **second person**.

The pronouns which represent the person or thing as **spoken of** are said to be in the **third person**.

Nouns are also in the **first person** when they name the **speaker**, in the **second person** when they name the person **spoken to,** and in the **third person** when they name the person or thing **spoken of.**

543. *Turn to the poem "In School Days" (page 247), and find all the pronouns.*

Mention the noun to which each pronoun refers, and tell whether the pronoun represents the speaker, the person spoken to, or the person or thing spoken of.

Tell whether each noun or pronoun is in the first, the second, or the third person.

544. *Tell whether each personal pronoun is in the first, second, or third person. Give your reasons.*

1. I chatter, chatter, as I flow.
2. It is I, be not afraid.
3. We are seven.
4. It is we who are to blame.
5. Thou shalt love thy neighbor as thyself.
6. It is thou who art chosen to rule.
7. Fun and frolic no more he knows.
8. It was he whom I called.
9. Down the dale she tripped.
10. It is she to whom the blackbird sang.
11. They were my friends.

SECTIONS 545–547

545. *Make a list of all the personal pronouns that you have found.*

Arrange them in two columns.

In the first column write all the pronouns which may refer to a noun in the singular number.

In the second column write the pronouns which may refer to a noun in the plural number.

Point out all the pronouns in your lists that are of the masculine gender; of the feminine; of either the masculine or the feminine; of the neuter gender.

546. The personal pronouns have the following forms : —

THE PRONOUN OF THE FIRST PERSON : *I*

	SINGULAR		PLURAL
Nominative	I	*Nominative*	we
Possessive	my *or* mine	*Possessive*	our *or* ours
Objective	me	*Objective*	us

THE PRONOUN OF THE SECOND PERSON : *thou*

	SINGULAR		PLURAL
Nominative	thou	*Nominative*	you *or* ye
Possessive	thy *or* thine	*Possessive*	your *or* yours
Objective	thee	*Objective*	you *or* ye

THE PRONOUN OF THE THIRD PERSON : *he, she, it*

	SINGULAR			PLURAL
	Masculine	*Feminine*	*Neuter*	*Masculine, Feminine, and Neuter*
Nominative	he	she	it	they
Possessive	his	her *or* hers	its	their *or* theirs
Objective	him	her	it	them

547. Except in poetry and in solemn language, *you, your,* and *yours* do the work of the **singular** number as well as that of the **plural.** Thus, —

> *You* are the best scholars in the class. [Plural.]
> *You* are the best scholar in the class. [Singular in sense.]

When *you* and *your* (or *yours*) are used in a singular sense, they are often said to be in the singular number. Yet *you*, whether singular or plural in sense, always takes the verb-forms that are used with plural subjects. Thus,—

> *You act* strangely, John.
> Mary, you *speak* indistinctly.
> *You were* my friend.
> *You were* my friends.

Such an expression as *you was* is a gross error. It is best, therefore, to describe *you* as always **plural in form**, but as **singular in sense** when it refers to a single person.

SECTIONS 548–550

Adjective Pronouns

This knife is sharp.	*This* is my knife.
These knives are sharp.	*These* are our knives.
That apple is red.	*That* is a red apple.
Those apples are red.	*Those* are red apples.

The italicized words are used in the first column as **adjectives.** Why?

In the second column, the same words are used as **pronouns.** Why?

Some words are used either as adjectives or as pronouns. Such words are called adjective pronouns.

549. *Point out each adjective pronoun. Tell whether it is used as a pronoun or an adjective. Tell its gender, person, number, case. Give reasons.*

1. This poem was written by Thomas Bailey Aldrich.
2. This is a delightful poem.
3. That is my uncle Charles.
4. These are very fine peaches.
5. Those mountains are wrapped in mist.
6. These soldiers have fought bravely.
7. That officer rides well.
8. Each man has his faults.
9. Each of us has his faults.
10. Some of our lessons are very easy.
11. Some children are not fond of study.

550. Do not use *them* for *these* or *those.* In the following sentences the three words are used correctly : —

These plums are ripe. We will gather *them.*

Those plums are not ripe. We must not gather *them.*

Do not use *here* after *this* or *these.*

Fill the blanks with this, these, that, those, *or* them, *taking care to use each word correctly.*

1. —— girls go to my school.
2. I know —— all.
3. I like —— kind of apples.
4. I have learned two of —— poems.
5. How do you like —— story ?
6. I like it better than —— story about the picnic.
7. —— stories are all interesting.
8. I have read every one of ——.

Write fifteen sentences, using this, that, these, those, *correctly.*

SECTION 551

You have a friend of your own age who has never studied physiology. Somebody has told him that he ought not to buy candy that is kept in unscreened or uncovered boxes. He does not understand why, and, knowing that you have a course in physiology in your school, he writes to ask you to explain the matter.

Write your friend's letter.

Write a reply, explaining the reasons for caution.

SECTION 552

What do you understand by an *emergency?* Look up the word in your dictionary and see if you really know what it means.

Then tell a story about some girl's wise and prompt action in an emergency.

Let the story be part of a letter to a friend of your own age. Imagine that he is travelling in the West, and that you are sending him the latest news from home.

SECTION 553

Write your friend's reply to the letter in Section 552.

He tells an experience of his own to match your story of the girl who had her wits about her at a critical time.

He confesses that he did not act with such coolness and promptitude in *his* emergency.

SECTION 554

FOR STUDY

Observe the verbs in the following sentences : —

1. We walk to school every day.
   Mary walks to school every day.
   She walks to school every day.
2. They run fast.
   The boy runs fast.
   He runs fast.
3. The farmers sow wheat.
   The farmer sows wheat.
   He sows wheat.

In the first group of sentences the same verb *walk* is used in all three examples.   In two of them, however, it appears in a different form, *walks*.   In the second group we find *run* and *runs ;* in the third group, *sow* and *sows*.

This form of the verb, ending in *s*, is sometimes called the *s-form*.

Read the following rule, then study the examples.

The s-form of the verb is used only when the subject is a noun or pronoun in the third person and singular number.

Never use the s-form of the verb with a plural subject.

~~~~~~~~~~

Use the following verbs correctly in sentences.

comes   goes   tries   carries   follows   brings
falls   works   speaks   studies   learns   plays

NOTE. — *Is, was, has,* and *does* always follow the rule which you have just learned.

SECTION 555

Change the subject of each sentence to a noun, or to a pronoun of the third person, and observe the necessary change in the form of the verb.

Example : —
1. I see the pine boughs waving in the wind.
2. He sees the pine boughs waving in the wind.

1. I see the dew on the daisies and clover.
2. I watch the sun as it sinks in the west.
3. I know a bank where the wild thyme blows.
4. I bring fresh showers for the thirsting flowers.
5. I enjoy many happy days.
6. I know a shady hollow near the brook.
7. I use acorn cups for saucers.
8. I like a boy who tells the truth.
9. I call the ocean my friend.
10. I have a plan for our summer excursion.
11. I think John does his best.
12. I do all that I can to please you.

SECTION 556

Use the following verbs correctly in sentences of your own. In every case let the word be a part of a verb-phrase in the predicate.

Example : — I *have broken* my kite.

Blown, chosen, come, done, drawn, drunk, driven, eaten, fallen, flown, forgotten, frozen, given, grown, known, risen, shaken, seen, sunk, spoken, stolen, torn, worn, written.

SECTION 557

THE CLAUSE

A sentence may contain more than one subject and one predicate.

Study the following sentences: —

1. Lowell wrote the *Biglow Papers.*
2. You know that Lowell wrote the *Biglow Papers.*
3. Lowell wrote the *Biglow Papers,* and Longfellow wrote *Evangeline.*

In the first sentence "Lowell" is the subject, and "wrote the *Biglow Papers*" is the complete predicate.

The second sentence tells about a person, "you." "You" is the subject of the sentence, and "know that Lowell wrote the *Biglow Papers*" is the complete predicate. "That Lowell wrote the *Biglow Papers*" is a part of the predicate — telling *what* you know.

In this case a **part of a sentence** contains a subject and predicate. Such a part of a sentence is called a **clause.**

You will find two **clauses** in each of the following sentences.

1. The winds roared and the lightning flashed.
2. Man proposes, but God disposes.
3. We have met the enemy, and they are ours.
4. We shall meet, but we shall miss him.
5. The bell rang, and the train moved on.
6. Winter has come, and the fields are covered with snow.

SECTION 558

Kinds of Sentences

Observe the following sentences : —

1. The apple trees have blossomed.
2. When May comes, the apple trees will blossom.
3. May is here, and the apple trees are in blossom.

How many clauses does the first sentence contain? the second? the third?

A sentence that contains but one clause is a **simple sentence**. Compare the second and third sentences. Separate the clauses in the second sentence and read them alone by themselves. Which clause makes sense by itself? What is true of the other clause? *When May comes* is a **dependent clause**. It needs the help of another clause to make complete sense. This clause **modifies** *will blossom*, or, as we sometimes say, **depends upon** *will blossom*.

A sentence which contains a dependent clause is a complex sentence.

The third sentence contains two clauses independent of each other. Standing alone, either clause makes sense.

A sentence which consists of two or more independent clauses is a compound sentence.

Make ten complex sentences, like the second example above.

Make ten compound sentences, like the third example above.

SECTION 559

Study the following sentences.

Tell whether each sentence is simple, complex, or compound. Give your reasons.

1. The stormy March is come at last.
2. Speak clearly if you speak at all.
3. The voyager noticed the light smoke curling up from a village whose shining roofs gleamed among the trees.
4. All that glitters is not gold.
5. Brevity is the soul of wit.
6. They that touch pitch will be defiled.
7. As he approached the village, Rip Van Winkle met a number of people.
8. The summer came, and all the birds were dead.
9. My heart leaps up when I behold
   A rainbow in the sky.
10. Laugh, and the world laughs with you.
11. Whether we look or whether we listen,
    We hear life murmur, or see it glisten.
12. The little bird sits at his door in the sun.
13. It was lovely summer weather in the country, and the golden corn, the green oats, and the haystacks in the meadows looked beautiful.
14. Ali Baba found the cave where the Forty Thieves hid their treasure.
15. He was dressed all in furs from his head to his foot,
    And his clothes were all tarnished with ashes and soot.

SECTIONS 560–561

An Explanation or Exposition

OUR VOCABULARY

Every one naturally uses words which belong to his experience. The sailor's language tells of the sea, and is filled with references to ships and their belongings. The engineer thinks and speaks of machines and engines. The farmer thinks and speaks about nature and her laws.

Each man is known by his language. His errors in speech tell something of his education or lack of it; his choice of words shows whether he is widely read. The stock of words which a person has for use in speaking and writing is called his *vocabulary*. Have you a large vocabulary or a small one?

You can improve your vocabulary by reading and by thinking about what you read. The dictionary will assist you. It will be particularly helpful in adding to your vocabulary words which are nearly alike in meaning, but which have shades of difference. Such words are called *synonyms*.

Study this explanation (or exposition) according to the following outline: —

1. Every one has his own vocabulary or stock of words.
2. A person's vocabulary shows his training.
3. How we may improve our vocabulary.

561. *Repeat the explanation orally, in your own words.*

Write a definition of vocabulary; *of* synonym.

Write the explanation, in three paragraphs.

SECTIONS 562–564

SYNONYMS

562. *Use these synonyms in sentences, consulting your dictionary as you write.*

permission	consent
clothing	apparel
affection	liking
victory	success
quiet	silence
bold	daring
price	cost
say	talk
tell	speak
common	customary
old	aged

563. *Make sentences in which you use six pairs of synonyms that you have found in your dictionary.*

564. *Find and use at least one synonym for each of the following words :* — mistake, fault, try, work, conquer, battle, journey, fame, sorrow, get, shrink, sea, see, tell, drag, forest, find, shadow, town, view, lonely, correctly, jump, stream.

To the Teacher. — The following words will afford opportunity for further study of synonyms: — proud, haughty; truth, honesty; brave, foolhardy; road, street; ride, drive; idle, lazy; strange, queer, odd; pretty, beautiful; friend, acquaintance; robber, thief; wise, learned. The resemblances in meaning and the differences may be brought out by oral exercises, followed by the writing of sentences.

The following pairs of words are examples, not of proper synonyms, but of words often misused or confused : — most, almost; fix, mend (or repair); team, wagon; lie, lay; sit, set; learn, teach; person, party; guess, think; awfully, very; fire, throw; love, like; mad, angry; strange, funny; expect, suppose; house, home; whole, all; father-in-law, stepfather; smart, clever, skilful. They may be used, at the teacher's discretion, in oral and written sentences that shall bring out the correct meaning and application of each word.

SECTION 565

ADJECTIVE CLAUSES

Examine the following sentences : —

A *courageous* man
A man *who has courage* } will not desert his friends.

These two sentences express exactly the same thought, but in different ways.

In the first sentence, the subject noun (*man*) is modified by the adjective *courageous*.

In the second, the clause *who has courage* is a modifier which does the work of the adjective (*courageous*). It is therefore called an **adjective clause.**

A clause that modifies a noun or pronoun is called an adjective clause.

SECTION 566

ADVERBIAL CLAUSES

Examine the following sentences : —

The boy awoke { *early.*
when day dawned.

In the first sentence, the predicate verb *awoke* is followed by a modifier, the adverb *early.*

In the second, the clause *when day dawned* is a modifier which does the work of the adverb (*early*). It is therefore called an **adverbial clause.**

A clause that serves as an adverbial modifier is called an adverbial clause.

SECTIONS 567-571

RELATIVE PRONOUNS

567. *Study these complex sentences, and see if you clearly understand the use of the italicized words :* —

1. The man *who* borrowed my hoe has brought it back.

2. The song *which* she sang was one of my favorites.

3. The lesson *that* we learn to-day will be useful to-morrow.

In the first sentence, the subject noun (*man*) is followed by a **modifier,** — the clause *who borrowed my hoe.* What is the clause that modifies the subject noun in the second sentence? in the third?

The italicized words (*who, which, that*) have a double work to do. (1) Each one stands for a noun, and is therefore a **pronoun.** (2) Each one also **connects a clause** with the noun which the clause modifies.

Such pronouns are called **relative pronouns.**

The chief relative pronouns are *who, which,* and *that.* *Who* changes its form to *whose* in the possessive case and to *whom* in the objective.

568. *Find the relative pronouns :* —

1. The evil which men do lives after them.

2. Every hour that fleets so slowly has its task.

3. He brought the message which saved the king.

4. Where is the mother who watched o'er my play?

5. The song of the lark, which was poured down from heaven, seemed to him a promise of good things.

6. The men who work know the value of an hour.

7. Those girls who stand at my right may be in the first party.

569. *Find the dependent clauses which the relative pronouns introduce in Section 568.*

Such clauses are called **relative clauses.**

The noun to which the relative pronoun refers is called its **antecedent.**

A relative pronoun must agree with its antecedent in gender, number, and person.

Find the antecedent of each relative pronoun.

570. *Fill the blanks with* who, whose, whom, which, *or* that.

REMEMBER: — *Who* and *whom* refer only to **persons**; *which* refers only to **things**; *that* may refer to **either persons or things.**

1. The boy —— won the prize was named Tom.
2. The prize —— Tom won was a medal.
3. The girl —— hat blew off was my sister.
4. The house in —— Jack lives is in James Street.
5. The neighbor to —— I lent the axe has returned it.
6. The trees —— grow in the yard are elms.
7. The book from —— I copied the poem is lost.
8. The friend from —— you received the letter has come.
9. The soldiers —— you see are cavalry.
10. The coat —— I ordered last month has just come.
11. The tailor from —— I ordered it has been slow.
12. A friend in —— you can trust is a treasure.
13. The law —— the Assembly passed is a good one.

571. *Make ten sentences in each of which you use a relative pronoun. Underline each relative clause. Point out the antecedent of each pronoun.*

SECTION 572

Interrogative Pronouns

The interrogative sentence is often introduced by an **interrogative pronoun,** as in the following examples : —

1. Who wrote " Barbara Frietchie " ?
2. Who discovered the Hudson River ?
3. By whom was the Erie Canal built ?
4. For whom was Raleigh's cloak thrown down ?
5. To whom was Pennsylvania granted ?
6. With whom did Roger Williams make his home ?
7. Whose name is associated with kite-flying ?
8. Which hero of American history do you like best ?

Find the pronouns for yourselves. Then make a definition for an interrogative pronoun.

Whom is correctly used in the examples above. *Make twenty sentences in which you use* whom *as an interrogative pronoun.*

SECTION 573

You have studied four classes of pronouns.

Review these classes in the following order : — (1) personal, (2) relative, (3) interrogative, (4) adjective.

Observe that nouns and pronouns are similar in many ways.   Both have **gender** (masculine, feminine, and neuter), **person** (first, second, and third), **number** (singular and plural), and **case** (nominative, possessive, and objective).

In reviewing, be ready to answer questions about the gender, person, number, and case of pronouns.

SECTION 574

MODELS FOR PARSING

When you mention the form of a particular word and tell how the word is used in the sentence, you are said to **parse** the word. You may use the models below in your exercises in **parsing.**

The *lumbermen* seized their axes. They used *them* skilfully.

The teamster to *whom* the accident happened has recovered.

Lumbermen is a common noun of the third person, masculine gender, and plural number. It is in the nominative case, being the subject of the verb *seized*.

Them is a personal pronoun of the third person, neuter gender, and plural number. It is in the objective case, being the object of the verb *used*.

Whom is a relative pronoun of the third person, masculine gender, and singular number, agreeing with its antecedent, *teamster*. It is in the objective case after the preposition *to*.

SECTION 575

COMPARISON OF ADJECTIVES AND ADVERBS

1. The violet is *sweet*.
2. The rose is *sweeter* than the violet.
3. The lily is the *sweetest* of all flowers.

You know that *sweet* is an **adjective.**

You now see it in its three forms, which are used in **comparing** sweet things.

When **two** persons or things are compared, *sweeter* is used. When **more than two** are compared, we must use *sweetest*.

Use the following adjectives in the same way, and make a similar rule for their use in comparing persons or things.

good	better	best
fine	finer	finest
heavy	heavier	heaviest
rich	richer	richest
much (many)	more	most

Many adjectives of two syllables, and most adjectives of three or more syllables, are compared by means of *more* and *most*.

> beautiful
> more beautiful (of two)
> most beautiful (of three or more)

The three forms of the adjective are called **degrees of comparison,** — the **positive,** the **comparative,** and the **superlative degree.**

POSITIVE	COMPARATIVE	SUPERLATIVE
small	smaller	smallest
red	redder	reddest
thin	thinner	thinnest
happy	happier	happiest
merry	merrier	merriest
far	farther	farthest
little	less	least
bad	worse	worst
dangerous	more dangerous	most dangerous

Adverbs are usually compared by means of *more* and *most*, but some are compared by means of the endings *er* and *est*, and a few are irregular.

1. Tom works *industriously*.
   Jack works *more industriously* than Tom.
   Ned works *most industriously* of all.
2. Mary studies *hard*.
   Helen studies *harder* than Mary.
   Jane studies *hardest* of the three.
3. Emma writes *well*.
   Frances writes *better* than Emma.
   Ruth writes *best* of all.

Do not say tallest *when you mean* taller *or* best *when you mean* better. *Or, in other words,* —

Do not use the superlative form when the comparative is required.

SECTION 576

Copy " Before the Rain " (Selections, page 40), and learn the poem by heart.

What was the " vapory amethyst " of the marshes and swamps and fens ? Have you seen an amethyst ? What is its color like ? Was the amethyst of the mist hard and clear like the stone, or soft and delicate ?

Have *you* ever seen the " sun drawing water " ? Where does the rain come from ? and how ? Does the poet speak truth as well as beauty ?

What have you seen that seems like the description of the grain ? What is amber ? When does the grain look like amber ? How does it " shrink " in the wind ?

SECTION 577

NOTE OF INVITATION AND REPLY

Mrs. Mason requests the pleasure of Miss Newton's company at dinner on Thursday, October ninth, at seven o'clock.
1574 Roberts Avenue.
Monday, September 29.

REPLY (ACCEPTING)

Miss Newton accepts with pleasure Mrs. Mason's kind invitation to dinner on Thursday, October ninth, at seven o'clock.
49 Irwin Street.
Tuesday, September 30.

REPLY (DECLINING)

Miss Newton regrets that serious illness in her family prevents her accepting Mrs. Mason's kind invitation to dinner on Thursday, October ninth.
49 Irwin Street.
Tuesday, September 30.

These models may be used in writing a formal invitation and a reply.

SECTION 578

Write a note of invitation, and a reply, accepting.

SECTION 579

Write an informal note of invitation to an old friend and a formal note to an acquaintance.

SUBJECTS FOR ORAL AND WRITTEN COMPOSITION

The following subjects for description, narration, character portrayal, and exposition are based upon the pupils'
study of history, or on books with which they are likely to
be familiar. The list affords wide opportunity for selection
by the teacher.

(1) Why the Massachusetts Colonists left England. (2) The Purchase
of Manhattan Island. (3) Wampum. (4) Why Governor Stuyvesant was
called "Headstrong Peter" (character). (5) Why Pennsylvania was Set-
tled. (6) Anecdote of William Penn. (7) Franklin's First Day in Philadelphia. (8) The Defeat of General Braddock. (9) How Sir William
Johnson became an Indian Chief. (10) How Order is Kept in a Village
(or City).

(1) The Boston Tea Party. (2) Washington at Valley Forge (char-
acter). (3) Why we Celebrate the Fourth of July. (4) A Tory. (5) The
Boyhood of Andrew Jackson. (6) "I would rather be right than be Presi-
dent." (7) Daniel Webster on the Farm. (8) Webster at School. (9) The
Cotton Gin. (10) The Sewing Machine. (11) The Erie Canal. (12) A
Half-faced Camp. (13) The Rail-Splitter. (14) The First Telegraph Line.

"Robinson Crusoe" (by Daniel Defoe). — (1) Crusoe Finds Friday.
(2) Character of Crusoe before the Shipwreck. (3) Character of Crusoe
after the Shipwreck. (4) Character of Friday. (5) Life in the Island.
(6) Robinson Crusoe's Castle. (7) The Footprint in the Sand. (8) How
Robinson Crusoe Looked.

"Secrets of the Woods" (by William J. Long). — (1) Describe Tookhees
washing his face (Chapter I). (2) How Tookhees Got the Big Crumb.
(3) A Wilderness Byway (description) (Chapter II). (4) Describe the
otters fishing in the ice-fringed pool (Chapter III). (5) The Otters' Slide.
(6) Meeko and the Robins (Chapter V). (7) Old Ben's Pointing (Chapter
VI). (8) The Camp on Deer Pond (description) (Chapter VII).

"The Birds' Christmas Carol" (by Kate Douglas Wiggin). (1) Description of Carol's room, "The Bird's Nest" (Chapter III). (2) How Larry
was Lost (Chapter VI). (3) The Christmas Dinner.

"Squirrels and Other Fur-Bearers" (by John Burroughs). — (1) How
Squirrels Fly (Chapter I). (2) How Squirrels Live through the Winter.
(3) Describe a chipmunk carrying food into his den (Chapter II). (4) Nig
and the Chipmunk. (5) Describe a woodchuck (Chapter III). (6) Cuff and
the Chipmunk. (7) How to Trap Foxes (Chapter VII). (8) The Weasel
and the Chickens (Chapter VIII). (9) The Weasel's Character. (10) How
a Porcupine Defends Itself (Chapter XI).

Review of Rules and Definitions

NOUNS AND PRONOUNS

1. A proper noun is the name of a particular person, place, or thing.

A common noun is a name which may be applied to any one of a class of persons, places, or things.

2. Gender is distinction according to sex.

A noun or pronoun denoting a male being is of the masculine gender.

A noun or pronoun denoting a female being is of the feminine gender.

A noun or pronoun denoting a thing without animal life is of the neuter gender.

3. Nouns and pronouns may be of the first, the second, or the third person.

The first person denotes the speaker; the second person, the person spoken to; the third person, the person or thing spoken of.

4. Nouns or pronouns which denote a single object are said to be in the singular number.

Nouns or pronouns which denote two or more objects are said to be in the plural number.

5. There are three cases, — the nominative, the possessive, and the objective.

A noun or pronoun is in the nominative case (1) when it is the subject of a sentence, (2) when it is used in direct address or as an exclamation, (3) when it is used as a predicate nominative, (4) when it is in apposition with the subject, (5) when it is used in the absolute construction.

The possessive case denotes ownership or possession.

The object of a verb or preposition is in the objective case.

PRONOUNS

Pronouns may be divided into four classes: —

1. Personal pronouns (as, *I, thou, you, he, she, it*).

2. Relative pronouns (as, *who, which, that*).

3. Interrogative pronouns (as, *who, which, what*).

4. Adjective pronouns (as, *this, that*).

1. The personal pronouns serve to distinguish (1) the speaker, (2) the person spoken to, and (3) the person or thing spoken of.

2. Relative pronouns connect dependent clauses with main clauses by referring directly to a noun or pronoun in the main clause.

A clause introduced by a relative pronoun is called a relative clause.

The noun or pronoun to which a pronoun refers is called its antecedent.

A relative pronoun must agree with its antecedent in gender, person, and number.

3. The pronouns *who*, *which*, and *what* are often used in asking questions. In this use they are called interrogative pronouns.

4. *This*, *that*, *those*, *these*, and some other words are called adjective pronouns. They may be used either as pronouns or as adjectives.

CLAUSES AND COMPLEX SENTENCES

A clause is a group of words that forms part of a sentence and that contains a subject and a predicate.

A clause may do the work of a part of speech. Such clauses are said to be dependent or subordinate.

A clause may do the work of an adjective or an adverb.

A clause that modifies a noun or pronoun is called an adjective clause.

A clause that serves as an adverbial modifier is called an adverbial clause.

All clauses that serve as modifiers are said to be dependent (or subordinate).

A complex sentence consists of two or more clauses, at least one of which is dependent (or subordinate).

APPENDIX

RULES FOR THE USE OF PUNCTUATION MARKS AND CAPITAL LETTERS *

CAPITAL LETTERS

I. Every sentence begins with a capital letter.
II. Every proper noun or abbreviation of a proper noun begins with a capital letter.
    An adjective derived from a proper noun is usually written with a capital letter.
III. Every direct quotation begins with a capital letter.

This rule does not apply to quoted fragments of sentences.

IV. In the titles of books, etc., the first word, as well as every important word that follows, begins with a capital letter.
V. The interjection *O* and the pronoun *I* are always written in capitals.

MARKS OF PUNCTUATION

The common marks of punctuation are the period, the interrogation point, the exclamation point, the comma, the semicolon, the colon, the dash, the hyphen, the apostrophe, marks of parenthesis, and quotation marks. Of these, the period, the interrogation point, and the exclamation point are used at the end of sentences.

I. The period is used after —
    1. A declarative or an imperative sentence.
    2. An abbreviation or the initial of a name.
II. The interrogation point is used after a direct question.
III. The exclamation point is used after an interjection or an exclamatory phrase or sentence.
IV. The comma is used —
    1. After nouns of address.
    2. To separate a direct quotation from the rest of the sentence.

* This summary is intended for reference only. It includes the common rules for punctuation marks and capital letters. If the teacher wishes to use the summary as a review of the subject of punctuation, the illustrative sentences and selections contained in the book will afford sufficient material for study and practice.

    3. To separate the parts of a series of words that have the same construction.

    4. To indicate transposition in the order of a sentence.

    5. To set off a modifier which explains or identifies a noun (an "appositive").

    6. In general, to break up a sentence into parts so that its meaning may be clear to the reader.

V. The semicolon (;) is used —

    1. To separate the parts of a compound sentence when no conjunction is expressed.

    2. To separate the parts of a long compound sentence the clauses of which are broken by commas.

VI. The colon (:) is less frequently used than formerly.

    1. It sometimes follows the name or title of a person addressed, as at the beginning of a speech or letter (as, — "Mr. Chairman : — The question under discussion is —"; "Dear Sir : —").
       In such cases it is usually followed by the dash.

    2. It sometimes precedes an enumeration or list, especially after "as follows," "namely," and the like. Here again the dash is commonly used.

VII. The dash (—) is sometimes used —

    1. Instead of the comma, to set off an expression which breaks the thought of a sentence. The marks of parenthesis are used in the same way.

    2. After the comma following the name of a person addressed, as in a letter (as, — "Dear Mary, —").

    3. To indicate an incomplete or broken construction.

VIII. Quotation marks are used to enclose every direct quotation, and each part of a broken quotation. A quotation within a quotation is included in single marks.

NOTE. — When a quotation includes several paragraphs, quotation marks are put at the beginning of each paragraph, but at the end of the last one only.

IX. The apostrophe is used —

    1. To mark the omission of a letter or letters in contractions.

    2. As a sign of the genitive or possessive.

    3. To indicate the plural of letters, signs, etc.

X. The hyphen is used—

    1. When the parts of a word are separated in writing.

    2. Between the parts of some compound words. (See the Dictionary in each case.)

INDEX

[*The references below are to* pages; f. *signifies "and following* page"; ff. *signifies "and following* pages."]

339

SELECTIONS TO BE COMMITTED TO MEMORY

PRESCRIBED FOR THE

FOURTH, FIFTH, AND SIXTH YEARS

BY THE

EDUCATION DEPARTMENT OF THE STATE OF NEW YORK

Several of the selections in the following pages have been so often printed without collation with authorized copies that various inaccuracies have become more or less current. In the present volume great care has been taken to give the correct text in every instance.

Acknowledgments are due to authors and publishers for allowing the use of copyright material: to Messrs. Charles Scribner's Sons for Eugene Field's "Night Wind"; to Messrs. D. Appleton & Company for Bryant's "Robert of Lincoln"; to Messrs. Little, Brown & Company for two poems by Mrs. Helen Hunt Jackson and for one by Miss Nora Perry; to the J. B. Lippincott Company for "Sheridan's Ride"; to Miss Susan Hartley Swett for two poems; to Mrs. Emily Huntington Miller for one poem; to Mr. Henry Holcomb Bennett for one poem; to Mr. Clinton Scollard for one poem. Selections from Longfellow, Whittier, Emerson, Lowell, Holmes, Aldrich, Björnson, Celia Thaxter, and Mr. Frank Dempster Sherman are used by permission of, and by special arrangement with, Houghton Mifflin Company.

2

SELECTIONS TO BE COMMITTED
TO MEMORY

FOURTH YEAR

SWEET AND LOW

Sweet and low, sweet and low,
  Wind of the western sea,
Low, low, breathe and blow,
  Wind of the western sea!
Over the rolling waters go,
Come from the dying moon, and blow,
  Blow him again to me;
While my little one, while my pretty one sleeps.

Sleep and rest, sleep and rest,
  Father will come to thee soon;
Rest, rest, on mother's breast,
  Father will come to thee soon;
Father will come to his babe in the nest,
Silver sails all out of the west
  Under the silver moon;
Sleep, my little one, sleep, my pretty one, sleep.

ALFRED, LORD TENNYSON.

3

FAIRY FOLK *

(A CHILD'S SONG)

Up the airy mountain,
　Down the rushy glen,
We dare n't go a-hunting
　For fear of little men;
Wee folk, good folk,
　Trooping all together;
Green jacket, red cap,
　And white owl's feather!

Down along the rocky shore
　Some make their home,
They live on crispy pancakes
　Of yellow tide-foam;
Some in the reeds
　Of the black mountain-lake,
With frogs for their watchdogs,
　All night awake.

High on the hilltop
　The old King sits;
He is now so old and gray
　He 's nigh lost his wits.
With a bridge of white mist
　'Columbkill he crosses,
On his stately journeys
　From Slieveleague to Rosses;
Or going up with music
　On cold starry nights,

* From the author's revised text.

To sup with the Queen
Of the gay Northern Lights.

They stole little Bridget
For seven years long;
When she came down again
Her friends were all gone.
They took her lightly back,
Between the night and morrow,
They thought that she was fast asleep,
But she was dead with sorrow.
They have kept her ever since
Deep within the lakes,
On a bed of flag-leaves,
Watching till she wakes.

By the craggy hillside,
Through the mosses bare,
They have planted thorn-trees
For pleasure here and there.
Is any man so daring
As dig them up in spite,
He shall find their sharpest thorns *
In his bed at night.

Up the airy mountain,
Down the rushy glen,
We dare n't go a-hunting
For fear of little men;

* An earlier version has —

"Is any man so daring
To dig one up in spite,
He shall find the thornies set".

Wee folk, good folk,
    Trooping all together;
Green jacket, red cap,
    And white owl's feather!

WILLIAM ALLINGHAM.

THE NIGHT WIND*

Have you ever heard the wind go "Yooooo"?
   'T is a pitiful sound to hear!
It seems to chill you through and through
   With a strange and speechless fear.
'T is the voice of the night that broods outside
   When folk should be asleep,
And many and many's the time I've cried
To the darkness brooding far and wide
   Over the land and the deep:
"Whom do you want, O lonely night,
   That you wail the long hours through?"
And the night would say in its ghostly way:
      "Yooooooooo!
      Yooooooooo!
      Yooooooooo!"

My mother told me long ago
   (When I was a little lad)
That when the night went wailing so,
   Somebody had been bad;
And then, when I was snug in bed,
   Whither I had been sent,

With the blankets pulled up round my head,
I'd think of what my mother'd said,
    And wonder what boy she meant!
And "Who's been bad to-day?" I'd ask
    Of the wind that hoarsely blew,
And the voice would say in its meaningful way:
            "Yooooooooo!
            Yoooooooo!
            Yoooooooo!"

That this was true I must allow—
    You'll not believe it, though!
Yes, though I'm quite a model now,
    I was not always so.
And if you doubt what things I say,
    Suppose you make the test;
Suppose, when you've been bad some day
And up to bed are sent away
    From mother and the rest—
Suppose you ask, "Who has been bad?"
    And then you'll hear what's true;
For the wind will moan in its ruefulest tone:
            "Yoooooooo!
            Yoooooooo!
            Yoooooooo!"

                                EUGENE FIELD.

THE FROST

The Frost looked forth one still, clear night,
And whispered, "Now I shall be out of sight;
So through the valley and over the height,
    In silence I'll take my way;

I will not go on like that blustering train,
The wind and the snow, the hail and the rain,
Who make so much bustle and noise in vain,
  But I 'll be as busy as they ! "

Then he flew to the mountain and powdered its crest;
He lit on the trees, and their boughs he dressed
In diamond beads; and over the breast
  Of the quivering lake he spread
A coat of mail, that it need not fear
The downward point of many a spear,
That he hung on its margin, far and near,
  Where a rock could rear its head.

He went to the windows of those who slept,
And over each pane like a fairy crept;
Wherever he breathed, wherever he stepped,
  By the light of the morn were seen
Most beautiful things: there were flowers and trees;
There were bevies of birds and swarms of bees;
There were cities with temples and towers; and these
  All pictured in silver sheen!

But he did one thing that was hardly fair —
He peeped in the cupboard, and finding there
That all had forgotten for him to prepare,
  " Now, just to set them a-thinking,
I 'll bite this basket of fruit," said he,
" This costly pitcher I 'll burst in three;
And the glass of water they 've left for me
  Shall ' tchick ' to tell them I 'm drinking!"

                              HANNAH FLAGG GOULD.

SEPTEMBER *

The golden-rod is yellow;
  The corn is turning brown;
The trees in apple orchards
  With fruit are bending down.

The gentian's bluest fringes
  . Are curling in the sun;
In dusty pods the milkweed
  Its hidden silk has spun.

The sedges flaunt their harvest
  In every meadow nook;
And asters by the brook-side
  Make asters in the brook.

From dewy lanes at morning
  The grapes' sweet odors rise;
At noon the roads all flutter
  With yellow butterflies.

By all these lovely tokens
  September days are here,
With summer's best of weather,
  And autumn's best of cheer.

But none of all this beauty
  Which floods the earth and air
Is unto me the secret
  Which makes September fair.

* Copyright, 1892, by Roberts Brothers.

'T is a thing which I remember;
    To name it thrills me yet:
One day of one September
    I never can forget.

HELEN HUNT JACKSON.

THE VILLAGE BLACKSMITH

Under a spreading chestnut-tree
    The village smithy stands;
The smith, a mighty man is he,
    With large and sinewy hands;
And the muscles of his brawny arms
    Are strong as iron bands.

His hair is crisp, and black, and long,
    His face is like the tan;
His brow is wet with honest sweat,
    He earns whate'er he can,
And looks the whole world in the face,
    For he owes not any man.

Week in, week out, from morn till night,
    You can hear his bellows blow;
You can hear him swing his heavy sledge
    With measured beat and slow,
Like a sexton ringing the village bell,
    When the evening sun is low.

And children coming home from school
    Look in at the open door;
They love to see the flaming forge,
    And hear the bellows roar,

And catch the burning sparks that fly
   Like chaff from a threshing-floor.

He goes on Sunday to the church,
   And sits among his boys;
He hears the parson pray and preach,
   He hears his daughter's voice,
Singing in the village choir,
   And it makes his heart rejoice.

It sounds to him like her mother's voice,
   Singing in Paradise!
He needs must think of her once more,
   How in the grave she lies;
And with his hard, rough hand he wipes
   A tear out of his eyes.

Toiling, — rejoicing, — sorrowing,
   Onward through life he goes;
Each morning sees some task begin,
   Each evening sees its close;
Something attempted, something done,
   Has earned a night's repose.

Thanks, thanks to thee, my worthy friend,
   For the lesson thou hast taught!
Thus at the flaming forge of life
   Our fortunes must be wrought;
Thus on its sounding anvil shaped
   Each burning deed and thought.

HENRY WADSWORTH LONGFELLOW.

THE CHILDREN'S HOUR

Between the dark and the daylight,
 When the night is beginning to lower,
Comes a pause in the day's occupations,
 That is known as the Children's Hour.

I hear in the chamber above me
 The patter of little feet,
The sound of a door that is opened,
 And voices soft and sweet.

From my study I see in the lamplight,
 Descending the broad hall stair,
Grave Alice, and laughing Allegra,
 And Edith with golden hair.

A whisper, and then a silence:
 Yet I know by their merry eyes
They are plotting and planning together
 To take me by surprise.

A sudden rush from the stairway,
 A sudden raid from the hall!
By three doors left unguarded
 They enter my castle wall!

They climb up into my turret
 O'er the arms and back of my chair;
If I try to escape, they surround me;
 They seem to be everywhere.

They almost devour me with kisses,
 Their arms about me entwine,

Till I think of the Bishop of Bingen
   In his Mouse-Tower on the Rhine!

Do you think, O blue-eyed banditti,
   Because you have scaled the wall,
Such an old mustache as I am
   Is not a match for you all?

I have you fast in my fortress,
   And will not let you depart,
But put you down into the dungeon
   In the round-tower of my heart.

And there will I keep you forever,
   Yes, forever and a day,
Till the walls shall crumble to ruin,
   And moulder in dust away!

             HENRY WADSWORTH LONGFELLOW.

THE BLUEBIRD *

I know the song that the bluebird is singing,
Out in the apple-tree where he is swinging.
Brave little fellow! the skies may be dreary,
Nothing cares he while his heart is so cheery.

Hark! how the music leaps out from his throat!
Hark! was there ever so merry a note?
Listen awhile, and you'll hear what he's saying,
Up in the apple-tree, swinging and swaying:

* By permission of the author.

"Dear little blossoms, down under the snow,
You must be weary of winter, I know;
Hark! while I sing you a message of cheer,
Summer is coming, and springtime is here!

"Little white snowdrop, I pray you, arise;
Bright yellow crocus, come, open your eyes;
Sweet little violets hid from the cold,
Put on your mantles of purple and gold;
Daffodils, daffodils! say, do you hear?
Summer is coming, and springtime is here!"

EMILY HUNTINGTON MILLER.

THE WIND AND THE MOON *

Said the Wind to the Moon, "I will blow you out!
          You stare
          In the air
          As if crying 'Beware,' †
Always looking what I am about:
I hate to be watched; I will blow you out!"

The Wind blew hard, and out went the Moon.
          So, deep
          On a heap
          Of clouds, to sleep,
Down lay the Wind, and slumbered soon,
Muttering low, "I've done for that Moon!"

* From the author's revised version. Some of the superseded readings
are given in the notes.
† The earlier reading was "Like a ghost in a chair," but this was after-
wards changed by the author.

He turned in his bed: she was there again!
>On high
>In the sky,
>With her one ghost-eye
The Moon shone white and alive and plain:
Said the Wind, "I will blow you out again!"

The Wind blew hard, and the Moon grew slim.*
>"With my sledge
>And my wedge
>I have knocked off her edge!
I will blow," said the Wind, "right fierce and grim,
And the creature will soon be slimmer than slim!" †

He blew and he blew, and she thinned to a thread.
>"One puff
>More's enough
>To blow her to snuff!
One good puff more where the last was bred,
And glimmer, glimmer, glum will go that thread!"

He blew a great blast, and the thread was gone.
>In the air
>Nowhere
>Was a moonbeam bare;
Larger and nearer the shy stars shone: ‡
Sure and certain the Moon was gone!

* The earlier version has "dim."
† The earlier version has —
>"If only I blow right fierce and grim,
>The creature will soon be dimmer than dim."
‡ The earlier version has —
>"Far off and harmless the shy stars shone."

The Wind he took to his revels once more;
>> On down
>> And in town,
>> A merry-mad clown,
He leaped and holloed with whistle and roar —
When there was that glimmering thread once more!*

He flew in a rage — he danced and blew;
>> But in vain
>> Was the pain
>> Of his bursting brain,
For still the Moon-scrap the broader grew
The more that he swelled his big cheeks and blew.†

Slowly she grew — till she filled the night,
>> And shone
>> On her throne
>> In the sky alone,
A matchless, wonderful, silvery light,
Radiant and lovely, the queen of the night.

Said the Wind: "What a marvel of power am I!
>> With my breath,
>> In good faith,
>> I blew her to death! —
First blew her away right out of the sky,
Then blew her in: what a strength am I!"

---

* The earlier version has —

>> "'What's that?' The glimmering thread once more!"

† The earlier version has —

>> "For still the broader the moon-scrap grew
>> The broader he swelled his big cheeks and blew."

But the Moon she knew naught of the silly affair;
        For, high
        In the sky,
        With her one white eye,
Motionless miles above the air,
She never had heard the great Wind blare.

GEORGE MacDONALD.

JIM CROW *

O, say, Jim Crow,
Why is it you always go
With a gloomy coat of black
The year long on your back?
Why don't you change its hue,
At least for a day or two,
To red or green or blue?
And why do you always wear
Such a sober, sombre air,
As glum as the face of Care?
I wait for your reply,
    And into the peaceful pause
There comes your curious, croaking cry, —
    "O, because! 'cause! 'cause!"

O, say, Jim Crow,
Why, when the farmers sow,
And the corn springs up in the row,
And the days that once were brief
Grow long, and laugh into leaf,
Do you play the rascally thief?

* From "The Lyric Bough" (Sherman, French & Co.). By permission of the author.

I can see by the look in your eye, —
Wary and wise and sly, —
    That you know the code in vogue;
Why will you, then, O, why,
    Persist in the path of the rogue?
I hearken for your reply,
    And into the empty pause
There rings your graceless, grating cry, —
    " O, because! 'cause! 'cause!"

And say, Jim Crow,
With all of the lore you know, —
    Lore of the wood and field,
Lore of the clouds, and the clear
Depths of the atmosphere,
    To our duller ken concealed, —
Why is it you ever speak
With a mingled squawk and a squeak?
You, with your talents all,
    And your knowledge of this and that,
Why must you sing like a squall,
    And talk like a perfect "flat"?
I listen for your reply,
    But in the lapse and the pause
All I hear is your impudent cry, —
    " O, because! 'cause! 'cause!"

                                    CLINTON SCOLLARD.

THE SANDPIPER

Across the narrow beach we flit,
    One little sandpiper and I,
And fast I gather, bit by bit,
    The scattered driftwood bleached and dry.

The wild waves reach their hands for it,
 The wild wind raves, the tide runs high,
As up and down the beach we flit, —
 One little sandpiper and I.

Above our heads the sullen clouds
 Scud black and swift across the sky;
Like silent ghosts in misty shrouds
 Stand out the white lighthouses high.
Almost as far as eye can reach
 I see the close-reefed vessels fly,
As fast we flit along the beach, —
 One little sandpiper and I.

I watch him as he skims along,
 Uttering his sweet and mournful cry.
He starts not at my fitful song,
 Or flash of fluttering drapery.
He has no thought of any wrong;
 He scans me with a fearless eye.
Stanch friends are we, well tried and strong,
 The little sandpiper and I.

Comrade, where wilt thou be to-night,
 When the loosed storm breaks furiously?
My driftwood fire will burn so bright!
 To what warm shelter canst thou fly?
I do not fear for thee, though wroth
 The tempest rushes through the sky:
For are we not God's children both,
 Thou, little sandpiper, and I?

CELIA THAXTER.

THE BAREFOOT BOY

Blessings on thee, little man,
Barefoot boy, with cheek of tan!
With thy turned-up pantaloons,
And thy merry whistled tunes;
With thy red lip, redder still
Kissed by strawberries on the hill;
With the sunshine on thy face,
Through thy torn brim's jaunty grace;
From my heart I give thee joy, —
I was once a barefoot boy!
Prince thou art, — the grown-up man
Only is republican.
Let the million-dollared ride!
Barefoot, trudging at his side,
Thou hast more than he can buy
In the reach of ear and eye, —
Outward sunshine, inward joy:
Blessings on thee, barefoot boy!

Oh for boyhood's painless play,
Sleep that wakes in laughing day,
Health that mocks the doctor's rules,
Knowledge never learned of schools,
Of the wild bee's morning chase,
Of the wild-flower's time and place,
Flight of fowl and habitude
Of the tenants of the wood;
How the tortoise bears his shell,
How the woodchuck digs his cell,
And the ground-mole sinks his well;
How the robin feeds her young,

How the oriole's nest is hung;
Where the whitest lilies blow,
Where the freshest berries grow,
Where the ground-nut trails its vine,
Where the wood-grape's clusters shine;
Of the black wasp's cunning way,
Mason of his walls of clay,
And the architectural plans
Of gray hornet artisans!
For, eschewing books and tasks,
Nature answers all he asks;
Hand in hand with her he walks,
Face to face with her he talks,
Part and parcel of her joy, —
Blessings on the barefoot boy!

Oh for boyhood's time of June,
Crowding years in one brief moon,
When all things I heard or saw,
Me, their master, waited for.
I was rich in flowers and trees,
Humming-birds and honey-bees;
For my sport the squirrel played,
Plied the snouted mole his spade;
For my taste the blackberry cone
Purpled over hedge and stone;
Laughed the brook for my delight
Through the day and through the night,
Whispering at the garden wall,
Talked with me from fall to fall;
Mine the sand-rimmed pickerel pond,
Mine the walnut slopes beyond,

Mine, on bending orchard trees,
Apples of Hesperides!
Still as my horizon grew,
Larger grew my riches too;
All the world I saw or knew
Seemed a complex Chinese toy,
Fashioned for a barefoot boy!

Oh for festal dainties spread,
Like my bowl of milk and bread;
Pewter spoon and bowl of wood,
On the door-stone, gray and rude!
O'er me, like a regal tent,
Cloudy-ribbed, the sunset bent,
Purple-curtained, fringed with gold,
Looped in many a wind-swung fold;
While for music came the play
Of the pied frogs' orchestra;
And, to light the noisy choir,
Lit the fly his lamp of fire.
I was monarch: pomp and joy
Waited on the barefoot boy!

Cheerily, then, my little man,
Live and laugh, as boyhood can!
Though the flinty slopes be hard,
Stubble-speared the new-mown sward,
Every morn shall lead thee through
Fresh baptisms of the dew;
Every evening from thy feet
Shall the cool wind kiss the heat:
All too soon these feet must hide

In the prison cells of pride,
Lose the freedom of the sod,
Like a colt's for work be shod,
Made to tread the mills of toil,
Up and down in ceaseless moil:
Happy if their track be found
Never on forbidden ground;
Happy if they sink not in
Quick and treacherous sands of sin.
Ah! that thou couldst know thy joy,
Ere it passes, barefoot boy!

JOHN GREENLEAF WHITTIER.

LUCY GRAY, OR SOLITUDE

Oft I had heard of Lucy Gray:
    And, when I crossed the wild,
I chanced to see at break of day
    The solitary child.

No mate, no comrade Lucy knew;
    She dwelt on a wide moor, —
The sweetest thing that ever grew
    Beside a human door!

You yet may spy the fawn at play,
    The hare upon the green;
But the sweet face of Lucy Gray
    Will never more be seen.

"To-night will be a stormy night —
    You to the town must go;

And take a lantern, child, to light
  Your mother through the snow."

"That, father, will I gladly do:
  'T is scarcely afternoon —
The minster-clock has just struck two,
  And yonder is the moon!"

At this the father raised his hook,
  And snapped a fagot-band;
He plied his work, — and Lucy took
  The lantern in her hand.

Not blither is the mountain roe:
  With many a wanton stroke
Her feet disperse the powdery snow,
  That rises up like smoke.

The storm came on before its time:
  She wandered up and down,
And many a hill did Lucy climb,
  But never reached the town.

The wretched parents all that night
  Went shouting far and wide;
But there was neither sound nor sight
  To serve them for a guide.

At daybreak on a hill they stood
  That overlooked the moor;
And thence they saw the bridge of wood,
  A furlong from their door.

They wept, and, turning homeward, cried,
  "In heaven we all shall meet";
When in the snow the mother spied
  The print of Lucy's feet.

Then downwards from the steep hill's edge
  They tracked the footmarks small;
And through the broken hawthorn hedge,
  And by the long stone-wall;

And then an open field they crossed:
  The marks were still the same;
They tracked them on, nor ever lost;
  And to the bridge they came.

They followed from the snowy bank
  Those footmarks, one by one,
Into the middle of the plank;
  And further there were none!

Yet some maintain that to this day
  She is a living child;
That you may see sweet Lucy Gray
  Upon the lonesome wild.

O'er rough and smooth she trips along,
  And never looks behind;
And sings a solitary song
  That whistles in the wind.

WILLIAM WORDSWORTH.

FIFTH YEAR

THE BROOK

I come from haunts of coot and hern,
  I make a sudden sally,
And sparkle out among the fern,
  To bicker down a valley.

By thirty hills I hurry down,
  Or slip between the ridges,
By twenty thorps, a little town,
  And half a hundred bridges.

Till last by Philip's farm I flow
  To join the brimming river,
For men may come and men may go,
  But I go on forever.

I chatter over stony ways,
  In little sharps and trebles,
I bubble into eddying bays,
  I babble on the pebbles.

With many a curve my banks I fret
  By many a field and fallow,
And many a fairy foreland set
  With willow-weed and mallow.

I chatter, chatter, as I flow
  To join the brimming river,
For men may come and men may go,
  But I go on forever.

I wind about, and in and out,
   With here a blossom sailing,
And here and there a lusty trout,
   And here and there a grayling,

And here and there a foamy flake
   Upon me, as I travel
With many a silvery water-break
   Above the golden gravel,

And draw them all along, and flow
   To join the brimming river,
For men may come and men may go,
   But I go on forever.

I steal by lawns and grassy plots,
   I slide by hazel covers;
I move the sweet forget-me-nots
   That grow for happy lovers.

I slip, I slide, I gloom, I glance,
   Among my skimming swallows;
I make the netted sunbeam dance
   Against my sandy shallows.

I murmur under moon and stars
   In brambly wildernesses;
I linger by my shingly bars,
   I loiter round my cresses;

And out again I curve and flow
   To join the brimming river,
For men may come and men may go,
   But I go on forever.

               ALFRED, LORD TENNYSON.

ROBERT OF LINCOLN *

Merrily swinging on brier and weed,
  Near to the nest of his little dame,
Over the mountain-side or mead,
  Robert of Lincoln is telling his name:
    " Bob-o'-link, bob-o'-link,
    Spink, spank, spink;
Snug and safe is that nest of ours,
Hidden among the summer flowers.
              Chee, chee, chee."

Robert of Lincoln is gayly dressed,
  Wearing a bright black wedding-coat;
White are his shoulders and white his crest.
  Hear him call in his merry note:
    " Bob-o'-link, bob-o'-link,
    Spink, spank, spink;
Look, what a nice new coat is mine,
Sure there was never a bird so fine.
              Chee, chee, chee."

Robert of Lincoln's Quaker wife,
  Pretty and quiet, with plain brown wings,
Passing at home a patient life,
  Broods in the grass while her husband sings:
    " Bob-o'-link, bob-o'-link,
    Spink, spank, spink;
Brood, kind creature; you need not fear
Thieves and robbers while I am here.
              Chee, chee, chee."

* From Bryant's " Poems." Copyright by D. Appleton & Company.
Reprinted by permission of the publishers.

Modest and shy as a nun is she;
  One weak chirp is her only note.
Braggart and prince of braggarts is he,
  Pouring boasts from his little throat:
  " Bob-o'-link, bob-o'-link,
    Spink, spank, spink;
Never was I afraid of man;
Catch me, cowardly knaves, if you can!
          Chee, chee, chee."

Six white eggs on a bed of hay,
  Flecked with purple, a pretty sight!
There as the mother sits all day,
  Robert is singing with all his might:
  " Bob-o'-link, bob-o'-link,
    Spink, spank, spink;
Nice good wife, that never goes out,
Keeping house while I frolic about.
          Chee, chee, chee."

Soon as the little ones chip the shell,
  Six wide mouths are open for food;
Robert of Lincoln bestirs him well,
  Gathering seeds for the hungry brood
  " Bob-o'-link, bob-o'-link,
    Spink, spank, spink;
This new life is likely to be
Hard for a gay young fellow like me.
          Chee, chee, chee."

Robert of Lincoln at length is made
  Sober with work, and silent with care;

Off is his holiday garment laid,
  Half forgotten that merry air:
    " Bob-o'-link, bob-o'-link,
    Spink, spank, spink;
Nobody knows but my mate and I
Where our nest and our nestlings lie.
          Chee, chee, chee."

Summer wanes; the children are grown;
  Fun and frolic no more he knows;
Robert of Lincoln 's a humdrum crone;
  Off he flies, and we sing as he goes:
    " Bob-o'-link, bob-o'-link,
    Spink, spank, spink;
When you can pipe that merry old strain,
Robert of Lincoln, come back again.
          Chee, chee, chee."

                          WILLIAM CULLEN BRYANT.

THE TREE *

The Tree's early leaf-buds were bursting their brown:
" Shall I take them away ? " said the Frost, sweeping down
        " No, leave them alone
        Till the blossoms have grown,"
Prayed the Tree, while he trembled from rootlet to crown.

The Tree bore his blossoms, and all the birds sung:
" Shall I take them away ? " said the Wind as he swung.
        " No, leave them alone
        Till the berries have grown,"
Said the Tree, while his leaflets quivering hung.

* From "Arne." By permission of Houghton Mifflin Company.

The Tree bore his fruit in the midsummer glow:
Said the girl, " May I gather thy berries or no ? "
    " Yes, all thou canst see, —
    Take them ; all are for thee,"
Said the Tree, while he bent down his laden boughs low.

BJÖRNSTJERNE BJÖRNSON.

TO-DAY

So here hath been dawning
    Another blue day ;
Think, wilt thou let it
    Slip useless away ?

Out of Eternity
    This new day is born ;
Into Eternity,
    At night, will return.

Behold it aforetime
    No eye ever did ;
So soon it forever
    From all eyes is hid.

Here hath been dawning
    Another blue day ;
Think, wilt thou let it
    Slip useless away ?

THOMAS CARLYLE.

OLD IRONSIDES

Ay, tear her tattered ensign down !
    Long has it waved on high,
And many an eye has danced to see
    That banner in the sky ;

Beneath it rung the battle shout,
   And burst the cannon's roar; —
The meteor of the ocean air
   Shall sweep the clouds no more.

Her deck, once red with heroes' blood,
   Where knelt the vanquished foe,
When winds were hurrying o'er the flood,
   And waves were white below,
No more shall feel the victor's tread,
   Or know the conquered knee; —
The harpies of the shore shall pluck
   The eagle of the sea!

Oh, better that her shattered hulk
   Should sink beneath the wave;
Her thunders shook the mighty deep,
   And there should be her grave;
Nail to the mast her holy flag,
   Set every threadbare sail,
And give her to the god of storms,
   The lightning and the gale!

               OLIVER WENDELL HOLMES.

OCTOBER'S BRIGHT BLUE WEATHER *

O suns and skies and clouds of June,
   And flowers of June together,
Ye cannot rival for one hour
   October's bright blue weather,

When loud the bumblebee makes haste,
   Belated, thriftless vagrant,

And golden-rod is dying fast,
  And lanes with grapes are fragrant;

When gentians roll their fringes tight
  To save them for the morning,
And chestnuts fall from satin burrs
  Without a sound of warning;

When on the ground red apples lie
  In piles like jewels shining,
And redder still on old stone walls
  Are leaves of woodbine twining;

When all the lovely wayside things
  Their white-winged seeds are sowing,
And in the fields, still green and fair,
  Late aftermaths are growing;

When springs run low, and on the brooks,
  In idle golden freighting,
Bright leaves sink noiseless in the hush
  Of woods, for winter waiting;

When comrades seek sweet country haunts,
  By twos and twos together,
And count like misers, hour by hour,
  October's bright blue weather.

O·sun and skies and flowers of June,
  Count all your boasts together,
Love loveth best of all the year
  October's bright blue weather.

                              HELEN HUNT JACKSON.

THE SHIP OF STATE *

Thou, too, sail on, O Ship of State!
Sail on, O Union, strong and great!
Humanity with all its fears,
With all the hopes of future years,
Is hanging breathless on thy fate!
We know what Master laid thy keel,
What Workmen wrought thy ribs of steel,
Who made each mast, and sail, and rope,
What anvils rang, what hammers beat,
In what a forge and what a heat
Were shaped the anchors of thy hope!
Fear not each sudden sound and shock,
'T is of the wave and not the rock;
'T is but the flapping of the sail,
And not a rent made by the gale!
In spite of rock and tempest's roar,
In spite of false lights on the shore,
Sail on, nor fear to breast the sea!
Our hearts, our hopes, are all with thee,
Our hearts, our hopes, our prayers, our tears,
Our faith triumphant o'er our fears,
Are all with thee, — are all with thee!

                    HENRY WADSWORTH LONGFELLOW

THE BUILDERS

All are architects of Fate,
    Working in these walls of Time;
Some with massive deeds and great,
    Some with ornaments of rhyme.

* From "The Building of the Ship."

Nothing useless is, or low;
  Each thing in its place is best;
And what seems but idle show
  Strengthens and supports the rest.

For the structure that we raise,
  Time is with materials filled;
Our to-days and yesterdays
  Are the blocks with which we build.

Truly shape and fashion these;
  Leave no yawning gaps between;
Think not because no man sees,
  Such things will remain unseen.

In the elder days of art,
  Builders wrought with greatest care
Each minute and unseen part;
  For the gods see everywhere.

Let us do our work as well,
  Both the unseen and the seen;
Make the house, where gods may dwell,
  Beautiful, entire, and clean.

Else our lives are incomplete,
  Standing in these walls of Time,
Broken stairways, where the feet
  Stumble as they seek to climb.

Build to-day, then, strong and sure,
  With a firm and ample base;

And ascending and secure
　　Shall to-morrow find its place.

Thus alone can we attain
　　To those turrets where the eye
Sees the world as one vast plain,
　　And one boundless reach of sky.

HENRY WADSWORTH LONGFELLOW.

HOME, SWEET HOME

'Mid pleasures and palaces though we may roam,
Be it ever so humble, there's no place like home!
A charm from the sky seems to hallow us there,
Which, seek through the world, is ne'er met with elsewhere!
　　Home, home! sweet, sweet home!
　　　　There's no place like home!
　　　　There's no place like home!

An exile from home, splendor dazzles in vain.
Oh, give me my lowly thatch'd cottage again!
The birds singing gayly, that came at my call, —
Give me them, — and the peace of mind dearer than all!
　　Home, home! sweet, sweet home!
　　　　There's no place like home!
　　　　There's no place like home!

JOHN HOWARD PAYNE.

WARREN'S ADDRESS TO THE AMERICAN SOLDIERS

Stand! the ground's your own, my braves!
Will ye give it up to slaves?
Will ye look for greener graves?
　Hope ye mercy still?

What's the mercy despots feel?
Hear it in that battle-peal!
Read it on yon bristling steel!
  Ask it, — ye who will.

Fear ye foes who kill for hire?
Will ye to your homes retire?
Look behind you! they're afire!
  And, before you, see
Who have done it! — From the vale
On they come! — And will ye quail? —
Leaden rain and iron hail
  Let their welcome be!

In the God of battles trust!
Die we may, — and die we must; —
But, O, where can dust to dust
  Be consigned so well,
As where Heaven its dews shall shed
On the martyred patriot's bed,
And the rocks shall raise their head,
  Of his deeds to tell!   JOHN PIERPONT.

LULLABY FOR TITANIA

FIRST FAIRY

You spotted snakes with double tongue,
  Thorny hedgehogs, be not seen;
Newts and blind-worms, do no wrong,
  Come not near our fairy queen.

CHORUS

Philomel, with melody
Sing in our sweet lullaby:
Lulla, lulla, lullaby; lulla, lulla, lullaby!

Never harm,
Nor spell, nor charm,
Come our lovely lady nigh.
So good night, with lullaby.

FIRST FAIRY

Weaving spiders, come not here;
Hence, you long-legg'd spinners, hence!
Beetles black, approach not near;
Worm nor snail, do no offence.

CHORUS

Philomel, with melody
Sing in our sweet lullaby:
Lulla, lulla, lullaby; lulla, lulla, lullaby!
Never harm,
Nor spell, nor charm,
Come our lovely lady nigh.
So good night, with lullaby.

SECOND FAIRY

Hence, away! now all is well.
One aloof stand sentinel!

WILLIAM SHAKSPERE, "A Midsummer Night's Dream."

THE BLUE JAY *

O Blue Jay up in the maple-tree,
Shaking your throat with such bursts of glee,
How did you happen to be so blue?

* By special arrangement with the author.

Did you steal a bit of the lake for your crest,
And fasten blue violets into your vest?
    Tell me, I pray you, — tell me true!

Did you dip your wings in azure dye,
When April began to paint the sky,
    That was pale with the winter's stay?
Or were you hatched from a bluebell bright,
'Neath the warm, gold breast of a sunbeam light,
    By the river one blue spring day?

O Blue Jay up in the maple-tree,
A-tossing your saucy head at me,
    With ne'er a word for my questioning,
Pray, cease for a moment your "ting-a-link,"
And hear when I tell you what I think, —
    You bonniest bit of the spring.

I think when the fairies made the flowers,
To grow in these mossy fields of ours,
    Periwinkles and violets rare,
There was left of the spring's own color, blue,
Plenty to fashion a flower whose hue
    Would be richer than all and as fair.

So, putting their wits together, they
Made one great blossom so bright and gay,
    The lily beside it seemed blurred;
And then they said, "We will toss it in air;
So many blue blossoms grow everywhere,
    Let this pretty one be a bird!"

SUSAN HARTLEY SWETT.

SIXTH YEAR

BEFORE THE RAIN

We knew it would rain, for all the morn,
   A spirit on slender ropes of mist
Was lowering its golden buckets down
   Into the vapory amethyst

Of marshes and swamps and dismal fens, —
   Scooping the dew that lay in the flowers,
Dipping the jewels out of the sea,
   To sprinkle them over the land in showers.

We knew it would rain, for the poplars showed
   The white of their leaves, the amber grain
Shrunk in the wind, — and the lightning now
   Is tangled in tremulous skeins of rain!

             THOMAS BAILEY ALDRICH

THE FLAG GOES BY *

   Hats off!
Along the street there comes
A blare of bugles, a ruffle of drums,
A flash of color beneath the sky:
   Hats off!
The flag is passing by!

Blue and crimson and white it shines,
Over the steel-tipped, ordered lines.
   Hats off!

     * By special arrangement with the author.

The colors before us fly;
But more than the flag is passing by.

Sea-fights and land-fights, grim and great,
Fought to make and to save the State:
Weary marches and sinking ships;
Cheers of victory on dying lips;

Days of plenty and years of peace;
March of a strong land's swift increase;
Equal justice, right, and law,
Stately honor and reverend awe;

Sign of a nation, great and strong
To ward her people from foreign wrong;
Pride and glory and honor, — all
Live in the colors to stand or fall.

    Hats off!
Along the street there comes
A blare of bugles, a ruffle of drums;
And loyal hearts are beating high:
    Hats off!
The flag is passing by!

HENRY HOLCOMB BENNETT.

THE YEAR'S AT THE SPRING

The year's at the spring
And day's at the morn;
Morning's at seven;
The hillside's dew-pearled;

The lark's on the wing;
The snail's on the thorn:
God's in his heaven —
All's right with the world.

ROBERT BROWNING.

CONCORD HYMN

(SUNG AT THE COMPLETION OF THE BATTLE MONUMENT,
APRIL 19, 1836)

By the rude bridge that arched the flood,
    Their flag to April's breeze unfurled,
Here once the embattled farmers stood,
    And fired the shot heard round the world.

The foe long since in silence slept;
    Alike the conqueror silent sleeps;
And Time the ruined bridge has swept
    Down the dark stream which seaward creeps.

On this green bank, by this soft stream,
    We set to-day a votive stone;
That memory may their deed redeem,
    When, like our sires, our sons are gone.

Spirit, that made those heroes dare
    To die, and leave their children free,
Bid Time and Nature gently spare
    The shaft we raise to them and thee.

RALPH WALDO EMERSON.

THE FIRST SNOW-FALL

The snow had begun in the gloaming,
  And busily all the night
Had been heaping field and highway
  With a silence deep and white.

Every pine and fir and hemlock
  Wore ermine too dear for an earl,
And the poorest twig on the elm-tree
  Was ridged inch deep with pearl.

From sheds new-roofed with Carrara
  Came Chanticleer's muffled crow,
The stiff rails softened to swan's-down,
  And still fluttered down the snow.

I stood and watched by the window
  The noiseless work of the sky,
And the sudden flurries of snow-birds,
  Like brown leaves whirling by.

I thought of a mound in sweet Auburn
  Where a little headstone stood;
How the flakes were folding it gently,
  As did robins the babes in the wood.

Up spoke our own little Mabel,
  Saying, "Father, who makes it snow?"
And I told of the good All-father
  Who cares for us here below.

Again I looked at the snow-fall,
  And thought of the leaden sky

That arched o'er our first great sorrow,
  When that mound was heaped so high.

I remembered the gradual patience
  That fell from that cloud like snow,
Flake by flake, healing and hiding
  The scar that renewed our woe.

And again to the child I whispered,
  "The snow that husheth all,
Darling, the merciful Father
  Alone can make it fall!"

Then, with eyes that saw not, I kissed her;
  And she, kissing back, could not know
That *my* kiss was given to her sister,
  Folded close under deepening snow.

JAMES RUSSELL LOWELL.

THE COMING OF THE SPRING *

There's something in the air
That's new and sweet and rare —
A scent of summer things,
A whir as if of wings.

There's something too that's new
In the color of the blue
That's in the morning sky,
Before the sun is high.

And though on plain and hill
'T is winter, winter still,

* Copyright by Little, Brown & Company.

There's something seems to say
That winter's had its day.

And all this changing tint,
This whispering stir and hint
Of bud and bloom and wing,
Is the coming of the spring.

And to-morrow or to-day
The brooks will break away
From their icy, frozen sleep,
And run and laugh and leap.

And the next thing, in the woods,
The catkins in their hoods
Of fir and silk will stand,
A sturdy little band.

And the tassels soft and fine
Of the hazel will untwine,
And the elder branches show
Their buds against the snow.

So, silently but swift,
Above the wintry drift,
The long days gain and gain,
Until, on hill and plain,

Once more, and yet once more
Returning as before,
We see the bloom of birth
Make young again the earth.

NORA PERRY.

SHERIDAN'S RIDE *

Up from the south at break of day,
Bringing to Winchester fresh dismay,
  The affrighted air with a shudder bore,
  Like a herald in haste, to the chieftain's door,
  The terrible grumble, and rumble, and roar,
  Telling the battle was on once more,
And Sheridan twenty miles away.

And wider still those billows of war
Thundered along the horizon's bar;
And louder yet into Winchester rolled
The roar of that red sea uncontrolled,
Making the blood of the listener cold,
As he thought of the stake in that fiery fray,
With Sheridan twenty miles away.

But there is a road from Winchester town,
A good broad highway leading down;
And there, through the flush of the morning light,
A steed as black as the steeds of night
Was seen to pass, as with eagle flight,
As if he knew the terrible need;
He stretched away with his utmost speed;
Hills rose and fell; but his heart was gay,
With Sheridan fifteen miles away.

Still sprung from those swift hoofs, thundering south,
The dust, like smoke from the cannon's mouth;
Or the trail of a comet, sweeping faster and faster,

* From "The Poetical Works of Thomas Buchanan Read." By permission of the publishers, J. B. Lippincott Company.

Foreboding to traitors the doom of disaster.
The heart of the steed and the heart of the master
Were beating like prisoners assaulting their walls,
Impatient to be where the battlefield calls;
Every nerve of the charger was strained to full play,
With Sheridan only ten miles away.

Under his spurning feet the road
Like an arrowy Alpine river flowed,
And the landscape sped away behind
Like an ocean flying before the wind,
And the steed, like a bark fed with furnace ire,
Swept on, with his wild eyes full of fire.
But lo! he is nearing his heart's desire;
He is snuffing the smoke of the roaring fray,
With Sheridan only five miles away.

The first that the general saw were the groups
Of stragglers, and then the retreating troops.
What was done? what to do? A glance told him both;
Then, striking his spurs, with a terrible oath,
He dashed down the line, 'mid a storm of huzzas,
And the wave of retreat checked its course there, because
The sight of the master compelled it to pause.
With foam and with dust the black charger was gray;
By the flash of his eye, and the red nostril's play,
He seemed to the whole great army to say,
"I have brought you Sheridan all the way
From Winchester, down to save the day!"

Hurrah! hurrah for Sheridan!
Hurrah! hurrah for horse and man!

And when their statues are placed on high,
Under the dome of the Union sky, —
The American soldiers' Temple of Fame, —
There with the glorious general's name,
Be it said, in letters both bold and bright,
  "Here is the steed that saved the day,
By carrying Sheridan into the fight
  From Winchester, twenty miles away!"

THOMAS BUCHANAN READ.

PUCK AND THE FAIRY

Puck. How now, spirit! whither wander you?
Fairy. Over hill, over dale,
  Thorough bush, thorough brier,
Over park, over pale,
  Thorough flood, thorough fire,
I do wander everywhere,
Swifter than the moon's sphere;
And I serve the Fairy Queen,
To dew her orbs upon the green.
The cowslips tall her pensioners be:
In their gold coats spots you see;
Those be rubies, fairy favors,
In those freckles live their savors.
I must go seek some dewdrops here,
And hang a pearl in every cowslip's ear.
Farewell, thou lob of spirits, I'll be gone.
Our Queen and all her elves come here anon.

WILLIAM SHAKSPERE, "A Midsummer Night's Dream."

MERCY

The quality of mercy is not strain'd:
It droppeth as the gentle rain from heaven
Upon the place beneath. It is twice blest:
It blesseth him that gives and him that takes.
'T is mightiest in the mightiest; it becomes
The thronèd monarch better than his crown:
His sceptre shows the force of temporal power,
The attribute to awe and majesty,
Wherein doth sit the dread and fear of kings;
But mercy is above this sceptred sway,
It is enthronèd in the hearts of kings;
It is an attribute to God himself,
And earthly power doth then show likest God's
When mercy seasons justice. Therefore, Jew,
Though justice be thy plea, consider this,
That, in the course of justice, none of us
Should see salvation. We do pray for mercy,
And that same prayer doth teach us all to render
The deeds of mercy.

WILLIAM SHAKSPERE, "The Merchant of Venice."

MAY *

May shall make the world anew;
Golden sun and silver dew,
Money minted in the sky,
Shall the earth's new garments buy.
May shall make the orchards bloom;
And the blossoms' fine perfume

* From "Little-Folk Lyrics." By permission of Houghton Mifflin Company.

Shall set all the honey-bees
Murmuring among the trees.
May shall make the bud appear
Like a jewel, crystal clear,
'Mid the leaves upon the limb
Where the robin lilts his hymn.
May shall make the wild flowers tell
Where the shining snowflakes fell,
Just as though each snowflake's heart,
By some secret, magic art,
Were transmuted to a flower
In the sunlight and the shower.
Is there such another, pray,
Wonder-making month as May?

FRANK DEMPSTER SHERMAN.

JULY *

When the scarlet cardinal tells
  Her dream to the dragon fly,
And the lazy breeze makes a nest in the trees,
  And murmurs a lullaby,
        It is July.

When the tangled cobweb pulls
  The cornflower's cap awry,
And the lilies tall lean over the wall
  To bow to the butterfly,
        It is July.

When the heat like a mist veil floats,
  And poppies flame in the rye,

* By special arrangement with the author.

And the silver note in the streamlet's throat
   Has softened almost to a sigh,
         It is July.

When the hours are so still that time
   Forgets them, and lets them lie
'Neath petals pink till the night stars wink
   At the sunset in the sky,
         It is July.

When each finger-post by the way
   Says that Slumbertown is nigh;
When the grass is tall, and the roses fall,
   And nobody wonders why,
         It is July.

                SUSAN HARTLEY SWETT.

THE BURIAL OF SIR JOHN MOORE

Not a drum was heard, not a funeral note,
   As his corse to the rampart we hurried;
Not a soldier discharged his farewell shot
   O'er the grave where our hero we buried.

We buried him darkly, at dead of night,
   The sods with our bayonets turning;
By the struggling moonbeam's misty light,
   And the lantern dimly burning.

No useless coffin enclosed his breast,
   Not in sheet or in shroud we wound him;
But he lay like a warrior taking his rest,
   With his martial cloak around him.

Few and short were the prayers we said,
  And we spoke not a word of sorrow;
But we steadfastly gazed on the face that was dead,
  And we bitterly thought of the morrow:

We thought, as we hollowed his narrow bed,
  And smoothed down his lonely pillow,
That the foe and the stranger would tread o'er his head,
  And we far away on the billow!

Lightly they'll talk of the spirit that's gone,
  And o'er his cold ashes upbraid him, —
But little he'll reck, if they let him sleep on
  In the grave where a Briton has laid him.

But half of our heavy task was done
  When the clock struck the hour for retiring;
And we heard the distant and random gun
  That the foe was sullenly firing.

Slowly and sadly we laid him down,
  From the field of his fame fresh and gory;
We carved not a line, and we raised not a stone —
  But we left him alone with his glory!

                                        CHARLES WOLFE.

LIST OF SELECTIONS

FOURTH YEAR

FIFTH YEAR

SIXTH YEAR